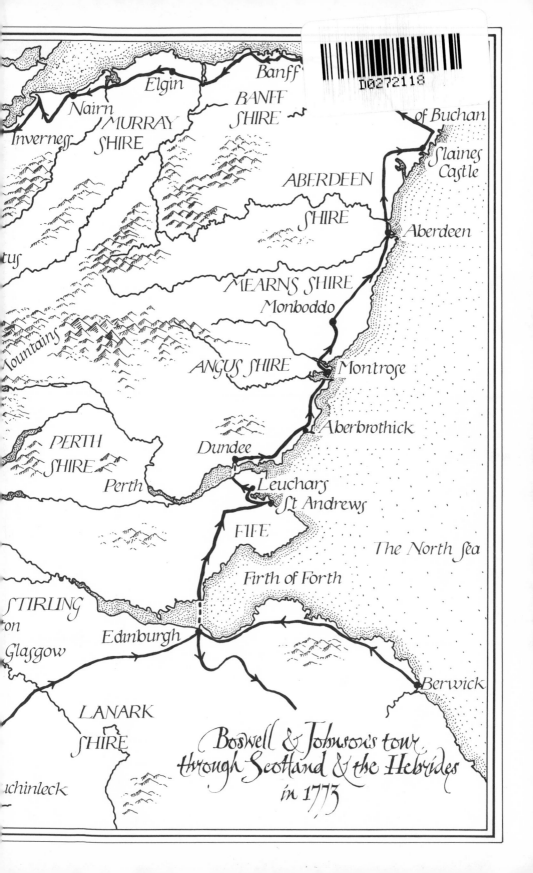

Boswell & Johnson's tour through Scotland & the Hebrides in 1773

A Walk to the Western Isles

By the same author

FRANK DELANEY

A

WALK

TO THE

WESTERN
ISLES

AFTER
BOSWELL & JOHNSON

HarperCollins*Publishers*

For Douglas, Charlotte and Lola

HarperCollins*Publishers*
77–85 Fulham Palace Road,
Hammersmith, London W6 8JB

Published by HarperCollins*Publishers* 1993

1 3 5 7 9 8 6 4 2

Copyright © Frank Delaney 1993

Frank Delaney asserts the moral right to be
identified as the author of this work

A catalogue record for this book is available
from the British Library

ISBN 0 246 13745 2

Photoset in Linotron Bembo by
Rowland Phototypesetting Ltd
Bury St Edmunds, Suffolk

Printed in Great Britain by
HarperCollinsManufacturing Glasgow

CONTENTS

LIST OF ILLUSTRATIONS

Isle Oronsay, Skye (*Scotland in Focus*)
Dunvegan Castle, Skye (*Scotland in Focus*)
Waterfall at Dunvegan (*Scotland in Focus*)
Inner Hebrides (*Scotland in Focus*)
The Island of Coll (*Scottish Tourist Board*)
St. Columba's Bay, Iona (*Scotland in Focus*)
Post Office at Lochbuie (*Frank Delaney*)
Lochbuie, Island of Mull (*Scotland in Focus*)
Inveraray Castle (*Scotland in Focus*)
Rest-and-be-Thankful (*Scotland in Focus*)
Eglinton Castle (*Scotland in Focus*)
Auchinleck House, Ayrshire (*Scotland in Focus*)
Auchinleck Signpost (*Scotland in Focus*)

ACKNOWLEDGMENTS

The author wishes to acknowledge practical or imaginative indebtedness to the following: the University of Aberdeen; John Bailey; James Beattie; C. H. Bennett; Alan Bold; James Boswell; and the present James Boswell; Sue Bradbury; Michael Brander; A. M. Broadley; Edmund Burke; Thomas Campbell; the Rev. and Mrs Cassells of Leuchars; Baldesar Castiglione; Robert Chambers; R. W. Chapman; J. L. Clifford; William Cobbett; Susan Collier-Delaney; Derek Cooper; Iain Crichton-Smith; Conor Cruise O'Brien; Anne P. Scott Davis; Daniel Defoe; Lord Elibank; Katherine Everett; Robert Fergusson; George Gale; David Garrick; Janet R. Glover; Oliver Goldsmith; Sir Peter Hall; F. E. Halliday; Melanie Haselden; Seamus Heaney; Christopher Hibbert; George Birkbeck Hill; Richard Holmes; Holyrood House; Quintus Horatius Flaccus; David Hume; Huntly House Museum; Professor and Mrs A. N. Jeffares; Paul Johnson; Richard Johnson; Dr Samuel Johnson; William Jolly; James Joyce; Hugh Kingsmill; Ladystairs Museum; Peter Levi; E. L. MacAdam; Mairi MacArthur; Alexander Macgregor; R. F. Mackenzie; Moray Maclaren; Fitzroy Maclean; James Macpherson; Edward Malone; Martin Martin, Gent.; Douglas Matthews and the staff of the London Library; George Milne; Lord Monboddo; Jan Morris; Arthur Murphy; the National Library of Scotland; William R. Ober; Hesketh Pearson; Thomas Pennant; F. W. Pottle; John Prebble; Peter Quennell; Janice Robertson; Pat Rogers; Thomas Rowlandson; Sir Walter Scott; William Shakespeare; Michael Shaw; Bill Simpson; Major and Mrs Patrick Telfer Smollett; T. C. Smout; Leslie Southwick; Robert Louis Stevenson; Bram Stoker; William Temple; David Thomson; Hester Thrale-Piozzi; C. B. Tinker; Edward Topham; Nigel Tranter; Publius Virgilius Maro; C. E. Vuillamy; John Wain; T. H. White; W. B. Yeats.

Chronology of the Journey
of Dr Johnson and Mr Boswell through
Scotland in 1773

A Walk to the Western Isles

CHAPTER I

'To find simplicity and wildness'

D R JOHNSON HAD BEEN ANNOYING me for years. I had never read him – nor his biographer, James Boswell, and eventually they constituted an irritating vacuum in my reading. I had not been introduced to them. When I grew up in Ireland, writers unsympathetic to the race always got short educational shrift, and Johnson would not have been forgiven the truth of his comment, 'The Irish are a fair people: they never speak well of one another.'

It was worse than that. Notwithstanding an honorary Doctorate of Laws from Trinity College, Dublin in 1765 – awarded 'on account of the egregious elegance and usefulness of his writings' – Johnson never showed a fraction of interest in visiting Ireland. He did not travel to receive the degree, and in 1779, six years after their Hebridean jaunt, when Boswell suggested an excursion, Johnson replied, 'It is the last place where I should wish to travel.'

BOSWELL: Should you not like to see Dublin, sir?
JOHNSON: No, sir! Dublin is only a worse capital.
BOSWELL: Is not the Giant's Causeway worth seeing?
JOHNSON: Worth seeing? Yes, but not worth going to see.

And in 1791 he wrote to a friend, 'Dublin, though a place much worse than London, is not so bad as Iceland' (which he had not visited either).

Then I found what felt like an inconsistency: he loved one of the dearest Irishmen of letters, Oliver Goldsmith, poor, impossible, adorable Noll Goldsmith, at whose hacked appearance and monkey-ish walk the children threw stones in the street; Johnson

3

protected him, bailed him out, applauded him and mourned him and missed him. And still, insisted my mind's shorthand-taker, Dr Samuel Johnson, although brilliant in his conversation, in his letters and his lexicography, was an opinionated xenophobe; and Boswell, according to all similar impressions, a libidinous toady.

To possess such short-changed knowledge of any man so present more than two centuries after his death is a fact bound to aggravate. How many writers from the past appear almost daily in our newspapers? Three names dominate: Shakespeare, Oscar Wilde – and Samuel Johnson, and he seems to crop up so often and with such aptness: 'That which is written without effort is in general read without pleasure.' It eventually felt acutely uncomfortable to tolerate such a superficial knowledge of this famous subject and his biographer.

Where and how to seek the fullest remedy? There is only one method of discovery better than reading a book on a subject – and that is by writing one. Johnson's *A Journey to the Western Islands of Scotland* appeared in 1775: Boswell's *The Journal of a Tour to the Hebrides with Samuel Johnson LL.D.*, a decade later, in September 1785, by which time Johnson had been dead twenty months. The two books brought both men together in a crucial unity: to judge from a glance at the chronology, Boswell travelled through Scotland with Johnson long before he wrote much of his famous *Life of Johnson*. Therefore, biographically speaking, might not Boswell's story of their Scottish travels have been the rehearsal of his extraordinary *modus operandi* – the great man's thoughts, habits, pronouncements and attitudes noted down, often in astonishing detail, by his watchful, bouncy companion?

'Discovering' them by following in their footsteps grew more and more appealing. On the Hebridean journey, the pair became Life itself and Life's recorder, and pursuing them thus could I not unveil them gradually and very fully? In their accounts of this tour, they characterised themselves as fully as if in fiction – because they encountered identical matters, never leaving each other's company from Edinburgh to the north and west and back to Edinburgh, yet their descriptions of the expedition differ significantly. Johnson's, half the length of Boswell's, is cerebral, incisive, acute and powerful: Boswell's a more humanitary record.

Once settled upon such an absorbing way of investigating the most famous double act in literature, advantages began to proliferate. Few literary journeys may be so utterly traced: their accessible and entertaining accounts contain detail far beyond mere clues. What they saw could not have changed too much out of recognition: a landscape of Scotland's power and magnitude does not alter; her towns and cities have long been fairly stable. Therefore, I could judge the two men from how they responded to what they viewed. Spending so much time in their company would implant them so clearly in my mind that any further reading would, for the rest of my life, be done against a background of 'first-hand' personal knowledge. I would absorb them almost without knowing – acquaintance by osmosis, and my tongue not too far from my cheek.

Disadvantageously, the idea seemed to lack originality. Culling an egregious figure from the flock of history, and tracing any footsteps he or she may have taken, has grown into a not uncommon writerly practice. Ancient literary roads are now crisscrossed with men and women wearing notebooks; indeed, this would be my own third or fourth such enterprise. And several writers had followed Johnson and Boswell to the Hebrides: the exercise seems to get repeated every generation or so. I thought to accommodate that substantial precedent by setting out on my own journey of enquiry. At the end of it I would know whether I would love or dislike, revere or shrug off, the two of English Literature's most famous creatures about whom I felt I proportionately knew least. This 'quest' factor also helped me over another difficult fence: Johnson's sacredness. He has been the preserve of two centuries of scholars, with, I supposed, a bibliography not much shorter than that of Shakespeare. If James Joyce went into exile with as his weapons 'silence, exile and cunning', then surely I could go rooting in the hallowed ground of Johnson and Boswell armed only with enthusiastic, uninformed curiosity?

Finally, when I began to accuse myself of wanting to write a book about a book, the criticism was defused immediately by the discovery that the books they wrote about their northern adventure are jointly and severally a joy. Anyway, Johnson himself, as I was to find out, spent much of his life writing about writing.

I was comforted further (if impertinently) by the discovery that Johnson's reasons for travelling to Scotland also had a literary root, even if he does begin with the statement, 'I had desired to visit the Hebrides, or Western Islands of Scotland, so long, that I scarcely remember how the wish was originally excited.' Boswell remembered for him. In the opening paragraph of his own *Journal of a Tour to the Hebrides* Boswell refers twice to an earlier study of the Hebrides: 'Martin's *Account* of those islands'; and – 'he [Johnson] told me, in summer, 1763, that his father put Martin's Account into his hands when he was very young, and that he was much pleased with it.'

Martin Martin, Gent., a university-educated employee of the Macleods of Dunvegan and a *protégé* of the Geographer Royal, had written:

A Description of the Western Islands of Scotland, circa 1695, Containing a Full Account of their situation, Extent, Soils, Product, Harbours, Bays, Tides, Anchoring Places, and Fisheries. The Ancient and Modern Government, Religion and Customs of the Inhabitants, particularly of their Druids, Heathen Temples, Monasteries, Churches, Chappels, Antiquities, Monuments, Forts, Caves and other Curiosities of Art and Nature. Of their admirable and Expeditious way of Curing most Diseases by Simples of their own Product. A Particular Account of the Second Sight, or Faculty of foreseeing things to come, by way of Vision, so common among them. A Brief Hint of Methods to Improve Trade in that Country, both by Sea and Land. With a New Map of the whole, describing the Harbours, Anchoring Places, and dangerous Rocks, for the benefit of Sailers. To which is added a brief description of the Isles of Orkney, and Schetland.

Johnson reportedly carried a copy of Martin in his luggage to the Hebrides, and his fondness for the book may have caused a misapprehension that little had changed, that he could view near-medieval circumstances. Although Boswell, who at that time lived in Edinburgh, would have us believe that the trip was owed entirely to invitations he had been issuing for years, Johnson went because he believed, having read Martin Martin, Gent., that in the Hebrides he would make a journey backwards through Time, that he could discover what life had been at least a century earlier; and that he would encounter, and so conveniently near to England, a people as rudimental and unchanging as the mountains. He did not quite state that the Highlanders and Hebrideans might prove as anthropologically interesting as far-off savages, but his publicly-expressed view of the Scots, about whom he was denigrating, patronising and racist, and the observations he afterwards collated in his *Journey to the Western Islands of Scotland*, repeatedly compare Scotland with the greater state of civilisation – meaning, naturally, London.

Boswell confirms Johnson's hopes that '. . . we might there contemplate a system of life almost totally different from what we had been accustomed to see; and, to find simplicity and wildness, and all the circumstances of remote time or place, so near . . .'

Johnson seems not to have challenged the datedness of Martin's Account, and perhaps the memory of it gave him reason to expect a more primitive life than he actually found. The Jacobite Rebellion in 1745 had a tragic and apocalyptic outcome for the Scottish clans, and so was Scotland altered utterly. In his many references to the economy of Scotland, did Johnson measure accurately the degree to which landlord and tenant relationships had changed? He saw and heard about emigrant ships, met able-bodied men who would soon be obliged to depart for America – an option which barely existed in the times of Martin Martin, Gent. Admittedly, of all the regions 'comfortably' near at hand, the Western Isles certainly numbered among those parts of Britain that had least changed – but in the autumn of 1773, was it as primitive and unchanged as Johnson, since boyhood, had expected?

With Boswell's *Journal of a Tour*, we are in more straightforward company. If these two were Literature's master and servant, from Boswell we get the 'below stairs' version of intellectual observation. His prose, though attractive, never reaches the majesty of Johnson's; he informs, where Johnson creates ideas; he holds the candle up to light Johnson's paintings. Where we are immediately interested in what Johnson thought, and how he used what he encountered to make sense of his life and of Scotland, to absorb it into his powerful mill and inform the rest of his large contemplation – Boswell interests us in whom they met, and what they saw, and the things they said.

In this Boswell illuminates Johnson's greatness and provides enough information for the reader easily to take a position – whereas Johnson's account has a dominant authority. Johnson always makes you think: Boswell usually makes you see and hear. Boswell's accompaniment, a big, fussy gloss on their travels, is the value added to Johnson's account. The qualitative gulf between them makes itself plain. If, as Cyril Connolly put it, 'literature is the art of writing something that will be read twice: journalism what will be grasped at once,' then you read Johnson five times and Boswell three; Johnson, as it were, the rigorous portraitist, Boswell the gossipy wedding photographer forever arranging people; Johnson lepidopterising the moment of observation, Boswell plumping up the cushions around it.

I planned to walk their route, bearing a rucksack. Unlike them, I would lunch – not dine – at mid-day, and dine – not sup – at night. The one-volume edition of their enjoyable texts, and all who sail in them, were to be my main guide and handbook; I also packed a paperback of Boswell's *Life of Johnson*, and promised myself that at journey's end, having seen the pair against the backdrop of Scotland, I would augment from other sources – Johnson's letters from Scotland, the observations and opinions of others, contemporary anecdotes and impressions of them both: hence this book.

Their journey lasted from Saturday, 14 August, to Monday, 22 November 1773, a hundred days in all kinds of weather, with some escapades mildly dangerous. For, obviously, his own social reasons, as well as for the entertainment of his great friend, Boswell had arranged that Johnson should have only the very best of Scottish company, and Boswell, like an *impresario*, booked every intellectual and conversational act on whom he could lay hands. With many such promises in hand, Johnson left London on Friday, 6 August 1773 by post-chaise; if a private vehicle it would have been a costly transport, equal today to an executive limousine. He had independent means, having been awarded an official pension of three hundred pounds a year in 1762, in respect of his writing and the approval it had received; he was in his sixty-fourth year. Comparatively speaking, Johnson hurried, and he had company all the way to Edinburgh. From London to Newcastle, Robert Chambers sat alongside him, a thirty-six-year-old barrister, a member of Johnson's famous Literary Club, 'a man whose purity of manners and vigour of mind,' said Johnson, 'are sufficient to make every thing welcome that he brings.'

This dash northwards is well documented. They travelled seventy-one miles the first day, intending to stay overnight at Stamford in Lincolnshire, but Johnson felt unwell and they stopped, a stage short, at Stilton, a dozen miles south-west of Peterborough. Next day, Saturday the seventh, they drove through Stamford and Grantham, lunched at Newark and on Saturday night stayed at Doncaster, a day's total of eighty-seven miles; they went to church next morning and took up a lunch invitation. This delayed their departure from Doncaster, and on Sunday afternoon and early evening they made only thirty-seven miles to reach York on Sunday night, where on Monday morning Johnson did a little sightseeing – York Minster, the ruins of the Abbey and the jail. They lunched in York, and then stayed overnight at Northallerton, a distance of thirty-two miles. On Tuesday, 10 August, Johnson and Chambers travelled forty-three miles from Northallerton to Newcastle, and took a day to do so. At Darlington the livery stables put fresh horses between the shafts.

Johnson felt out of sorts while travelling north, passing up the opportunity to visit a fine church at Darlington, using pressure of time as an excuse for lack of energy, although in Durham he did view the cathedral and its library – in his letters he said he found it 'mean and scanty'. Also in Durham, 'beside all expectation', he bumped into an old friend, a Miss Fordice, now a doctor's wife: Johnson found her 'much decayed', but, knowing that her husband had recently experienced severe money troubles he believed he saw in her 'withered features more impressions of sorrow than of time'.

In Newcastle, while Johnson rested for three days, Robert

Chambers disembarked: he had come to say goodbye to his relatives before taking up a judgeship in India. Another friend, Mr William Scott, took his place in Johnson's coach. Scott, whom Sir Walter Scott described as 'one of the pleasantest men I ever knew', later became Lord Stowell, eventually one of Johnson's executors, to whom Sam bequeathed some of his books. In the coach with Johnson on Friday morning, Scott, aged twenty-eight, soon complained of a headache. Johnson replied, 'At your age, sir, I had no headache.'

I travelled from London to Edinburgh by British Rail, not perhaps as rattly, but just as dirty and as haphazard in matters of food and serenity. The train touches most of the main dots on Johnson's route, and no matter how appealing it might have been to linger in one or two, I had to recognise that Johnson's time in Scotland, not his means of getting up there, was the object of my exercise. Just south of the Border, I began to savour the long run-in up along Northumberland's shank. Travel is so frequently so boring that all the mind's tools are needed for a survival kit. From somewhere in my memory, I rummaged out the (hitherto irrelevant) fact that in 1746, a Scottish landlord in Newcastle-upon-Tyne dropped dead of a broken heart on the morning news came through of Culloden, with its implicit message of final calamity. And, since we are in Northumberland – Hotspur was named Henry Percy after his father, the first Duke: 'A son who is the theme of honour's tongue/Among a grove the very straightest plant.' Hotspur never became Duke of Northumberland because at Shrewsbury in 1403, he had to 'brook the loss of brittle life' and predeceased his father, leaving Hotspur's son, the third Henry Percy, to inherit eventually.

With the sun on my right hand, we neared, according to the map, Alnwick – Hotspur country. Johnson spent the afternoon of Friday, 13 August 1773 at Alnwick castle, seat of the Duke of Northumberland, and, he wrote in a letter, 'went through the apartments, walked on the wall and climbed the towers'.

School jokes returned: perhaps Hotspur was as fat as Falstaff? 'This earth that bears thee dead,' says Hal, 'bears not alive so *stout* a gentleman.' Amid laughter, discuss. An inspired teacher brought to the classroom the extra-curricular *Henry IV Part 2* so that we might understand Hotspur's characterisation even better – as he told us – 'by the Irish method, that is, through what others said of him'. It was a case of *de mortuis nil nisi bonum* as, praise-singing her 'heart's dear Harry', the teacher read aloud Lady Percy's grief: 'He was the mark and glass, copy and book/ That fashion'd others. And him, O wondrous him! O miracle of men.' A Percy belonged in Johnson's set, Thomas Percy, a clergyman who became Bishop of Dromore and chaplain to the Duke of Northumberland. Percy was a song-collector, balladmaker, translator and antiquarian; Johnson visited him in his vicarage at Easton Maudit near Northampton for a holiday in the summer of 1764.

Once, Percy complained to Johnson about travel writers, in particular their contemporary, Thomas Pennant, who, Percy said, had mis-described Alnwick castle and its gardens. Percy chose difficult ground on which to fight Johnson, who admired Pennant: 'He's the best traveller I ever read; he observes more things than anyone else does.' Pennant, a Welshman from Flintshire, made writing tours of Ireland, Wales, the Continent and – whence Johnson's especial interest – Scotland and the Hebrides. Moses Griffith, taken along as an *amanuensis*, illustrated Pennant's works in watercolours, and this earlier pair of travellers became, and remain, well-regarded.

Except in the eyes of Percy who, knowing Pennant's reputation as a natural historian (he corresponded with, and influenced, Gilbert White of Selborne), complained to Johnson, 'He pretends to give the natural history of Northumberland, and yet takes no notice of the immense number of trees planted there of late.' Johnson corrected him. 'That, sir, has nothing to do with *natural* history; that is *civil* history. A man who gives the natural history of the oak, is not to tell how many oaks have been planted in this place or that. A man who gives the natural history of the cow, is not to tell how many cows are milked at Islington. The animal is the same whether milked in the Park or at Islington.' The argument grew heated – in Boswell's words, 'inflammable particles were collecting for a cloud to burst,' and in the interests of amelioration Percy had to shake Johnson's hand.

*　　　*　　　*

Northumberland is firm, entrancing countryside. Had Johnson digressed a little farther to the west between Newcastle and Alnwick, he could have walked Otterburn. The historian Raphael Holinshed suggested that Hotspur, who was routed here in August 1388 as night fell, was 'surnamed for his often pricking, as one that seldome times rested, if there were anie service to be doone abroad'. Was it the same impetuousness that led Hotspur to attack the Scots under James Douglas at twilight? It cost him the battle. The field of action, or as much as is known accurately of it, may be viewed from the Jedburgh road to the north-west of Otterburn village. Hotspur lost under a full moon, even though the Scots had a smaller army, and Douglas actually died of his wounds on the field, but his canny generals hid his body under the high ferns to protect morale. Conveniently for ballad-makers (and for me too, bearing in mind the destination of Boswell and Johnson), Douglas's last words rhymed:

> I had a dream, a dreary dream, beyond the isle of Skye
> I saw a dead man win a fight: I think that man was I.

The pleasure of travel by train through Britain today has more or less evaporated and I need distraction in depth to assuage irritations. Along with Boswell's *Life* and the one-volume edition of Boswell's and Johnson's Scottish books, I had packed a plump old notebook compiled over two or three journeys around these parts, filled with remarks to myself, snippets from guide-books, local newspaper cuttings, song-books, church histories, and so on. The map now confirmed the notebook – that, off to the left, that is to say the west, the signposts will point to the 'hams – Ugham: Edlingham; Whittingham; Eglingham; Chillingham of the white cattle, where on the Tankerville estate grazes a herd whose pedigree predates Christ, wild, unapproachable animals bred by the Druids for sacrifice; and at Norham on the banks of the Tweed, Turner, re-visiting, bowed low to the ruins of the castle in memory of a particularly good drawing he had made there many years earlier.

Out by the sea on the right stands the fairytale of Bamburgh Castle, due east of Belford, Johnson's last overnight resting-place in England before his Scottish adventures. Bamburgh was confiscated from Robert Bruce and given to a Hotspur ancestor; it needs only long pennants streaming from its battlements, or a Russian Shakespeare production, to perpetuate the drama. With habitual inexplicableness, the train stopped on the line, as 'unwontedly' as in Edward Thomas's poem 'Adlestrop', and there we sat by the north-eastern coast. Some childhood annual or other, it may have been *The Eagle*, told the story in pictures of Grace Darling, the Longstone lighthouse-keeper's daughter, who rowed a boat in a wild equinoctial storm to save the crew of a steamer run aground; and even though the local folk of the day grumbled that she had received too much credit, that others had been much more heroic, now she has become immortal via generations of schoolteachers and her own museum in Bamburgh. In the early 1960s in Dublin, I took down the words of a ballad:

'Twas on the Longstone lighthouse, there dwelt an English maid
Pure as the sky above her, of danger unafraid;
One morning just at daybreak, a storm-tossed crew she spied;
But oh, to try seemed madness to breast the angry tide.

I can only recall the first four lines, and now that I have written them down, I shall probably never remember them again.

When the train's shuffles became more than a promise of motion, the dots of the Farne Islands appeared, with their marvels of names: I had been here before, too, and I remembered the names of many of them, but had written them all down. The Irish poet, Seamus Heaney, has referred to the music of the weather forecast, Rockall, Malin, Hebrides, Faroes, south-east Iceland; Cromarty, Forth, Viking, Dogger, Fisher, German Bight. Might not Heaney's wonderful gifts, or even the roughness of a local balladeer, make terrific music out of that Farne list? Great Whin Sill, Gun Rock, Clove Car, Cuthbert's Gut, Glororum Shad, Wide-opens, Nameless Rock, Oxscar, The Brownsman, The Churn, Fang, Elbow, Knivestone. Then, as I craned forward to glimpse it, the line of thin spittle materialised, the North Sea surf at Holy Island, Lindisfarne, the name of a rock music band, and – equally designed to promote trance – the Lindisfarne Gospels in the British Museum, with their cross-hatchings and trumpets and spirals and whorlings, the work of four holy authors, Eadfrith, Ethelwald, Billfrith (a jeweller, really: he built the casing) and the translator, Aldred. At Holy Island, always watch out for otters: they swam in from the sea to watch St Cuthbert at his morning ablutions, and he blessed their little brown heads.

I find it odd that Johnson did not visit here, or Otterburn; odder still knowing his interest in history, that he also by-passed Flodden Field, south-west of Berwick, below Coldstream. Five years ago, the climb through a parting in the combed corn to view the battle-fields filled my nose with pollen. Every August, according to my notebook, in a commemoration at Branxton, a piper plays 'The Flowers of the Forest', Scotland's renowned lament. The men who fell at Flodden: the deans of Glasgow and Edinburgh, two bishops and two abbots, a dozen lords, not far off a score of earls, and the sons of the great Scottish families, including one of Boswell's ancestors – they, presumably, were the flowers of the forest, and they were trampled at Flodden in the afternoon of 9 September 1513, when the larger army of James IV took on forces raised on the instructions of Henry VIII, and the English soldiers took their boots off on the slippery hill and routed the Scots: they seem to have been doing it ever since, one way and another. James's body, later discovered on the battlefield, was taken to London for a ceremonial funeral promised by Henry VIII, which never took place, and James's embalmed head was later scooped out and the skull used like an apothecary's jar by a court glazier for mixing his ingredients.

In Edinburgh, fearing immediate invasion from England, the city fathers in panic began the Flodden Wall, and for the many years of its building, did not dare move outside it, thus beginning the tradition of tall buildings within the city. Pennant, Johnson's favourite travel writer, visited Edinburgh in 1769 and called the place 'A city that possesses a boldness and grandeur of situation beyond any that I have ever seen. It is built on the edges and sides of a vast sloping rock, of a great and precipitous height at the upper extremity, and the sides declining very quick and steep into the plain. The view of the houses at a distance strikes the traveller with wonder; their own loftiness, improved by their almost aerial situation, gives them a look of magnificence . . .'

*   *   *

In a field near Berwick, plover gathered, a bird with a reputation for bringing ill-luck. The plover is a betraying bird – the thin scream and scared beating of wings told Redcoat soldiers that someone was hiding in the long grass. I have never seen more plover in my life than in these fields beneath the Cheviots: will I see them again in this fine weather, and will they bring me good or bad luck up here in the north? Johnson, on his northern tour, drove along the dotted line of Scotland's unfortunate history – by Otterburn and Flodden to Culloden near Inverness, the last battle fought for Scotland.

Rivers and their crossings belong in all our mythologies. Styx; Rubicon; Ganges; Cornishmen feel safe only when back across the Tamar; in Ireland Cromwell did not cross the Shannon. The river Tweed blinks in the sunlight. From here on the verge of Scotland, the pilots, looking for Edinburgh airport, think about lowering their wheels. Outside the train window, the water flows along broadly and respectably, silvery where it evades the shadows. About fifteen years ago, the good people of Cork, Ireland's Yorkshiremen, shrewd, commonsensical and proud of it, were taken in by, and gave Mass offerings to, a gentleman who told them he was the Bishop of Somewhere – Birmingham, I think; closer scrutiny unfrocked him as a wine waiter from Berwick-upon-Tweed, a town of arches. The chaise's wheels must have splashed the Tweed, or made rough, trundling noises on the bridge, especially if carrying a heavy man such as Dr Samuel Johnson: 'His person was large,' wrote Boswell, 'robust, I may say approaching to the gigantick, and grown unwieldy from corpulency.'

'Unwieldy from corpulency'? One should know as much as possible about one's travelling companions. Do they smell? Do they drink? Are they punctual? Will they make you miss the train? Reading for essential preliminary information before setting out, I settled for a few major biographical details and copious personal observations. The rest, in keeping with true voyages of discovery, would transpire *en route*, and could be amplified at the end. All I needed to establish were some principal visions of the man and his companion; I needed to fix them physically in my imagination's eye.

According to all biographical and anecdotal reports, Johnson was built for the stationary rather than the mobile; overweight and slovenly, he had breathing difficulties. His intellectual reputation aside for the moment, that an ageing man of doubtful, if not raddled, physique, and less than perfect general health, contemplated that damp, clanking journey, must make Johnson some kind of hero to our coddled age.

First impressions of him always surprised people: big bones, an awkward demeanour, six feet tall, stout and stooped; difficult, that is, messy, hair arrangements: over a crop of wiry, incapable-of-being-kempt frizz, he wore varying, ill-fitting wigs in unfetching shades of grey, added to which acute shortsightedness led to his reading so close to lamps and candles that his wigs and forehead frequently bore scorchmarks. Below his defective and thyroidic eyes stood an overwhelming nose. His cheeks and neck bore smallpox and scrofula markings; he had an unwieldy tooth formation, and he habitually opened and shut his mouth as if chewing. Notoriously forthright, he hectored when faced with cant, egotism or insincerity, but he said to the novelist Fanny Burney, 'You must not mind me, Madam; I say strange things, but I mean no harm.'

Whinnying like a horse, he made alarmingly sudden movements: sometimes he laughed out of all proportion to a witticism; he often waved his hands and arms in elaborate, unfounded gestures. Eloquent of speech, elegant of mind, he was careless of hygiene; like Newton, his fame and genius excused certain personal matters, stains, odours and such, although women in particular remarked upon his unusually dirty hands, linen and hose. Sam rocked as he sat, ate noisily, argued fiercely, and, glancing along his knife, fork or spoon as if down the barrel of a gun, colonised whole dining-rooms with his lack of decorum. He may have had nothing outward or cosmetic to help him in the daily truck with life, but this sluggish, scarred and large man wrote, they say, and talked, prose of celestial perfection, a hero of the English language.

Such a travelling companion as I have therefore found: noisome and noisy, no connection between his appearance and his spirit. But he had a power that would sustain for longer after his death than he would ever have attributed to himself – because for all his arrogance he had a wide streak of modesty. Reading him, John Ruskin, born a generation after Johnson's death, 'at once and for ever recognized in him a man entirely sincere, and infallibly wise in the view and estimate he gave of the common questions, business and ways of the world. I valued his sentences not primarily because they were symmetrical, but because they were just and clear . . . He taught me carefully to measure life, and distrust fortune . . .'

Nor will Johnson, for all the rationale his era introduced, be a companion on an even keel: he crowned his physical unusualness with emotional difficulties. Of a melancholic father and an anxious mother, from youth Sam suffered fears of insanity. His routing of such feelings accounts in part for his huge literary output – he worked with an almost deranged commitment in order to remain sane. Depression gave him the oxygen of genius – energy: it manifested itself in an astonishing range of capacities within a prodigious output: essays, the editing of magazines, his criticism, his poems – and a prototype Dictionary of the English language. His deep piety was frequently connected to his emotions – he burst into tears whenever he heard a well-sung *Dies Irae*. The religion which brought him succour also frightened him by its angers and dreads: he composed prayers to keep them at bay, and seems to have acknowledged within himself a genuine devoutness. When not comforted by his faith, he rushed around within a vicious circle of anxiety, bemoaning how badly he used his great drive. In common with many people prone to unresolved emotional pressures, Johnson made lists of what to do instead of actually doing them, yet, almost despite himself, he produced a large output.

Still, he seems to have travelled with enjoyment and cheerfulness, and fairly courteously, and with intelligent enquiry. He had large appetites for food, drink and social intercourse; acknowledging an appetite for journeys, he complained humorously that those with sufficient energy to travel never had enough inclination, while he, who had the means and intent, was growing too old. Nevertheless, he went to Wales, Paris, many places within England, and said he wanted to ramble through Poland, India and sundry other places. Many people loved him, and many more respected him; yet, a reputation for prejudice has clung to him, especially in Scotland: 'The noblest prospect which a Scotchman ever sees,' he told Boswell, 'is the high road that leads him to England.'

Most knowledge of Johnson comes from Boswell – to the displeasure of some. Ford Madox Ford, in the last of his many books, *The March of Literature*, argued that we have long been led to view Johnson inaccurately: 'the most tragic of all our major literary figures, a great writer whose still living writings are always ignored, a great honest man who will remain forever a figure of half fun because of the leechlike adoration of the greatest and most ridiculous of all biographers. For it is impossible to believe that, without Boswell, Johnson for us today would shine like a sun in the heavens . . .'

This is an interesting bind in which to find myself at the start of such an enterprise. I assumed in my unknowingness that Boswell would be the key to Johnson: do I now have to see around Boswell, rather than through him? Certainly I cannot avoid him, because he seems never to have left Johnson's side, a position of immortality to which he generally elected himself.

A dark-eyed and dark-haired, chubby and busy little person, Boswell stood about five feet six inches tall and had a flirtatious appearance. He cultivated his capacity to be well liked, and behaved cheerfully enough when it backfired. One of his friends, Lord Eglinton, told him (and Boswell recorded it in his *London Journal*), 'Jamie, you have a light head, but a damned heavy arse; and to be sure, such a man will run easily downhill, but it would be severe work to get him up.' Indeed: Boswell spent a lot of time down-ish, one way and another. In the thirty years between age twenty and fifty he suffered at least nineteen recorded venereal ailments, picked up in his multifarious priapics.

Caught somewhere between the skittish and the serious, Boswell's naiveness of face appealed, and his matching manner invited all comers – he was open, and forgiving, and habitually available for levity. If comedy consists in falling into the gap between aspiration and achievement, then, spiritually speaking, Boswell seems to have led a comic life. He attributed to himself fine feelings, principles and lofty ideals, but not a few in the world saw him (however much they may even have liked him) as idle, snobbish, toadying and lecherous. Every aspiration he raised ran the immediate risk of his hauling it down simultaneously. On the one hand he expressed a desire to become an officer in the Guards; on the other he hoped that the uniform might bring him into contact with women of 'quality, beauty and fortune'. He seemed built around no core, a psychological characteristic evidenced by the way he broke a rule immediately he had made it, dismasting his own ship the moment he had set sail. Thus, he swung like an out-of-control metronome between good and base behaviour, the reformer for whose reforms tomorrow never came. He eventually learned to justify such vacillations, rather as a thief only robs the most exclusive banks, with statements like, 'She was indeed a fine, strong, spirited girl, a whore worthy of Boswell, if Boswell must have a whore.' When Jamie caught the clap, it was his wife who dusted him down and sent him off to the doctor.

My journey will come to an end in the Ayrshire village of Auchinleck. Boswell's father, the martinet Lord Auchinleck, a Scottish judge, disputatious, sour, Calvinistic and disciplinarian, caused James genuine distress throughout childhood, adolescence and young manhood. James's response to his father's sharp-tongued and humiliating oppressions took a number of forms: when free of home he rejected all paternal principles – he even became a Roman Catholic for a time; he swiftly grew a libertine's appetite for flesh and carousing; and he sought the company of famous men, as if to overcome the utter denial he felt at his father's hands.

We had crossed the Border: I could now look forward to the hills of Lammermuir and a Stevenson dedication, from *Weir of Hermiston*. I learned it by heart years ago, I do not know why:

> I saw rain falling and the rainbow drawn
> On Lammermuir. Hearkening I heard again
> In my precipitous city beaten bells
> Winnow the keen sea wind.

Minutes away from the precipitous city, we rode through the heavy farms of East Lothian, in a countryside so rich in agriculture they called it the Klondike, where violent rocks as red as Australia rise above the acid-yellow fields of oil-seed rape. Out to sea on the right, there will rise the Bass Rock. 'Great enough to carve a city from,' Stevenson (Graham Greene's ancestor: on the Balfour side) said of it in *Catriona*, in which novel, a work he thought his 'high water mark', he imprisoned David Balfour on the Bass Rock and condemned him to listen to a long, rambling tale-within-a-tale from Andie Dale, his captor. In Leith, where Johnson eventually embarked for his travels proper, Stevenson walked, talked and surely must have done other things with 'robust, great-haunched, blue-eyed' prostitutes, his statement against Edinburgh's *bourgeois* demeanour. He rendered immortal one midnight madonna, Kate Drummond, by using her name for *Catriona*; it is even said that he wanted to marry her;

> I love night in the city
> The lighted streets and the swinging gaits of harlots.

In the city of Stevenson and Hume and Burke and Hare and Jekyll and Hyde and, by birth as it were, Sherlock Holmes and Dr Watson, see how digressions threaten my purity of intent, knock my eye off the ball. The discipline of selection will be my problem throughout this journey. I cannot resist battlefields and their connections, nor any old monastery of any kind, nor fortified ruins nor dykes, nor a castle, nor a spring well, nor, up here, the fortified houses of Scotland, nor the light from a heart of fire such as Stevenson's.

In such fashion this journey now begins to take me over, as history and songs and literature and folklore and memory and stories all swirl around in their habitual untidy magic inside my head. I have never quite understood how they came to make their home there, whether it be genetic, racial or environmental. Could I not have been content with the peace of, say, sporting memories, or mathematics, or the execution of the perfect golf-swing, or details about cars, or air and train schedules, or sex, or balance sheets, or memories of childhood, or money worries, or my children's future, or where the next meal is coming from, or the way of the world? I have all those too, but I also appear to have a more-than-partially-indexed anthology of seemingly unconnected matters, out of which fall from time to time (or, truthfully, very often hop up willingly when I reach for them) odd facts, and quotations long and short; and bizarre conjunctions, dreamlike images of the inventions of writers. Words and airs of songs old and new nudge me like useless ghosts. Yeats, at the height of his feyness (and that was high), asked an old man in Sligo if he ever saw the fairies? The gentleman replied, 'Amn't I annoyed with them?' *Exactly*. Several years ago, when a long kidnapping and siege in Ireland ended, I asked the victim, a Dutchman called Dr Tiede Herrema, how he had remained sane, held at gunpoint in a council-house bedroom the size of a tall cardboard box. He replied that every day, at a specific time, he closed his eyes and across the acres of his mind played eighteen holes of golf over the course near his home. Were I to find myself in similarly unfortunate circumstances I would run, I think, a contest with myself, to see how much I could recall of, say, 'Tintern Abbey': 'Five years have passed; five summers, with the length of five long winters! [Why was the exclamation-mark always both incongruous and important, like that at the end of *Oklahoma!*?] and again I hear these waters, rolling from their mountain-springs with a soft inland murmur . . .'

Johnson travelled forty-nine miles from Newcastle to Belford, and on the Saturday trundled the last seventy-one miles into Edinburgh. The hot bright weather may have contributed to his poorliness since leaving London; so may the hard-springed, rocking coach, even though Johnson loved such transport, as Boswell records on more than one occasion: 'As we were driven rapidly along in the post-chaise, he said to me "Life has not many things better than this"'; and, 'If I had no duties, and no reference to futurity [said Johnson], I would spend my life in driving briskly in a post-chaise with a pretty woman; but she should be one who could understand me, and would add something to the conversation.' Few people could afford the post-chaise on such a scale as a journey from London to Edinburgh, registered as 390 miles.

The costs included the hire of the horses; duty on each horse, charged by the mile; plus drivers' fees per stage of the journey; plus road toll charges; Johnson's trip has been estimated at having cost around twenty-two pounds, a good deal more expensive proportionately than taking a taxi on the same journey today. Heavy among the seats, he sat and talked in the coach, this overweight, squinting, thoughtful man whose gift was the compressing of his knowledge, via the valve of language, into precise meaning: did nothing come between him and what he accurately wanted to say?

I have a vision of him bowling and creaking along between the hedges of summer blossom, on rutted roads high with dust, in his brown clothes and frizzy bushy grey wig, hurtling up to Scotland. Here is a summary of that journey:

Friday, 6 August: London to Stilton: seventy-one miles; *7 August*: Stilton to Doncaster: eighty-seven miles; *8 August*: Doncaster to York: thirty-seven miles; *9 August*: York to Northallerton: thirty-two miles; *10 August*: Northallerton to Newcastle-upon-Tyne: forty-three miles; *13 August*: Newcastle-upon-Tyne to Belford: forty-nine miles; *14 August*: Belford to Edinburgh: seventy-one miles. Two hundred and eighteen years before my train terminated, he came in to Edinburgh by road late on Saturday evening, 14 August 1773.

CHAPTER II

'All was literature and taste'

THE RUCKSACK SAGS BY MY FEET on Waverley, the bridge named for the printing presses that once stood here and hammered out Sir Walter Scott's Waverley novels. Scott's monument, an echo of the Albert Memorial in London, wears massive bandages this year, while they wipe the black grime from it; when not shrouded, his statue can be seen sitting inside the edifice at the bottom, a little lost. A half-mile away as the crow flies over this windy and civilised, bright and dour, frosty, misty and sunny city, a plaque in the cobbled ground near St Giles' Cathedral marks Scott's Heart of Midlothian.

Leerie the Lamplighter, Kidnapped and the rest of Robert Louis Stevenson will have long fixed any child's notion of Edinburgh – the tall gingerbread houses of its lower reaches; the coils and intrigues of the lanes and nooks; the secure, smooth Georgian firmness of the New Town. Everyone who lives in Edinburgh is obliged to look up from birth – to the castle all empirical flags and battlements, and to the ancient Celtic fort of Arthur's Seat. Dun Aedynn, or Dinas Eidynn, home of the the tribe in the epic poem *The Gododdin*, became Edwinesburgh; Dunedin in New Zealand grew from the same linguistic family. 'Edinburgh pays cruelly for her high seat in one of the vilest climates under the heaven,' wrote Stevenson, in 1878. 'She is liable to be beaten upon by all the winds that blow, to be drenched with rain, to be buried in cold sea fogs out of the east, and powdered with the snow as it comes flying southward from the Highland hills. The weather is raw and boisterous in winter, shifty and ungenial in summer, and downright meteorological purgatory in the spring.'

Venice controls people with water: Edinburgh with steepness.

23

The climb from Waverley bridge to the old enclave where Boswell lived works best by using the stairs towards one of the residential courts. When bearing a rucksack, leaning far forward becomes the only means of not falling back down the granite ridges of steps. On the narrow stairway, arched and heavy-vaulted like some chilly northern *bodega*, the doorbells shine with flavoured names – Munro, Mackenzie, Reid, Anderson. Boswell trod here; as did the real Stevenson and his fictional Alan Breck, David Balfour and Catriona Drummond. If history is largely geography, how much time has to have elapsed before history becomes fiction? These two whom I follow: how much was real, how much invented? I will assume both told the truth.

When considering Stevenson's complaints about the 'meteorological purgatory', allow for his ailing bronchia. Then enjoy the climate's contribution to the romance of Edinburgh: granite streets in a November yellow-lit fog; the closes and courts near the castle on a warm sunny afternoon; on a midnight of northern-lights brightness, visit the graveyard to find Stevenson's father's tomb. As the one o'clock gun is fired at the castle, the timeball across on Calton Hill, high above the city, drops down along its rod, so that the mariners out in the Firth of Forth can set their chronometers. Such a pleasure to find the universality of James Joyce's Ulyssean Dublin expressed once again: 'Mr Bloom moved forward raising his troubled eyes . . . After one. Timeball on the ballast office is down.'

Since Johnson spent the entire journey to the Highlands and the west uncoiling ideas from his observations, we have Boswell for the unexceptional details of everyday life, the signposts. After an enjoyable preamble, he begins at the beginning, the moment he had angled towards for years – Johnson's arrival. 'On Saturday the fourteenth of August 1773, late in the evening, I received a note from him, that he was arrived at Boyd's Inn, at the head of the Canongate. I went to him directly.'

Johnson and Boswell originally met on Monday, 16 May 1763, in the back-parlour of a Covent Garden bookshop run by an actor. After some initial verbal reverses, Boswell thereafter vigorously cultivated the (in this case) compliant Johnson. He had earlier tried his luck on a fellow Edinburgher, the philosopher David Hume, and, a little later, Laurence Sterne, Voltaire and Rousseau. All proved either dull or unwilling to endure the attention Boswell seemed likely to foist upon them – vehemently so, in the case of Voltaire, who feigned a swoon in order to detach himself from the Scotsman's attentions, but when he 'came round' he found Boswell before him, as ever was, in full unnoticing flow.

Throughout the 1760s, in their many London conversations, Boswell often advanced to Johnson the idea of a Scottish journey. In April 1771, he put it in writing from Edinburgh; 'I gave him an account of my comfortable life as a married man, and a lawyer in practice at the Scotch bar; invited him to Scotland, and promised to attend him to the Highlands, and Hebrides.' Johnson's reply did not dispel the possibility: 'Whether we climb the Highlands or are tost among the Hebrides . . . I hope the time will come when we may try our powers both with cliffs and water.'

Boswell's main fear, as he expresses it in the early paragraphs of his Hebrides *Journal*, had been that the great man would find any company outside London unstimulating and beneath him. Hoping to melt any such possible objections, and therefore to clinch the visit, Boswell had already touted a number of impress-ive invitations. He wrote manipulative letters to some of the Highland chieftains, and then to three significant citizens whose standing and interests would surely prove enticing.

The first of these to reply, William Robertson, a fifty-two-year-old minister, chaplain and academic, had produced commended histories of Scotland, and of the Emperor Charles V, and would settle his reputation in 1777 with the publication of his *History of America*. Shamelessly, Boswell asked Robertson to promise John-son intellectual company. Robertson rose to it, seeking to tweak all at once Johnson's vanity, prejudices and competitiveness. 'He will meet with many persons here who respect him, and some whom I am persuaded he will think not unworthy of his esteem. I wish he would make the experiment. He sometimes cracks his jokes upon us; but he will find that we can distinguish between the stabs of malevolence, and [Robertson even flourished a psalm] *the rebukes of the righteous, which are like excellent oil, and break not the head.*'

Another of Boswell's letters went to James Beattie, a poet and essayist, who, at thirty-eight, had a reputation already. Here Boswell squeezed a different twist. Beattie had a beautiful wife, and Johnson, who had a well-known *penchant* for conversation with pretty women, admired her loveliness. Beattie wrote back saying he was actually about to set out for London, and that when he got there, he would do what he could.

Boswell chose his third intellectual dignitary equally well, a man, as with the Beatties, known to, and admired by, Johnson: 'I never was in Lord Elibank's company without learning something,' although Johnson typically tempered this by complaining that Elibank's conversation never contained anything 'conclusive'. The choice largely proved a good one for a further reason: Elibank, a man hailed by Smollett for his 'universal intelligence', was in the habit of bowing elaborately to Johnson. Aged seventy, he possessed sufficient years, charm and command of learning for Johnson to respect his stature, appreciate his company and even admire his translations.

Elibank replied to Boswell in a tone which forsook understatement: 'I could never forgive myself, nor deserve to be forgiven by others, if I was to fail in any mark of respect to that great genius. I hold him in the highest veneration . . . and though I should regret to let Mr Johnson go a mile out of his way on my account, old as I am, I shall be glad to go five hundred miles to enjoy a day of his company.' Writing to Johnson, he began as he meant to continue – with a lurch of sycophancy: 'I was to have kissed your hands at Edinburgh . . . I value you more than any King in Christendom . . . I can contribute but little to your entertainment; but my sincere esteem for you gives me some title to the opportunity of expressing it.'

For all his heaving, Lord Elibank cannot claim to have influenced Johnson's decision to travel north: his letters did not reach the travellers until they had arrived in Skye. Johnson then replied with a beautifully-judged note, keeping matters in his own proportion, while smoothly permitting Lord Elibank's deferences 'from a mind so well qualified to estimate characters and to deal out approbation in its due proportions'. It was a sort of 'How-clever-of-you-to-respect-that-I-am-brilliant' letter, although

Johnson did enter the courtesy of a demur: 'If I have more than my share [of approbation] it is your Lordship's fault; for I have always reverenced your judgement too much, to exalt myself in your presence by any false pretensions.'

Even without yet seeing Elibank's reply, Boswell believed that he now had his dance cards fully inscribed, and late on that August Saturday evening, he hurried down the High Street to Canongate to meet his great mentor. It seems to be the case with Johnson that he could never be predicted. Did he raise his unwieldy corpulence and embrace Boswell? Not quite. Mr Scott (of the headache) waited with Johnson at the inn, and in an aside mentioned to the eager Boswell an unhygienic experience. Having ordered lemonade in Boyd's, Dr Johnson had asked for it to be sweetened – 'upon which the waiter, with his greasy fingers, lifted a lump of sugar, and put it into it'. Johnson, furious, threw the lemonade out of the window. Boswell, who had invited Johnson as a house guest, had time to soothe his demi-god, and the couple, substance and its shadow, the one exactly twice as old as the other, left Boyd's and walked in the night up the Royal Mile to James's Court.

Newer buildings hide the eighteenth century on these hard, well-constructed streets. A grey plaque five feet above head height on a side wall reads: 'Boyd's Inn at which Samuel Johnson arrived in Edinburgh 14th August 1773 on his memorable tour to the Hebrides occupied the larger part of the site of this building.' Very Scottish, that: the precision of 'tour *to* the Hebrides', not 'tour *of*' : and it echoes Boswell's and Johnson's precision – they both used 'to', not 'of'. Time was when the best English was spoken in Scotland, in Inverness (although not according to James Joyce, who waved the flag for lower Drumcondra, a suburb of a Dublin suburb).

This street today contains, among other things, the ineluctable health-food shop, a *boutique*; and offices occupy the upper floors of the former Boyd's to the corner of the Royal Mile. Deacon Brodie stole all around here, and the two sides of his character, respectable businessman by day, thief by night, ultimately to die on a gallows trap of his own manufacture – he was, indeed, its test-pilot and it flew him surely to the next world – gave Stevenson

27

the metaphor for Dr Jekyll and Mr Hyde. Stevenson is everywhere in Edinburgh's air.

In the prevailing colour, grey – of stone and cloud – the citizens now keep these tourist streets excellently clean, as if determined to live down the folk memory of an insanitary reputation. Daniel Defoe, in his *Tour Through the Whole Island of Great Britain* fifty years before Johnson, wondered whether the people of Edinburgh 'delighted in Stench and Nastiness . . . In a morning, earlier than Seven o'Clock, before the human Excrements are swept away from the doors, it stinks intolerably; for after Ten at Night, you run a great Risque, if you walk the streets, of having Chamberpots of Ordure thrown upon your Head . . .'

This no longer happens (except sometimes in what passes for literary criticism), and Boswell claimed the 'peril is much abated', having long been ruled out of order by the magistrates. Yet, Captain Edward Topham, who visited the city a year after Johnson, wrote in his *Letters from Edinburgh*, 'they still continue these practices with impunity. Many an elegant suit of clothes has been spoiled; many a powdered, well-dressed maccaroni sent home for the evening.' And to conclude this period in Dr Johnson's own words, 'Many a full-flowing perriwig moistened into flaccidity.'

Whether Edinburgh had cleaned up its act by 1773, something invaded the famous nostrils that night. Unlike Cardinal Wolsey traversing London, Johnson did not possess an orange to hold to his nose, and, perhaps pretending teasingly to mistake Boswell for the High Street's open-sewered efflux, said, 'I smell you in the dark.' Traditionally Edinburgh's pet name of *Auld Reekie* comes from the smoke of the many chimneys as viewed from across the Forth by the people of Fife. One man over there is said to have timed his family's call to prayer by the appearance of the first plumes. But, given this famous odoriferousness, the term 'Reekie' may also have had a more personal root.

James's Court was named, not, as I had first hoped, after Boswell, but after its speculative builder, James Brownhill, who set it up as a prosperous enclave, guarded by a porter. The Court has an excellent public house called *The Jolly Judge*. Boswell's house no longer exists, destroyed by fire in 1857, eighty-four years

WALKING UP THE HIGH STREET.

after the great guest and his young host walked arm-in-arm into it.

Margaret Boswell, the wife, behaved towards Johnson with sublime courtesy. She had anticipated his strenuous liking for tea, and also insisted that 'she would give up her own bedchamber to him, and take a worse'. Not that she necessarily knew it yet, but she had just conceived, or was about to: their second child, Euphemia, was born in May 1774, and Boswell would be absent for the first three months of the pregnancy. Due to depart Edinburgh in a few days, he would not return from the islands until November, imperfect domesticity for a woman who had already miscarried twice in four years of marriage.

Boswell had wed (on 25 November 1769) his cousin, Margaret Montgomerie, two years older than him. A stable and loving woman, she had little money and few expectations. She showed a steadfast fondness for Boswell, despite his many excesses. For the first few years of their marriage, he remained faithful to her, and then, twelve months before Johnson arrived in Scotland, Boswell lapsed with an Edinburgh whore and emerged duly venerealised. Margaret's knowing commonsense overcame any distaste or hurt, and James embarked upon the habit of medical attention for his moving parts.

Not far from James's Court, in the Librarian's office at the National Library of Scotland, on loan from the Scottish Portrait Gallery, hangs a group portrait of the Boswell family. They numbered five at the time of sitting: from left to right – Boswell, his small son, an older girl, a baby and Mrs Boswell.

The children and Mrs Boswell are well and fashionably dressed, and James, brown-eyed, large-nosed, with a small but voluptuous mouth, is seedily prosperous. His wig needs a little repair (had it once been 'moistened into flaccidity' under a discharging chamber-pot?) The boy, aged seven or eight, his sister's arm draped over his right shoulder, wears a weskit under a green suit with large buttons, and carries in one hand a plum, or a ball, in the other a kaleidoscope or toy telescope. The girl, who looks doubtful and pensive, has some gold work on her dress with touches of pink in the white fabric, and broad bands of cream satin round the skirt: her bonnet resembles a pretty, upturned pot of white satin. She has long brown hair, and the bows and ringlets of a sweet and thoughtful pre-pubescent child; she and her brother resemble their father. The baby, a charming little thing in tiny red slippers, seems to be standing on its mother's lap, an arm around Mamma's shoulder. With none of the gravity of its siblings, it has a falling mop of auburn curls, one small hand raised between breast and throat; from a third of the way down, its dress has seven repeating bands of white satin. It could be a boy – or a girl: I wish we could bend low and look upwards as with dogs.

Not even the blandest artist could have avoided the strength of Mrs Boswell, the picture's greatest concern – she is direct, a firm and clear-eyed woman, if never a *belle*, nor fairylike, nor pert. A flat, slightly domed bonnet fronted with a silver-white satin bow sits on her frizzy grey hairstyle, pompadourish enough to be a wig. The bonnet is held in place by a thin black cord tied gently in a looped knot around her strong neck, the neck almost of a well-bred swan. At her breast, cream lace cascades in discreet folds; she wears a chocolate-brown dress of shiny fabric with lace at a cuff resting on mid-forearm. She shows a long, slender left wrist and hand, and on her ring finger a single, slim gold ring. Is that a thin bangle she wears above her elbow? Her right hand protects the small child, and rests on its right hip: of the group only the baby is not looking at the artist.

Resolute Mrs Boswell has a high and open face; she, too, has a long nose. An unvoluptuous mouth; she wears a light touch of rouge; a sturdy frame, although most of her upper body is lost within the folds of her dress and the dimness of the portrait; her wide, warding-off eyes say that she knows her chosen ground and will protect it vigorously, and is aware of what she must do in order to prevent life overwhelming her. So – Boswell satisfied his sense of reality in the woman he married, and his fantasies in the women with whom he cavorted? Johnson, in a letter to a friend who had evidently enquired as to his impression of Boswell's wife, described her as having 'the mien and manners of a gentlewoman, and such a person and mind as would not in any place either be admired or condemned. She is, in a proper degree, inferior to her husband; she cannot rival him, nor can he ever be ashamed of her.'

'Darling Peggie', however, came generally to associate her husband's excesses with his visits to London, to his great literary friend. Therefore, whatever her courtesy, she did not like Johnson. He was sufficiently disconcerted by her attitude to mention it in the third sentence of his very first letter to Boswell when the tour ended. From London on Saturday, 27 November 1773, he wrote to James, 'I know Mrs Boswell wished me well to go.'

For years afterwards Johnson continued to challenge Peggie's lukewarmth; it became a small obsession, obvious in even a brief audit of the many letters quoted in Boswell's *Life*.

29 January 1774: Make my compliments to Mrs Boswell, and tell her that I do not love her the less for wishing me away. I gave her trouble enough, and shall be glad, in recompense, to give her any pleasure.

5 March 1774: I hope Mrs Boswell and little Miss [Veronica, their oldest child] are well. When shall I see them again? She is a sweet lady, only she was so glad to see me go, that I have almost a mind to come again, that she may again have the same pleasure.

27 May 1775: Pray teach Veronica to love me. Bid her not mind mamma . . . Make my compliments to Mrs Boswell, though she does not love me. You see what perverse things ladies are . . . When she mends and loves me, there may be more hope for her daughters.

27 August 1775: Of Mrs Boswell, though she knows in her heart that she does not love me, I am always glad to hear any good, and hope that she and the dear little ladies [by now Euphemia had been born] will have neither sickness nor any other affliction. But she knows that she does not care what becomes of me, and for that she may be sure that I think her very much to blame.

16 November 1775: I know that she does not love me; but I intend to persist in wishing her well till I get the better of her.

23 December 1775: My compliments to Mrs Boswell, who does not love me.

Twelve months later, that is, three years after their Highland jaunt, the grape-shot still flew.

21 December 1776: I congratulate you on the increase of your family, and hope that little David is by this time well, and his mamma perfectly recovered. [Alas: the baby, born in November, died the following March.] If Mrs Boswell would but be friends with me, we might now shut the temple of Janus. [One of the many classical allusions with which Johnson so enjoyably illuminated his meanings: the ancient Romans opened the doors of the god Janus's temple when war broke out, closed them when peace descended.]

Early in 1777, a thaw began, and Boswell conveyed his wife's compliments: 'She is to send you some marmalade-of-oranges of her own making.' Johnson replied on 3 May : 'Tell Mrs Boswell that I shall taste her marmalade cautiously at first. *Timeo Danaos et dona ferentes*. ['I fear Greeks bearing gifts': Johnson's affection for Virgil.] Beware, says the Italian proverb, of a reconciled enemy. But when I find it does me no harm, I shall then receive it and be thankful for it, as a pledge of firm, and, I hope, unalterable kindness. She is, after all, a dear, dear lady.'

In summer another gift followed and on 22 July 1777, Johnson wrote to Mrs Boswell: 'I received it as a token of friendship, as a proof of reconciliation, things much sweeter than sweetmeats, and upon this consideration I return you, dear madam, my sincerest thanks. By having your kindness I think I have a double security for the continuance of Mr Boswell's, which is not to be expected that any man can long keep, when the influence of a lady so highly and so justly valued operates against him. Mr Boswell will tell you that I was always faithful to your interest, and always endeavoured to exalt you in his estimation.'

Even in the natural curriculum of courtesy to a friend's wife, how many people have ever used the English language with such sparing elegance as Johnson? And how touching that such a giant of thought and literature could not bear to be disliked by the wife of a friend.

Thereafter, any references Johnson makes to Mrs Boswell while corresponding with her husband have a softer ring to their tone. He refers to her as 'my dear enemy', and Boswell as 'my dear friend'; he proffers advice on Peggie's incipient tuberculosis: 'London is a good air for ladies; and if you bring her hither, I will do for her what she did for me – I will retire from my apartments for her accommodation' (this, five years after that first night they met in Edinburgh); and calls her Boswell's 'naughty lady' – surely a misplaced term, given Boswell's multifarious and poxy infidelities.

The journey to rapport had been slow and tactful. Margaret Boswell's antipathy certainly had its roots in associating Johnson with her husband's sexual misdeeds in London. She also disliked Johnson's household slovenliness. He let candlewax drop on her carpets – when the flame did not shine bright enough, he merely turned the candle upside down. Yet, Mrs Boswell played an enabling part in launching Johnson's Scottish tour comfortably. For three days she was hostess to the many people who called on the great man now sitting in her home: Boswell hauled them in like a barker to a sideshow, and his wife's role can be divined from sprinkles of detail in Boswell's account of the tour, although he did not, of his own admission, keep 'a regular full journal till some days after we had set out from Edinburgh'. (Johnson offered absolutely no account at all of his time in Edinburgh, calling it 'a city too well known to admit description'.)

On Sunday Mrs Boswell catered for visitors at breakfast, lunch and dinner, with cups of tea or glasses of wine in between. On Monday, she provided similarly: 'so far as wisdom and wit can be aided by administering agreeable sensations to the palate, my wife took care that our great guest should not be deficient.' For Tuesday's meals she had at least eight extra visitors, two at breakfast, five at lunch, one at supper. Johnson wrote to his great friend and near-*inamorata*, Mrs Hester Thrale of Streatham, '. . . There was such a Conflux of company that I could scarcely support the tumult. I have never been well in the whole Journey [so far], and am very easily disordered.'

One sympathises with Johnson, especially bearing in mind his physical size – small rooms cause a kind of compression of the shoulders in large men. We ought to sympathise even more with the woman of the house. When David Hume lived in rooms in the same block as Boswell (by 1773 he had moved to the open spaces of the New Town) he found the house 'very cheerful and elegant, but too small to display any talent for cookery' (his great passion – 'I have just now a receipt for making *Soupe à la Reine* copied with my own hand. For beef and cabbage and old claret nobody excels me.')

Down the Royal Mile from James's Court, in the Huntly House Museum, among the wooden water pipes of Boswell's day, and near the cathedral bells 'rung for the pleasure of the citizens during the dinner hour', a room of the period has been reconstructed, and it defines claustrophobia – low-ceilinged and crammed with furniture. Mrs Boswell endured the invasion of such a room during Johnson's stay, indulging her husband's passion for the company of famous people no matter how fetid Sam – and they – may have been.

When Johnson rose on the Sunday, his first morning in Scotland, he played with Boswell's daughter Veronica, then aged four months, and born on the March night of the premiere of Oliver

VERONICA A BREAKFAST CONVERSATION.

Goldsmith's *She Stoops to Conquer*. Is she the girl in the portrait –
the boy being Alexander, and the baby Euphemia? The Boswells
had five children who lived: three girls, Veronica, Euphemia and
the youngest child, Betsy; and two boys, Sandie, later Sir Alexander, and James junior. Dr Johnson told his friends that he considered himself a bad prospect as a parent, and never wished to
father; nevertheless, he frequently showed that he found small
children attractive, calling them 'pretty dears'. He played easily
with little Veronica Boswell, a glow of intimacy which sent the
child's father dangerously close to ecstasy: 'She would be held
close to him; which was a proof from simple nature, that his figure
was not horrid. Her fondness for him endeared her still more to
me, and I declared she should have five hundred pounds of
additional fortune.' For Heaven's sake, Boswell – pull yourself
together! The child may have been fascinated with the novelty
of such a face as Johnson's. Anyway, will you surely have five
hundred pounds in your estate when you die?

Breakfast guests included Mr Scott (of the headache), and Sir William Forbes of Pitsligo. A year older than Boswell, a banker and in due course Boswell's executor, Forbes also became a writer, with a life of James Beattie, and an autobiography, *Memoirs of a Banking House*. As it might well do in Scotland, the talk turned to law, with Forbes suggesting that 'an honest lawyer should never undertake a cause which he was satisfied was not a just one.' Johnson skittled Forbes's notion, with the first extended piece of aphoristic Johnsonian wisdom Boswell records. His summary of his views, exhibited in this, the first time Scotland encountered his conversation, might have been an exhibition piece designed especially to impress the Scots, and as it introduces me to Johnson's clarity and eloquence, it is worth quoting all Boswell's account of it.

'Sir,' said Mr Johnson [Boswell vacillated between calling Johnson 'Dr' and 'Mr', until he became more accustomed to the honorary doctorates bestowed upon Johnson by Dublin and Oxford], 'a lawyer has no business with the justice or injustice of the cause which he undertakes, unless his client asks his opinion, and then he is bound to give it honestly. The justice or injustice of the cause is to be decided by the judge. Consider, sir: what is the purpose of the courts of justice? It is, that every man may have his cause fairly tried, by men appointed to try causes. A lawyer is not to tell what he knows to be a lie: he is not to produce what he knows to be a false deed; but he is not to usurp the province of the jury and of the judge, and determine what shall be the effect of evidence, – what shall be the result of legal argument. As it rarely happens that a man is fit to plead his own cause, lawyers are a class of the community, who, by study and experience, have acquired the art and power of arranging evidence, and of applying to the points at issue what the law has settled. A lawyer is to do for his client all that his client might fairly do for himself, if he could. If, by a superiority of attention, of knowledge, of skill, and a better method of communication, he has the advantage of his adversary, it is an advantage to which he is entitled. There must always be some advantage, on one side or other; and it is better that advantage should be had by talents, than by chance. If lawyers were to undertake no causes till they were sure they were just, a man might be precluded altogether from a trial of his claim, though, were it judicially examined, it might be found a very just claim.'

As with Oscar Wilde a century later, did Johnson truly speak with such grammatical perfection? Perhaps Boswell edited him to advantage. Or did the pair of them go over and over what Johnson thought until Boswell finally wrote it down in the way Johnson wanted? My scant knowledge of them had at least told me that Boswell's biographical method occasioned recurrent literary discussion, that no writer of note would have embarked upon a career as biographer without contemplating what Boswell did and how, and all the pursuant questions of the distance between biographer and subject, the sympathy, empathy, antipathy, the path of objectivity through the minefield of subjectivity. Ahead of me, and throughout Boswell's *Journal of a Tour to the Hebrides*, lie clues that Johnson may have influenced what Boswell wrote about him.

First impressions of their relationship may be gleaned within paragraphs of Johnson's arrival. They had walked side-by-side, Boswell reported the tease about smelling, and Johnson meant to feel at home in Boswell's home. Boswell's text throws out compliments as a thurible puffs incense. As early as Edinburgh, we see an older man with an acolyte who, I sense, wants something – something more than just the pleasure and *cachet* of basking in Johnson's light. In which case, Boswell had long ago measured his man astutely. His *Life* confirms Johnson's attitude towards relationships, and to judge from the demeanour reported by Boswell in his Hebrides text, and even an early glance at his massive biography, he had long gauged that Johnson, for his own reasons, could be ideally accessible.

Johnson had no sons of his own; he had inherited a stepdaughter who, by the time he knew her, was already too grown for him to have a powerful say in her upbringing. Accordingly, he bestowed his affection paternally and altruistically on young men of Boswell's age – Mr Scott, for instance, and Robert Chambers who travelled as far as Newcastle with him, and many others. Such men exercised – in Boswell's case knowingly – the informal collegiateship of adding to one's education, fitting oneself better for life, by seeking the company of remarkable elders. This practice had come as directly into Johnson's society as if derived immediately from the same principle among the Greeks whom Johnson so much admired. He indulged it copiously; he never stinted with his knowledge – indeed he handed out advice based on his learning and experience whether or not the recipient had asked, and the tutorials of this social *academe* were often couched in affectionate terms. For example, seven years earlier, in July 1766, Boswell had finalised his legal studies; he passed his Scots law examinations, defended the required Latin *Thesis in Civil Law*, and thus became an advocate. Immediately after these accomplishments, he wrote a detailed account to Johnson, enclosing a copy of the thesis.

As a father might, Johnson began his reply with corrections of Boswell's Latin: 'In the beginning, *Spei alterae*, not to urge that it should be *primae*, is not grammatical: *alterae* should be *alteri*.' After this wristy flash of syntax, Johnson's letter becomes tender and congratulatory without surrendering authority: 'You have done exactly what I always wished, when I wished you best. I hope that you will continue to pursue it vigorously and constantly. You gain, at least, what is no small advantage, security from those troublesome and wearisome discontents, which are always obtruding themselves upon a mind vacant, unemployed, and undetermined.' If Johnson had such capacity for generosity and affection towards his friends, no wonder so many people surrounded him, whatever his irascibility and personal eccentricities – and conversely, no wonder Boswell was able to get so close.

The full list of folk who called upon Johnson at Boswell's house in those first few days represents the professional, academic and social establishment of Edinburgh at that time – a gauge of Johnson's pulling power. Today, towards what contemporary literary figure staying in one's house would one be able to attract such tides of eminent visitors as Johnson did at Boswell's? It also draws a picture of the vigour of Edinburgh's cultural firmament.

After breakfast on Sunday, Johnson went out to worship and met Scotland's most senior law officer, the Lord Chief Baron Orde, who accepted an invitation to lunch the following day.

Back at James's Court, still accompanied by Scott and Forbes, Johnson retired to his room for a short while, taking with him some pious reading matter, a book of sermons called *Ogden on Prayer*, which crops up so repeatedly in Boswell's *Journal of a Tour* that in Rowlandson's notorious cartoons it peeks out of Boswell's pocket. When Johnson emerged from Ogden, Boswell introduced him to a new arrival in the drawing-room, Robert Arbuthnot, a gentleman of a celebrated literary kinship: John Arbuthnot, his 'relation' (Boswell's word), was regarded by Johnson as pre-eminent among writers in Queen Anne's reign, a man of letters as potent, though never as famous, as his friends Swift and Pope.

The topics of conversation throughout the early part of Sunday ranged from that excellent disquisition on lawyers by Johnson, to emigration, at the time, as Johnson would increasingly discover, a noticeable social feature in post-Jacobite Scotland. Johnson produced an original view: he believed that emigration weakened the country of departure, that shrinking communities tended to make do, and thereby reduced the standard of their living. 'Men, thinly scattered, make a shift, but a bad shift, without many things. A smith is ten miles off: they'll do without a nail or a staple. A tailor is far from them: they'll botch their own clothes. It is being concentrated which produces high convenience.'

They discussed the philosopher David Hume, whom Johnson loathed for his atheism, his prose style, his hostility to the English, and his arguments. Johnson's faith depended profoundly upon the prospect of gaining the sight of God; Hume denied the possibility of such, or any, eternity. Throughout Johnson's barbed discourse, Boswell never once revealed (nor did anyone else in the room) that Hume had lived in the very same block. It would have been difficult to do so in the face of Johnson's fierceness: he said Hume's head had corrupted Hume's heart, '. . . or perhaps it [his heart] has perverted his head. I know not whether he has first been a blockhead and that has made him a rogue, or first a rogue and that has made him a blockhead.' Boswell suppressed the remark in his published *Journal*, calling it 'something much too rough'.

Peggie served veal; Messrs Scott, Forbes and Arbuthnot were joined by 'another gentleman', an unnamed student friend of

Boswell's. In the afternoon Dr William Robertson arrived, the clergyman and biographer to whom Boswell had appealed for help in luring Johnson north. Too late to eat with them, Dr Robertson accepted a glass of wine, and the talk turned to Edmund Burke, whom Johnson praised highly for his 'great variety of knowledge, store of imagery, copiousness of language', but maintained firmly that the man had not an ounce of wit – 'Burke never once made a good joke.'

This led to discussion of how men divided their capabilities, with Johnson unable to understand how a man could apply himself to one thing and not to another. While Robertson claimed it had to do with the difference between judgment and imagination, Johnson gave the opinion that it was a matter of how the mind came to be directed by its owner: 'Sir, the man who has vigour, may walk to the east just as well as to the west, if he happens to turn his head that way.' Later, Boswell ushered forward 'two good friends of mine, Mr William Nairne, advocate, and Mr Hamilton of Sundrum, my neighbour in the country'.

Now I begin to understand Boswell's everlasting fame: already, in the first twenty pages of his *Journal of a Tour*, the full, wide value of him begins to open up. Even though he concedes that he kept only sketchy accounts of these social encounters – 'I have preserved nothing of what passed' – he none the less wipes the grime from his window and lets us see into that eighteenth-century Edinburgh drawing-room. He may have written it all down for any number of reasons, some or all of which I hope to find out, but the by-product has been a huge literary and historical generosity: he makes voyeurs of us, his readers, and so we eavesdrop on that after-dinner conversation of a summer Sunday night in Edinburgh.

They talked of books and of the theatre, discussing Fielding, as a similar dinner table today might raise Graham Greene, or Gabriel García Márquez. Likewise, as a comparably interested *milieu* in the late twentieth century would debate Olivier's *Coriolanus*, or, say, contrast Jonathan Pryce's *Hamlet* with Ian Charleson's, over supper Johnson talked of current styles in tragic acting – of which he was contemptuous, but still managed to be amusing. He believed 'the action of all players in tragedy is bad. It should be

a man's study to repress those signs of emotion and passion, as
they are called.'

Few tourists stroll in and out of James's Court. As I reached
it, the sun cut a diagonal light across one high, bare wall. No
drawing-room windowpane to rub, and look through, breathing
condensation and nose whiteflattened against the glass, peering in
at the eighteenth-century talkers. The surrounding walls and other
courts fuel imaginings of that Sunday, when the company listened,
flattered no doubt to find themselves astride (if they were) Boswell's and Johnson's literary and theatrical references. These men
had heard of Johnson, as one has seen the light of a far-off star,
and here – the comet is landed in their company. Did their cheeks
flush a little; did they shine in the glow; did they nod and smile,
anxious to agree, or prepared courageously to counter; were they
stimulated, excited and, whatever their Scots prickly evenness and
commonsense, a little thrilled, Mr Nairne, and Mr Arbuthnot,
and Mr Hamilton of Sundrum? We are not told where Mrs
Boswell was during all of this fertile conversation: flitting in and
out, I suppose, supervising a maid with a tray, eyeing Johnson
discreetly but not un-severely, fretting over the temperature of
the syllable-heavy, claustrophobic room? And did they all – even
for the moment Peggie – forgive Boswell his act as Johnson's
straight man?

Waterproof clothing works both ways. Ergo, what is designed
to keep rain out, tends also to keep in perspiration, an arresting
little discovery after scaling Edinburgh's heights, hardly yet the
rough tundra of the Highlands. In the tall enclave of James's
Court, the sun and the north wind fought a draw. From Johnson's
and Boswell's diverse accounts of their 'jaunt', of what they had
seen and done and said on the Saturday night and Sunday, a timetable materialises of Johnson's movements, encounters and conversations. His stay in Boswell's house can be traced quite clearly,
and almost fully illustrated, from his arrival through to his departure on the Wednesday morning. Next day, Monday, Johnson
went forth after breakfast to view Edinburgh, and returned to
receive callers, and sit with guests at all meals. Tuesday reverted
to Sunday's shape, with Johnson staying indoors and holding forth

while Boswell wheeled them in. On Wednesday morning they went to the port of Leith, and sailed across the Firth of Forth, bound for points north and west.

Not everybody liked this famous pair. Boswell suffered many bites from those who saw him as a toady and parasite; his contemporary, the satirist Anthony Jasquin, commented:

> See Boswell – but who for such drudgery more fit? –
> Collect the vile refuse of poor Johnson's wit

and William Cobbett complained of 'Old dread-death and dread-devil Johnson, that teacher of moping and melancholy . . . If the writings of this time-serving, mean, dastardly old pensioner had got a firm hold of the people at large, the people would have been bereft of their soul. These writings, aided by the charm of their pompous sound, were fast making their ways, till light, reason and the French revolution confined them to the shelves of repentant, married old rakes and those of stock-jobbers with young wives standing in need of something to keep down their unruly ebullitions.' Cobbett had colleagues in opinion: what is the connection between critical intemperance and envy?

A little such hostility surfaced in Edinburgh, when they took Johnson to see the Parliament House on the Monday. Inside the courts, not sitting during August 1773, a local gentleman exacted a sly revenge on Boswell for Johnson's many and famous anti-Scottish remarks. Mr Henry Erskine was introduced to Johnson; a few minutes afterwards, as the little party moved off, Mr Erskine slipped a shilling quietly into Boswell's hand, as one tips a lackey, and whispered thanks for the introduction to his 'bear'.

Johnson's nickname had preceded him to Scotland. He had been given it by the poet Thomas Gray, whose 'Elegy in a Country Churchyard', odes and other poetic works were known not to have been well-regarded by Johnson. He called Gray 'a dull fellow', and his opinion would certainly have reached the poet in the tiny bullring of eighteenth-century London's literary gossip. Gray, obviously stung, gave shambling, brown-coated, ungainly Johnson the nickname *Ursa Major* – although followers of Johnson may also be pleased to interpret it as a sort of astronomical compliment. After the Highland trip ended, when Margaret Boswell boiled over with twin resentments – of Johnson's influence over her husband, and with dislike of the great man's ungainly appearance – she spat the nickname at her husband. 'I have seen many a bear led by a man,' she observed, 'but I never before saw a man led by a bear.'

Next on Monday, they took Johnson to see the Laigh Hall, under repair when I visited; a large undercroft, fit for a French cathedral (Cromwell used it as a stable), tall pillars, stone walls, rectangular vaulted ceilings and a huge fireplace. Johnson viewed politely the Advocates' Library, and by now the word was spreading that the great man (or Great Bear) had arrived and was perambulating around Edinburgh's most famous buildings. People gathered, both to look and to hear. Johnson did not fail them, and spoke for their benefit one of his most lasting remarks, which Boswell recorded both here and in the *Life* (where he related it to Johnson's weekly outpourings for *The Rambler*). 'There was, by this time, a pretty numerous circle of us attending upon him. Somebody talked of happy moments for composition; and how a man can write at one time and not at another. "Nay, (said Dr Johnson), a man may write at any time, if he will set himself doggedly to it."'

'Doggedly': it gives the impression of tediousness; as Johnson used it, he must have meant persistence and the kind of virtuous tenacity attributed to faithful hounds. Yet, his Dictionary gives 'dogged' as 'sullen, sour, morose, ill-humoured, gloomy', a definition range which brings new thought to bear upon the effort of writing as experienced by Johnson himself: did he mean that in order to write all the time, or as often as is needed to complete an individual work, or amass a large body of writings, a man must write regardless of his mood or emotional condition? This would answer to some extent my query formed early on in this growing acquaintance – of how Johnson managed to compile such a huge body of work when, as I am beginning to learn, he suffered both physiological and emotional indifferences. To support Johnson's seemingly curious usage, and the notion that he himself wrote whether feeling 'sullen, sour, morose, ill-humoured, gloomy', my rattle-bag mind whirrs and clicks, and out of the slot pops Trollope's old character in *The Last Chronicle of Barset*, who remarks, in a universally apt and by now familiar, perhaps famous, piece of advice, 'It's dogged as does it. It ain't thinking about it.' Johnson, perhaps even without thinking, found no obstacles to his writing and his conversation; Mozart, Blake and Joyce all made observations suggesting they enjoyed a similar unimpededness.

Now they showed Johnson 'the great church of St Giles', which at that time, Boswell says, had 'lost its original magnificence in the inside by being divided into four places of Presbyterian worship'. Later re-ordered and its appearance improved, the cathedral still feels as disappointing as Johnson found it. They next led him down the Post-house Stairs (long disappeared) and bade him look up from the Cowgate to the great heights of thirteen storeys whence he had just descended: the University; the Royal Infirmary; to Holyrood Palace, and home to Boswell's for a lunch of in-season grouse, attended by six others: they included the blind poet Thomas Blacklock, Burns's spiritual mentor, and the Duchess of Douglas, 'an old Lady [wrote Johnson to Mrs Thrale] who talks broad Scotch with a paralytick voice, and is scarce understood by her own countrymen; The Lord Chief Baron, Sir Adolphus Oughton, and many more.'

At table they discussed Swift, whom Johnson, as he always did, dismissed: 'Swift is clear, but he is shallow', and even suspected him of plagiarism: 'I doubt if the The Tale of a Tub was his.' An argument began regarding the authenticity of Ossian, the controversial *oeuvre* of James Macpherson. This, one of literary Scotland's (and England's) most vexed questions of the day, recurs throughout their journey: did Macpherson truly meet people in the remote hinterlands from whom he 'wrote down' Gaelic snatches of the works of a great ancient Celtic poet called Ossian? The poems had already caught on widely; philosophers, writers, European heads of state and artists embraced them long after Johnson and others had denounced them as forgeries. They captivated Napoleon, who read them on his campaigns. Owing to their effect upon the King of Sweden, at whose court the Dublin physician, Sir William Wilde, served, Oscar Fingal O'Flahertie Wills Wilde

44

received his first two names from Oscar, the grandson of Finn McCool, the giant hero-god of Celtic mythology, and Macpherson's title – *Fingal, an Epic Poem in Six Books.*

No record exists of any afternoon excursion into the streets of Edinburgh: guests may have lingered; and for supper, four people arrived, at Boswell's invitation: 'We had Dr Cullen, his son the advocate, Dr Adam Fergusson [head of the University: they had met him earlier in the day while out sightseeing] and Mr Crosbie, advocate.' The legal and academic circles of Edinburgh had already been well represented to Dr Johnson by Boswell: in any case, it was perfectly natural that Boswell's barrister-at-law colleagues and friends should have called. In Dr Cullen, Boswell introduced another stratum: he had a chair of Medicine at Edinburgh. More than a decade later, Boswell would appeal to him for medical advice when Johnson's life entered its last year.

Supper's talk rattled on haphazardly – witchcraft; sleepwalking; whether the oran-utang might be taught how to speak; the stage again: Johnson said that when he watched an actor whom he personally knew, the performance never seemed to transcend the actor's own personality. All round, he gave out a versatile catalogue of opinions. On witchcraft: 'If moral evil be consistent with the government of the Deity, why may not physical evil be also consistent with it?' Of somnambulism, a topic raised and dominated by Dr Cullen, Boswell regrets that he made no note. The oran-utang issue arose when somebody mentioned the unconventional, pre-Darwinian Lord Monboddo (whom we shall meet *en route*). Lord Monboddo had been known to believe that the oran-utang could be taught to speak, and Johnson offered a devastatingly terse reduction: 'But, sir, it is as possible that the oran-utang does *not* speak as *that* he speaks . . . I should have thought it not possible to find a Monboddo; yet *he* exists.'

James's Court today, though high and spacious, has no personality, but it is still possible to recapture the feel of Boswell's time in others nearby, and the next Court into which I walked, Ladystairs, has a museum in the Primrose family ancestral house to the memory of the great local writing trio, round-headed Walter Scott, long-faced Robert Burns and beloved Stevenson.

When entering narrow doors, a heavy rucksack surrenders much of its practical value. The stairs, says a museum notice, 'had been built with steps of varying heights', a canny protection against thieves, 'that persons unfamiliar with the dwelling might betray their presence by stumbling'. Above the wooden-galleried landing, with its model of the Scott Monument, hangs a modern tapestry of the famous three. The collections in the glass cases include a lock of Scott's hair, and a penny bank savings-box made in the shape of Burns's cottage; downstairs, the cabinets display articles of Stevenson's clothing which eerily appear in the photographs taken at his house in Samoa. A golf-ball dug up at Swanston Cottage, a boyhood retreat, had the initials 'RLS' carved on it. On the walls hang photographs of his French artistic haunts, Siron's Inn in Barbizon, and the other village in the Forêt de Fontainebleau, Grez-sur-Loing.

Seemingly, I cannot avoid Stevenson. Turn a corner through a court, to where I can see in the sunshine right across Edinburgh, and his phrases come to life. 'From their smoky beehives, ten stories high, the unwashed look down upon the open squares and gardens of the wealthy; and gay people sunning themselves along Princes Street, with its mile of commercial palaces all beflagged on some great occasion . . .'

In my head I have Johnson and Boswell, and for the moment Stevenson has my heart: between them I am directed to the mind and the spirit of this city, and although it has the second largest tourist population in the United Kingdom after London, not enough people can know of the variety of Edinburgh. If it stood alone in a marsh, it would always feel and look like a capital: less decrepitised than modern Dublin, immodestly aspiring towards the classicism of Rome and Athens, reluctant to be as intimate as Glasgow. The stones which built it, as cold and formed as Calvinism, also built the Bank of England and Buckingham Palace, quarried from the Pentland Hills in the distance. Should Scotland ever revolt in favour of republican status, conspirators could still flit in and out of the wynds, closes and lands that herringbone this Royal Mile. A 'wynd' is the one that twists between the sky-high houses; a 'close' logically does not have an opening at the other end; a 'land' was an Edinburgh apartment house as far back as the early seventeenth century, Gladstone's Land and Blackie's Land stand not far away from where Boswell lived. Johnson wrote to his friend Mrs Thrale in Streatham, 'Boswell has very handsome and spacious rooms level with the ground on one side of the house, and on the other four stories high.'

Conspiracy is the cornerstone of plot. From the inner streets of Venice, innumerable lanes dart like stilettoes into the shadows; some emerge with a sly grin on the Grand Canal, some never do, concluding in corners, or small courtyards hung with fronds, or blank walls with impassive doors and the little silver tongue of a fountain hanging from the wall. In London, Dickens's vapours still come off the river at Southwark bridge. Here in Edinburgh, I have found a conspirator's paradise – high windows for lookouts, narrow alleys for skulking, broad streets for pretence. Like David Balfour in the first two pages of *Catriona*, 'Here I was in this old, black city, which was for all the world like a rabbit-warren, not only by the number of its indwellers, but the complication of its passages and holes.' *Treasure Island*, they say, might have been the rock in the lake in the Heriot Row gardens, into which Robert Louis Stevenson could see from his bedroom window over in the New Town.

Let me reckon with Stevenson once and for all (on this trip, at any rate – I can always return to him). As the list of writers for whom I retain affection grows harshly shorter, my devotion to him cannot be as simple as a long gratitude for his services to my childhood, or admiration of his triumph over the adversity of poor health. Do I identify with his nature – capable equally of sunny friendliness and choleric irascibility? His impressive self-discipline appeals: after he had burned the first draft of *The Strange Case of Dr Jekyll and Mr Hyde* – though furious at his wife's criticism, he acknowledged the accuracy of her judgment – he then olympically wrote a new and final version, sixty-four thousand words in six days, took two more days to copy it, and sent it off to his publisher. Images from his life and writings: his engineers' family who built the Bell Rock lighthouse, a tourist attraction in its day; his dour father who charmed ladies in the New Town with dinner conversation; his ageing mother hoisting her skirts and standing in the warm surf of Samoa, and sitting in a wicker throne like the queen of the islands; the spy-glasses, revenue officers, lanterns and doubloons of *Treasure Island*; the House of Shaws in *Kidnapped*; Soledad and Silverado; Modestine the donkey in the Cevennes and her dogged pace, the gloom of his travels to and in America, and all his stardust facts, true or false. On the cobbles of Edinburgh I now resolved to get him out of my system as quickly as possible and get on with the job.

Stevenson's lifelong ill-health kept him in constant inward touch with two emotional forces – children's imaginations and awkward fatherly affections, both of which depend upon the view from the pillow, or, as he called it in a poem from *A Child's Garden of Verses*, 'The Land of Counterpane'. He began *Treasure Island*, originally called *The Sea Cook*, when, during rainy school holidays in Braemar, he helped his stepson, Lloyd Osbourne, with a drawing of an imaginary map. Other Stevenson works continued to appeared in publications such as *Young Folks* – appropriately, since they sprang straight from boyhood imagination. *Kidnapped*, for instance, specifically owed to early nightmares, and yarns of Jacobite intrigues a century earlier.

As for fatherly affections – although he and his puritanical father diverged severely in RLS's student days of hashish, sex and rejection of Scotland's typically intense religious faith, he remained faithful to the image of the man who routed the nightmare hag of childhood. Last night in London, I read again my favourite book dedication (a toss of a coin between it and Jan Morris's in *The Oxford Book of Oxford*, which she: DEDICATED GRATEFULLY TO THE WARDEN AND FELLOWS OF SAINT ANTONY'S COLLEGE OXFORD – *EXCEPT ONE*). Stevenson, in both *Kidnapped* and *Catriona*, addressed prefatory letters to his old drinking crony from Edinburgh days, Charles Baxter, and in the *Catriona* dedication, written in Samoa, Stevenson concluded with a moving paragraph which subliminally addresses his hundred-years-war between wanderlust and homesickness, and includes a manifest of tenderness.

> You are still [Charles] – as when first I saw, as when last I addressed you – in the venerable city which I must always think of as my home. And I have come so far; and the sights and thoughts of my

youth pursue me; and I see like a vision the youth of my father, and of his father, and the whole stream of lives flowing down there far in the north, with the sound of laughter and tears, to cast me out in the end as by a sudden freshet, on these ultimate islands. And I admire and bow my head before the romance of destiny.

This, and many other moments in Stevenson, pins Edinburgh to my mind, and give the place an excitement unseemly in a city of such restraint, and a warmth with which the place is not habitually credited. But other men's words are like prison guards, they make us hostage to 'the youth of my father and his father'; and on this journey, even though travelling in the lee of a giant such as Johnson (and a star, it has to be said, such as Boswell), and further prepared to be lured aside by myriad others, I hoped I should find it easier than ever to break out. So I dropped Stevenson back on the bookshelf, resisting the temptation to put him in the rucksack too. On the Royal Mile I now wrestle myself back to my two companions and their earlier times.

Johnson did not visit Edinburgh castle until his return from the Hebrides in November. Although large architectural changes have taken place, the general shape of this high part of the city remains the same – the broad Royal Mile runs for one mile and one hundred and six yards from Edinburgh Castle to Holyrood Palace. The tolbooths of Johnson's day, and the encroaching buildings narrowing the street at Netherbow Gate have been trimmed back, but he certainly saw the beams of John Knox's house (another gentleman outside the pale of Johnson's approval). On the way down the Canongate, the cemetery on the left contains the bones of two remarkable Scots, one of whom Johnson met, and never, regrettably, the other. 'Here are Deposited the remains of Adam Smith, *Author of the Theory of Moral Sentiments* and *The Wealth of Nations*. He was born 5th June 1723 and he Died 17th July 1790.'

Johnson knew him well, and struck good and bad sparks off him. When Boswell reported a criticism of *The Wealth of Nations* on the grounds that Adam Smith had never been in trade and therefore might be equated with 'a lawyer upon physick', Johnson replied, 'It is not necessary to have practised, to write well upon a subject.' On the other hand, when Adam Smith sang the praises of Glasgow too fulsomely for Johnson's astringent ear, he lunged at him, 'Pray, Sir, have you ever seen Brentford?'

Some yards away from Smith lies Robert Fergusson, a rakehell Scots poet already ill and a year away from mad death in the Bedlam at twenty-four years of age when Johnson visited Boswell, an occasion Fergusson 'commemorated':

> Welcome, thou verbal potentate and prince!
> To hills and valleys, where emerging oats
> From earth assuage our pauperty to bay,
> And bless thy name, thy dictionarian skill . . .

Robert Burns wrote Fergusson's epitaph; 'O thou, my elder brother in misfortune/By far my elder brother in the Muse.' Stevenson, born a century later, loved Fergusson as much for his vivacious life as for his verses: 'that poor white-faced drunken vicious boy from St Andrews . . . so clever a boy, so wild, of such a mixed strain, so unfortunate, born in the same town with me, and, as I always felt rather by express intimation than from evidence, so like myself . . .' Wishful thinking, born of independence and rebelliousness, and a shared uncertain physiology: Stevenson's Fergussonian identification swelled largest whenever his health worsened. This stone in Canongate graveyard was erected by Burns, and Stevenson wished to renovate it, but died too soon to do so, too soon for many things.

I keep looking for elegances and beauties that I know Johnson also experienced: the sunny view of the Forth from the top of the hill; the wonderful roof beams at Parliament House, like golden mace-tips or inverted chess-pieces overhead the port-faced barristers in their whispering robes; the satisfactoriness of the arduous cobbles; the eccentric gables and sagging lintels of the residential courts; the swoop of the city, visible at every wider corner; the high skies; and the earthen ramparts of Arthur's Seat; the crag and pile of the castle, irresistibly provocative.

He visited Holyrood House, whose serene frontage opens benignly. 'We surveyed,' wrote Boswell, 'that part of the palace appropriated to the Duke of Hamilton as Keeper, in which our beautiful Queen Mary lived, and in which David Rizzio was murdered.' Openings to the public are curtailed when the Queen comes to Holyrood every summer: other members of the royal family stay quite often: I take the tour. A well-constructed fairhaired woman leads us through many rooms and chambers: all the hangings and furnishings prove that monarchs must live with the past to affirm their future. My interest centres on Johnson's, and thus the lurid events of the dreadful night of 9 March 1566. A brass plaque marks the spot in a second-floor tower room where Rizzio, Mary's effective but conceited Italian secretary, died of 'fifty-six wounds with a dagger, which was left in him', inflicted by Mary's husband, Darnley, and a bunch of conspirators; Mary, several months pregnant with James VI of Scotland and James I of England, not twins, one and the same, fled. Johnson quoted the ballad of the occasion, 'And ran him through the fair body.' The tour party nods and smiles and looks up, yes, yes, wonderful ceilings and tapestries and bed hangings, such geniuses, the stuccodores of Holyrood. Out of all the tapestries of Diana the Huntress, the blue-and-white tiles of Delft along the fireplace, and the *baldacchino* hanging from chains above Queen Mary's glorious bed, I will longest remember faces from the royal portraits, especially Darnley, tall and haughty, like a member of some upper-class, late medieval rock-and-roll band.

'And we were too proud,' wrote Boswell, 'not to carry him to the Abbey of Holyrood House, that beautiful piece of architecture, but, alas! that deserted mansion of royalty.' I want to know whether Boswell told Johnson that the ancient ruined abbey at the side of the palace once offered succour to paupers and all other impecuniaries. Would Johnson have made a pointed and informed observation? Even in my short acquaintance with him, he often spoke better wisdom when drawing on the experience of others, and perhaps his own memories of poverty might have proven too sharp to give him objectivity. In 1756 and again in 1758 Johnson was placed under arrest for debt, and was bailed out by the people to whom he sent begging letters.

The old Infirmary has gone; only the gates remain, relocated in nearby Drummond Street; Johnson enjoyed the University library, and relished the conversation of the Librarian who doubled as Professor of Oriental Languages; the fine Adam Old Quad was in the process of being built, and Boswell reported the then College buildings as 'indeed very mean'. Johnson applied the same epithet more liberally when he summarised his walkabout to Mrs Thrale: 'Most of their buildings are very mean, and the whole town bears some resemblance to the old part of Birmingham.'

Part of the enjoyment I want from this journey will come from discoveries for my own life, outwith (as they say here: I wish it were used generally) Boswell and Johnson. Beneath the heights of the High Street and the Old Town, down in the deep wastes of the Cowgate, near Fishmarket Close and Stinking Vennel, I found on a wall a plaque put there a long time after Johnson, and nothing to do with him.

'To the memory of James Connolly, born June 5th, 1868, at 107 Cowgate. Renowned International Trade Union and Working Class leader. Founder of the Irish Socialist Republican Party. Member of the Provisional Government of the Irish Republic. Executed 12 May 1916 at Kilmainham.'

Predictably, one more writer intrudes on me:

> I write it out in a verse –
> MacDonagh and MacBride
> And Connolly and Pearse
> Now and in time to be,
> Wherever green is worn,
> All changed, changed utterly:
> A terrible beauty is born

– I fail to remember any more, only the lucid frightfulness of Yeats's refrain. So Connolly was born as he died – in the shadow of a jail. The last of the 1916 Leaders to be executed in Dublin, his death, propped up in a bath-chair, too gangrenous in the leg to stand, caused the outcry that led, after five more years of blood, to the Anglo—Irish Treaty.

'Tuesday, 17th August [this is Boswell]: Sir William Forbes came to breakfast, and brought with him Dr Blacklock' – again. The fifty-three-year-old poet's blindness gave rise to much speculation

Sir Joshua Reynolds's portrait of Dr Johnson: his 'countenance was the cast of an ancient statue . . . His person was large, robust, I may say approaching to the gigantick, and grown unwieldy from corpulency.' James Boswell, *Life of Johnson*

The first of William Daniell's aquatints: Armadale, where Johnson set foot on the Hebrides as the discomfited guest of Sir Alexander Macdonald who, according to Boswell, 'has disgusted all mankind by injudicious parsimony'.

Raasay, to which Johnson crossed from Skye: 'If I should tell at a tea table in London, that I have crossed the Atlantick in an open boat, how they'd shudder, and what a fool they'd think me to expose myself to such danger.'

Dunvegan Castle, where Dr Johnson wore his wig turned inside out as a night-cap and Lady Macleod said, 'I have often seen very plain people, but anything as ugly as Dr Johnson with his wig thus stuck on, I never have seen.'

Johnson wrote to Mrs Thrale from Skye, 'No part that I have seen is plain; you are always climbing or descending, and every step is upon rock or mire. A walk upon ploughed ground in England is a dance upon carpets, compared to the toilsome drudgery of wandering in Skye . . .'

George Willison's portrait of James Boswell: 'I gave [Johnson] an account of my comfortable life as a married man, and a lawyer in practice at the Scotch bar; invited him to Scotland, and promised to attend him to the Highlands, and Hebrides.'

among Johnson and his London contemporaries as to how he could write descriptively. Johnson, an answer for everything, ventured that as a lame man may be carried from room to room, Blacklock might exercise his poetry on the basis of the world as he had encountered it in the works of others. Now when they met, they engaged cordially, Johnson as ever at his humane best among afflicted people, and they talked of morality, of life's grand design, and of Johnson's plain belief that 'there is, and ever has been, an all-powerful intelligence.'

No sightseeing took place on the Tuesday. Five people came to lunch: Sir Alexander Dick; Lord Hailes; Mr Maclaurin, another fellow-advocate of Boswell; Dr Gregory, a physician; and Boswell's uncle, Dr John Boswell with his twin conflicting reputations – for libertinism and egregious religious zeal. Respectively, the guests again reflected Boswell's selection from the best Edinburgh could offer. Alexander Dick, older than Johnson, later corresponded with the Great Bear, offering him rhubarb when Johnson ailed, and telling him how, owing to Johnson's remarks on the general tree-lessness of Scotland, a local nurseryman could report that as a result of the publicity accruing to the publication of Johnson's Hebrides *Journey*, demand for trees and hedges had 'doubled, and sometimes tripled'. Lord Hailes, a law lord of the Dalrymple family, had an interest in philology which rendered him surrealistically pedantic on the bench: he once questioned the validity of a lawsuit on the grounds that the word 'justice' had been misspelt in one of the affidavits. He numbered among those lampooned by Boswell and the third luncheon guest, John Maclaurin, in a ragged ballad called 'Court of Session Garland':

> 'This cause,' cries Hailes, 'to judge I can't pretend,
> For *justice*, I perceive, wants an *e* at the end.'

Regarding the Tuesday, Boswell writes, 'This was one of Dr Johnson's best days. All was literature and taste, without any interruption.' Lord Hailes took the surest route to flattering Johnson, by telling him that he had unmasked the authorship of a piece Johnson wrote pseudonymously. Johnson: 'No one else knows it.'

Next, Hailes ticked off Johnson for misrepresenting in one of his poems the beauty of two royal mistresses, both of whom had been famously ugly. Boswell does not record Johnson's response; in any case, umbrage seems unlikely, since Hailes was giving Johnson what writers crave, the compliment of attentive reading.

John Maclaurin took up the baton of flattery, seeking the aid of Johnson's learning. 'He produced two epitaphs upon his father, the celebrated mathematician. One was in English, of which Dr Johnson did not change one word. In the other, which was in Latin, he made several alterations.' The later hours of Tuesday brought two more visitors. Another advocate, Alexander Murray, later Lord Henderland, 'did not venture to say any thing, that I remember,' observed Boswell, a little disappointedly, 'though he is certainly possessed of talents which would have enabled him to have shown himself to advantage, if too great anxiety had not prevented him'. One more Boswell relative rounded off the callers, Dr Alexander Webster, an Edinburgh clergyman, 'who, though not learned, had such a knowledge of mankind, such a fund of information and entertainment, so clear a head and such accommodating manners, that Dr Johnson found him a very agreeable companion'. And so, after three excessively sociable days, to bed: the two gentlemen had girt themselves to leave for the north and west next morning.

One last look at James's Court: if our atmosphere retains, somewhere in the skies above our heads, all the conversation that has ever been spoken, in the way the deeper mind is said to store all experience in its caverns, and if one day some physicist or psychic invents a divining rod to draw down and tape-record all that has ever been said, all the talk that still floats about up there like thermals or radio waves, then this is the place to set up the equipment. James's Court may be disappointing now, but for those three brilliant days it was the repository of worthwhile exchange, debate and Boswellian pride, and the best hospitality professional Edinburgh, then in a brilliant period, had to offer.

Through Milne's Court, I clopped with care down the vast steps again, towards the valley of Princes Street. Approaching the

National Gallery from the rear I stopped, pretending to look down at the railway as it led from Waverley Station, but in truth to watch surreptitiously a couple of buskers. One, with white spiky hair and the voice of a walrus, sang a Country & Western hymn called 'The Last Mile of the Day', in which I discerned only one line, 'If I walk in the pathway of duty'; the other, a face violent with methylated spirits, played a harmonica and produced more spittle than the waves along the shore of the Kingdom of Fife. The contrast quickens: back at Holyrood, I saw a picture of the Duke of Hamilton receiving the Order of the Thistle, the highest order of chivalry in Scotland.

In the National Gallery, I perk up at Bellotto's 'View of Verona with the Ponte delle Navi in 1745'. Johnson never got to Italy, though he much longed to. 'A man who has not been in Italy, is always conscious of an inferiority, from his not having seen what it is expected a man should see. The grand object of travelling is to see the shores of the Mediterranean. On those shores were the four great Empires of the world; the Assyrian, the Persian, the Grecian, and the Roman. All our religion, almost all our law, almost all our arts, almost all that sets us above savages, has come to us from the shores of the Mediterranean.' The gallery has a preponderance of Dutch painters, a collection in this Reformation city born of a fellow-feeling for the Protestant ethic, and links in law and education: Boswell, for example, studied law in Utrecht.

I came in to even the keel of my mood, to get away from royalty's excesses and the busker's spittle – and to chase up another Johnsonian connection, his dear friend Joshua Reynolds; and there he is, sure enough, with 'The Ladies Waldegrave' painted in 1780, 'for the sitters' great-uncle, Horace Walpole'. Even if William Blake hated him, Reynolds has always cut an attractive figure, not because of his Beethovenesque eventual blindness, or even for the swagger of his reds and blues, unheard-of until then in an English artist, nor even for his vision – he painted as if writing history – but for a reason whose risky sentimentality I acknowledge. It was the first fact I ever knew about Reynolds, and it is this: on the day he heard of Oliver Goldsmith's death, Reynolds threw down his brushes, burst into tears and could, he said, paint no more that day, not even the long noses of the Waldegraves, Laura, aged 20, Maria 19 and Horatia, 18.

Places first encountered in the literature of childhood never wholly surrender their innocence. Looking back from Princes Street, the Edinburgh houses reaching sheer up to the castle, as high as the towers of San Gimignano although less Florentine or ducal, still seem made of gingerbread. The city has a number of reputations; socially it can be as cold as failure; financially as precise as Euclid; politically as rough-edged as Detroit. The New Town in Edinburgh remains a sleek and peaceful demesne of glossy cobbles. Brass door furniture, high windows, tall doorways – everything has been painted or polished and ringed with confidence. A bird flying low over these roads of financial virtue might feel obliged to land carefully, like a guest placing boots on a white carpet. None the less, the New Town has an enchantment, especially in a winter twilight when the haar from the Firth sharpens the air, or the fog from a chapter of *Jekyll and Hyde* makes you watch out for Stevenson, in his wide-brimmed hat, with his fast-stepping nervous slouch, talkative, quicksilver Stevenson, on his way home to Heriot Row.

CHAPTER III

'The first experiment of unfrequented coasts'

THE WALK FROM THE NEW TOWN to the water of Leith takes half an hour – along oriental streets: Indian spiced food, a veterinary surgeon's storefront, pawnbroking, men's tailoring, a model railway shop. In W. Brown, Fishmonger's window, the black flat ray with the spiky teeth was as angry as could be; at close quarters, the drab plaice has a bright colour on every scale. A bakery breaks the heart, with eclairs, cream-crowned baps, coconut-flaked raspberry bomblets polished with glinting jam, and little currant buns smiling like demons, all smooth and buttery. In the bicycle shop flashed a helmet black and shiny as pornography.

The private houses belong in Stevenson's era rather than Johnson's, and beneath their prim cornices proliferates this appealing seediness; Leith is like the Dublin of *Ulysses* or the Limerick of my grandfather – a dingy port of small old radial streets, blind alleys and myopic warehouses. The Leith police dismisseth us; say that without lisping and you are deemed sober. Empty yards and small warmongering ships all grey and stencils; huge wooden supports at forty-five-degree angles against so many of these lovely old warehouse walls. You take my house when you do take the prop that doth sustain my house. 'Of the Merchant of Venice,' wrote Johnson, 'the style is even and easy with few peculiarities of diction or anomalies of construction. The comic part raises laughter and the serious fixes expectation.' How, oh how, can he get so much meaning into one short sentence? Perhaps by emulating his great hero, Dryden, who said of Shakespeare, 'He was the man who of all modern, and perhaps ancient poets, had the largest and most comprehensive soul.'

SETTING OUT FROM EDINBURGH.

I needed a boatman, to ferry me over the Forth into history, into Wednesday, 18 August 1773. In the aftermath of rain, I walked out, past the new oyster bars and yuppified warehouses of refurbished Leith, by Yardheads along long docks to the security men behind dense grilles at the entrance to a private dockyard. One, a burly and pleasant man with a single tooth pegged off-centre behind his upper lip, asked why go to Inch Keith, the place was full of rats. He showed no surprise at the explanation, and directed me to the Port Authority. Along the Port Road, another Farne Island materialised in *Oxscar*, the name of a small lights vessel moored behind a frigate. Rain threatened again; a man with a long beard, a hat, a gaberdine coat and a green scarf over one eye, looked at the sea and other things in an absent manner. He loped undirectedly in the open space: the bushy whiteness of his hair and whiskers made him look like a senile Arctic fox.

Times have changed at the water of Leith – here where Mary, Queen of Scots, came in, and where in the centuries past, these wharves teemed like insect colonies, as all great seaports did in the old tales of silk, kegs of brandy and tall-masted whalers, who once put out from here for the freezing North Sea. No wonder Stevenson wrote *Treasure Island*.

Johnson noticed that even then Leith had little enough bustle left in her. Already, Glasgow's docks had begun to triumph, and would further increase when mail to, and tobacco from, North America flourished. 'He observed of the Pier or Quay, "You have no occasion for so large a one: your trade does not require it: but you are like a shopkeeper who takes a shop, not only for what he has to put into it, but that it may be believed he has a great deal to put into it." ' They set sail for the coast of Fife, but 'Dr Johnson determined we should land on Inch Keith.'

As it will over and over again, Johnson's interest in the anthropological and social essence of Scotland now appears. He recounted detail only where it generated thought; his rigorous mind's second-best exercise (after his powerful drive of enquiry) was a natural capacity for editing out the superfluous. In this he was unquestionably English, as non-Celtic as can be.

A short chain of contacts produced a ferryman: Bill Simpson, taxidriver by day, fisherman by desire. He would take me to Inch Keith, but not until the morning. I spent the night in Leith, reading Johnson and Boswell. At one in the morning, still uninclined to go to bed, I went to the nearest open pub. People sat by a fire, quiet in their talk, no jukebox, no music, no pool table, no darts, just dim light and a few foreign voices, as well as the lilt of Leith. No smell of sandalwood, nor offers of mysterious trinkets from dark strangers with gleaming teeth; no 'tales, marvellous tales of ships and stars and isles where good men rest'. The sailors of Leith know colder waters: they go to Shetland and Orkney and Viking places, not Flecker's Samarkand or black Cyprus.

From the shore at Newhaven, just east of Leith, Inch Keith and Kinghorn, the pair's first joint destinations, may both appear clearly, weather permitting, as it did at ten o'clock next morning. To the right a long slipway reaches down to the water, and the harbour, with a high sustaining wall, feels safe; Bill Simpson has a refreshing face and nature. Upstream to the left, the Forth Bridge painters descend from Sisyphus rolling his stone uphill: no sooner have they finished than they must start again. Not a cloud in the sky: we were not to sail as Johnson and Boswell did: Bill Simpson warmed up an engined rubber inflatable. Inside it, we perched in tandem on a machine that looked like a motorbike without wheels. Luckily for the inflatable, I travelled alone, whereas they had with them Boswell's servant, Joseph Ritter, 'a Bohemian; a fine stately fellow above six feet high, who had been over a great part of Europe, and spoke many languages. He was the best servant I ever saw,' says Boswell. Mr Nairne the advocate went with them as far as St Andrews, earning himself one of Johnson's elegant compliments (for by now, and deliciously, we have at last entered Johnson's own account of the trip): Mr Nairne 'could stay with us only long enough to show us how much we lost at separation'.

Johnson lightened his load at Edinburgh. According to Boswell, 'from an erroneous apprehension of violence, Dr Johnson had provided a pair of pistols, some gun-powder and a quantity of bullets.' He must have expected bandits, or perhaps republicans, Jacobites, or some rabid sort of anti-Hanoverians; Culloden's lurid impressions. Reassured of safety, Johnson stowed his private munitions in a drawer at Boswell's house. He also left behind one of the most valuable books ever lost to literary history, 'one volume of a pretty full and curious *Diary of his Life*', later destroyed. Oh, how Boswell, the true biographer, wishes Peggie had used the three months of their absence to copy Johnson's *Diary* clandestinely. Honourableness often being counterproductive to any recorder of the lives of others, Boswell feels certain that 'the theft, *pro bono publico*, might have been forgiven.'

We growled out of the little harbour of Newhaven and then roared into the open Firth. Sunlight glinted on the purple rucksack as it lay like a stowaway in the bow of this rubber water-scooter; we were a huge dayglo red bug hurtling across the glassy water of the Firth, still a smooth sea, but hard under the boat's rapid keel, like a carpet without underlay on a concrete floor. The Firth is about five and a half miles wide at this point, and Inch Keith three miles away. Light spray fogged my vision, with no chance to wipe my glasses: otherwise a lovely morning. Along the Firth, the ramparted banks were built by the last war's POWs, who were also detained on Inch Keith. When the face gets extremely cold, the mouth begins to salivate automatically. A small formation of seabirds flew high above, like a flight of honour. Cormorants flapped lazily off; the Chinese ring their throats so that they cannot swallow the fish, and must therefore bring them home. In the distance, along the path of the sun, the tip of a wreck showed, foundered twenty years ago. The lighthouse on Inch Keith can be seen for twenty-two miles, and the beam flashes a white light every fifteen seconds.

Inch Keith straight ahead, we rounded a corner in the open sea and entered what felt like an ancient Napoleonic, even Elizabethan, harbour – cliff-high walls with a skin of the ocean's dragon-green. Immediately, the water calmed immensely. We drew up beside a powerful, rusting ladder, and a horde of barking dogs descended upon us; they smelt like a pit of mange, especially the greyhounds; one of these animals had three legs. The island would also yield some horses, and the largest imaginable pig, as big as a dirty pink whale – and one human inhabitant, a reclusive woman. Which of them is she – Prospero, Caliban or Ariel?

Whatever did Johnson think he was doing: ascending rough Scotland with the gadfly Boswell? 'Here, by climbing with some difficulty over shattered crags, we made the first experiment of unfrequented coasts. Inch Keith is nothing more than a rock covered with a thin layer of earth, not wholly bare of grass, and very fertile of thistles. A small herd of cows grazes upon it every summer. It seems never to have afforded to man or beast a permanent habitation.' Since then it has: prisoners of war, garrisons, lighthousemen, and now this female St Francis, saviour of infirm and unwanted animals.

If Inch Keith is to prove in any way typical of what Johnson said he wished to see in Scotland, then a man who combined intellect with, apparently, a sharp worldliness, may have had other reasons for coming so far – especially at his time of life. The suspicion, already forming in Edinburgh, began to harden. Did a mutual purpose, never stated or perhaps never recorded, underpin the relationship between Johnson and Boswell, a motive jointly and severally shrewd – but not necessarily honest? Accepted that Johnson had a huge natural curiosity, anthropological and otherwise, was it really strong enough to encourage him, with his creaking, wheezing physique, to places such as Inch Keith? Probably yes, but only up to a point. Did something other draw him north – the belief, perhaps, that he could control, or certainly influence, at least one major biography of himself? In accepting Boswell's invitation to tour Scotland, he could both appease his eager would-be biographer by paying him a three-months-long compliment, and at the same time plumb deeply the waters of Boswell's attitude towards him, sounding for insincerity or malice.

Certainly, Boswell did not write about Johnson in a wholly objective way; once his writing-in-transit began in earnest some time after their tiny invasion of Inch Keith, his *Journal of a Tour to the Hebrides* oozes admiration and obeisance. He bobs to his Great Bear, walking backwards ahead of him, strewing Johnson's pathway with compliments. Even on Inch Keith he saw to it that Johnson 'stalked like a giant among the luxuriant thistles and nettles'. Therefore – did Boswell learn to write so sycophantically, and at times so excellently, under Johnson's editorial eye?

A little along from the slimy jetty, Bill Simpson opened a garage and drew out a tractor. The whole island was not 'full of noises, sounds and sweet airs, that give delight and hurt not'; Prospero, for all his eventual sadness, had a better time of it. Did Shakespeare really write no more after *The Tempest* because he developed arthritis? This maimed rock, once useful, now a haven for rejected creatures, had no sound of its own on a calm morning; only an occasional gull, or a wheeling 'kitti-wake, kitti-wake'. No bell, no waterfall, no pleasant local music to leaven the disuse, to give some little honour to the senses in this gap-toothed place full of old buildings: Inch Keith is a miserable joint.

The tall oceangoing sailing ships once came in here to take on their fresh water from Inch Keith's three wells, and some comfort came from the picture of the high furled spars of the three-masters, *Hispaniola* and friends, sitting snooty and assured just outside the harbour waiting for their longboats to return. On a little scraggy shoulder of grass and rock stood a rescued horse with a tattered blue blanket thrown over him, and beyond him the world's biggest pig, a gargantuan, if shoddy, Empress of Blandings. 'Wallowing' feels too thin a term for this beginning-of-the-world-primordial-ooze creature. If it ever got up the speed to charge, it would, like Desperate Dan, burst a hole its own shape in the side of anything. It could carry a grubby Nabob ceremonially into town; this pig could feed one of those Highland weddings that last for three days.

The path to the lighthouse winds hard and steep. Each World War pressed Inch Keith into service: all the troop houses now have their rafters showing: they were truly 'jerrybuilt', both in the mistaken sense of having been built to fight 'Jerry' as in 'German', and in the true sense: the term derives from 'Jeremiah', as in 'doomy'. Up close, all lighthouses, even those no longer manned like Inch Keith, have an unexpectedly dramatic presence. Looking back from the tractor's perch, the sunlight danced on the water, and at the end of its pathway rose a wonderful Disney-ish view of Edinburgh, with the castle clearly visible. Down to the left of the island, towards the point, more dereliction, a wrecked landscape.

Dr Johnson, who 'found only the ruins of a small fort', made observations on 'the different appearance' Inch Keith would have made 'if it had been placed at the same distance from London, with the same facility of approach; with what emulation of price a few rocky acres would have been purchased, and with what expensive industry they would have been cultivated and adorned'. Boswell, showing up the early discrepancies between them in their accounts of the journey, quotes what Johnson actually said on Inch Keith: 'I'd build a house, make a good landing-place, have a garden and vines, and all sorts of trees. A rich man of a hospitable turn, here, could have many visitors from Edinburgh.' Throughout the journey, Johnson returns to the fantasy of owning an island home.

We reached the lighthouse, passing, by the gateway, the house where Catherine Allen, the hermitess, lives. Miss Allen has statues of little animals dotted around her pathways and her childlike garden. She discourages visitors. The last resident keepers of the Inch Keith light lived in a row of low buildings all along to our right, white walls, neat green woodwork; and behind them stagger the derelict houses of lighthouse families of a century ago.

From the great 'H' for 'helicopter' in the yard may be seen Inch Keith's clearest and most specific connection with the two eighteenth-century wanderers – an ancient notation over a doorway: 'The fort,' wrote Boswell, 'with an inscription on it, *Maria Re 1564*, is strongly built.'

Inside the yellow tower, exquisite brass still survives from the great lighthouse days when the Stevenson family became folk heroes for their building of lighthouses and beacons, the Bell Rock, the Skerryvore, and fifty others. A profound spiral stairwell, a wide benign corkscrew, leads to the light. Set in mercury in a large rectangular matte-black boxed grill a few feet deep, the Inch Keith light shines from rows and rows of silent, chrome-bright bulbs, through hedges of filters and flanges, a long way from the great paraffin candlepower of the original. However efficient the new technology, ancient forces will always have their say. On the outside of the light's glass, the keepers have strapped a little fierce statue of an owl – the only way they can hope to deter starlings and seabirds from crashing into the glass.

The hermitess Miss Allen, a young-ish and shy woman, stood on the quay when we descended, greeting men from Edinburgh ferrying provisions to her island. We shook hands; the privacy in her face obliged me to swallow the two hundred or so questions I wanted to ask her. What Allen was she (as if she might be Irish)? Did people intrude? What did she do in the evenings? In the winter? Did she ever go to the mainland, or did she feel, as the lighthousemen said of old, 'The land is the danger'? Standing alone within this small knot of people and animals, in her soft, hesitant non-metropolitan voice, she volunteered a smidgen about her concern for the animals, a three-legged dog being a nifty conversational ice-breaker. She spoke little, and I uncharacteristically even less, as if tongue-tied at the fortitude of her solitude.

Johnson called out to Boswell, 'Come, now, pay a classical compliment to the island on quitting it.'

'I happened, luckily,' says Boswell, pretending futilely not to preen, 'in allusion to the beautiful Queen Mary, whose name is upon the fort, to think of what Virgil makes Aeneas say, on having left the country of his charming Dido: *Invitus, regina, tuo de litore cessi.*' A portrait of the biographer as show-off: 'Reluctantly, O queen, I departed your shore.'

Our departing inflatable rounded the corner of Inch Keith's pier, and set its red bouncing snout towards the shore of Fife. The sun gave light, no warmth, on the hard Firth; by the time we reached the far shore, ten minutes away, a large, cool if bright, haze had dropped by. Kinghorn's little old harbour has a sandy beach, as well as a high wall. I paid the ferryman, and Bill Simpson wheeled and left, romping across the sparkling water back to Leith.

When the pair and company landed on that eighteenth-century August Wednesday, a chaise awaited, and after lunch – neither writer records where they ate, or whether they picnicked: Boswell merely says 'we dined at Kinghorn' – they set off, with Mr Nairne the advocate, and Joseph, Boswell's servant, riding alongside. Inch Keith can be seen more clearly from Kinghorn than from Edinburgh. 'We found it a Rock somewhat troublesome to climb,' wrote Johnson to Mrs Thrale, 'about a mile long and half a mile broad.' Hardly so, in length anyway. In the fort he 'measured two apartments of which the walls were entire and found them 27 feet long and 23 feet broad': Johnson carried a renowned walking stick (it grew famous in Scotland, as we shall discover) into which he had inserted measuring marks at a foot and a yard. 'The Rock had some grass and many thistles, both cows and sheep were grazing.' Did he mean the two species of animal, or that Inch Keith had only a pair of cows? 'There was a spring of water. The name is Inchkeith. Look on your maps. This visit took an hour. We pleased ourselves with being in a country all our own, and then went back to the boat, and landed at Kinghorn, a mean town, and travelling through Kirkaldie [*sic*], a very long town, meanly built, and Cowpar [*sic*], which I could not see because it was night, we came late to St Andrews, the most ancient of the Scotch universities, and once the See of the Primate of Scotland.' It was for them an unmemorable journey; it remains so, and one may be grateful to Kinghorn for not raising one's expectations with any undue grandeur.

Outside Kinghorn, the road lifts like a golf course, with, fortunately for a walker, footpaths, although they switch allegiances all the time, first one side of the road, then the other. On the grey sea of Fife to the right, a curiously-shaped ship sat doing nothing. Are there ship-spotters the way there are train-spotters? The blue spaces in the sky widened among muttons of cloud. This land undulates, knolly terrain, where the fields have a tailored quality, as smooth as human bodies. If Nature did not fashion the ground in this way, these rounded breasts and long shoulders may conceal tumulus graves full of Celtic, or, up here, Pictish, riches. On Inch Keith ten thousand years ago, someone used implements made from the antlers of red deer. Along this country, they buried their dead in stone-lined graves with a cup of mead, a weapon and a piece of personal jewellery such as a jet necklace. Thus, the deceased person could cross to the shore of the Next World, as we living souls hope to set forth each day – refreshed, equipped and presentable. From Kinghorn to Kirkcaldy these fields suggested all such things, and the view of them, and the wish to have a wonderful instrument with which to X-ray the deep earth, alleviated the sweating ups-and-downs of the roads.

Looking back, those four nights and three days that Johnson spent at Boswell's house in Edinburgh constitute something of a little *mirabilis* period in English letters. If such social occasions are not the actual foundations of literature, they at least decorate cultural history: Coleridge and Wordsworth walking the Quantocks drafting the first concepts of *The Ancient Mariner*; Henry James in correspondence with Stevenson on the art of fiction; Ford Madox Ford and Joseph Conrad in endless literary colloquy. That image of Johnson in Boswell's house has chiefly the value of display, but it is the display of a man at home in discussion of all manner of humanity – the law as well as literature, faith as well as witchcraft, and in general a sensibility of life in keeping with the soul of a great artist, who, in Johnson's case, seems to have talked his Art at least as much as he wrote it.

Once again, what I cannot yet divine is whether Johnson deliberately, artistically almost, strove to make his spoken sentences so lucid and economical, or whether Boswell rewrote them in the telling? Or whether, indeed, Johnson edited Boswell's re-telling, so that what we get in Boswell is a highly-wrought, refined 'literature' purporting to be reported speech? Every which way, we frequently receive Johnson's spoken thought and feeling in a fashion that encourages us to think again, or supports us in our efforts to make sense of our lives – the Art, truly, of conversation.

Kirkcaldy, the 'lang toon', was too lang for my liking, by at least a mile. On the right stretches a port of sorts, on the left some discos and sprinklings of night life, with names like 'Jackie O'. One finds the same dated charm on Greek islands, where their nightclubs are named for stars who fell, or faded out, or, like Mrs Onassis, departed the limelight a dozen years ago. The question of lunch began to rumble. At supper one night not long after they met, Johnson said to Boswell: 'Some people have a foolish way of not minding, or pretending not to mind, what they eat. For my part, I mind my belly very studiously, and very carefully; for I look upon it, that he who does not mind his belly will hardly mind anything else.' Other men in books who walked seem to have mastered the whole awkward business. Hazlitt, when going a journey, loved the prospect of taking his ease at an inn, having come to 'some old town, walled and turreted . . . or some straggling village, with the lights streaming through the surrounding gloom'. I bought an apple in Kirkcaldy, and by now the grey had begun to come home again to the sky. When Johnson stayed in Streatham with the Thrales, he proved as powerful a trencherman as that famous eater, Agatha Christie. Hester Thrale recorded in her diary, 'Mr Johnson's own Pleasures – except those of Conversation – were all coarse ones: he loves a good Dinner dearly, eats it voraciously & his notions of a good Dinner are nothing less than delicate: a Leg of Pork boiled until it drops from the bone almost, a Veal Pie with Plums and Sugar, & the outside Cut of a Buttock of Beef, are his favourite Dainties, though he loves made Dishes, Soups, &c., souses his own Plum Pudding with melted Butter, & pours Sauce enough into every Plate to drown all Taste of the Victuals.'

I knew only two things about Kirkcaldy before I walked into it – that it once possessed the world's largest linoleum industry, and that it gave birth to Adam Smith. Now I know that it must be the stringiest small town I have ever seen, notwithstanding one or two endless narrow villages on the edge of the Vendée, or that

long street of St Ninian's Whithorn, due west of here on the far
side of Scotland, over in Galloway; that the 'l' in Kirkcaldy is
silent; that the end of the lang toon lifts in a devilish sharp little
hill; that huge mills rise from it; and that I began to take a wrong
turning there. The error yielded one piece of fruit – Dysart, a
pretty little place with an East and West Quality Street, a Neuk
or two, and a Hot Pot Wynd. I did not work out my misnaviga-
tion until (lesson for life) I had gone too far. From Dysart I walked
onwards, on the A955, by West Wemyss, through Coaltown of
Wemyss and East Wemyss, into Buckhaven. Neither Johnson nor
Boswell mentioned any of these places, and the modern map now
suggested that they took an upper road from Kirkcaldy to Cupar.
Few roads perform such a service to drabness as the road from
Dysart to the Wemysses. Inside the broken walls, under the trees,
the National Detritus Association had been at work, assiduously
spreading old armchairs, discarded basins and saucepans, broken
sanitary ware, burst plastic bags yielding variegated rubbish, beer
cans and bottles and inexplicable spars of coloured sponge foam.
Occasionally a field had prettiness; otherwise, the blight of
departed energy blanketed the place. This had been coal country,
and under grass as thin as an old woman's hair, the black baldness
of the earth showed not, as I romantically wished, seams of coal,
but tips of slag. Lines of empty cottages – one was called *Plantation
Row* – made Coaltown of Wemyss even sadder, and the black and
brickwork architecture leaves the village in desperate need of a
colourist. At a bus stop I asked an elderly couple the simplest way
to Cupar from East Wemyss and they told me there was no simple
way, that 'the best method of getting to Cupar' was from Leven,
or 'go back to Kirkcaldy'.

'The roads are neither rough nor dirty; and it affords a southern
stranger a new kind of pleasure to travel so commodiously without the interruption of toll-gates.' Early in his travels, Johnson
found things to praise in Scotland, although a few days later he
complained that 'the roads of Scotland offer little diversion to the
traveller, who seldom sees himself either encountered or overtaken.' We begin, now, to become familiar with a refrain that
runs all through Johnson's Scottish journey – his views on trees:

'The variety of sun and shade is here utterly unknown. There is no tree for either shelter or timber. The oak and the thorn is equally a stranger, and the whole country is extended in uniform nakedness, except that in the road between Kirkaldy and Cowpar, I passed for a few yards between two hedges. A tree might be a show in Scotland, as a horse in Venice.'

The error had cost me several miles, and on the hill past the school at Kennoway on the upper road it began not so much to rain as to mist profusely. From behind a high hedge (perhaps one of the few growths of Johnson's time) a pleasant middle-aged woman with a dog queried my choice of walking weather, to which, lacking deific powers, I had no defence. And who are all these people sitting in their cars at the roadside, with no visible intent? They do not sleep, or eat, or drink, or read newspapers, they sit there, merely contemplating the windscreen. Another thing – why is it, that when the walker turns to face the oncoming traffic in order to give the driver a better view, the driver takes advantage and aims his vehicle at the walker – those wing mirrors, wide as a door, lethal as a club. The old Irish saying, 'That rain would wet you,' is not at all ludicrous; this mist drifted in everywhere. A car kindly stopped, the female representative of a vodka firm, with much arcane knowledge about pub competitions, where, several nights a month, she presents the prizes for the quiz, or the darts, or the pool table.

In the Kingdom of Fife, one may find travellers and other old systems. Early last century, a tinker found a great Viking hoard in the ground out here somewhere, and sold the silver to a clock-maker in Cupar. As a consequence, local people claimed that time was kept more accurately along this east-coast former peninsula than anywhere else in Scotland. The mist through which I had walked, and then the steaming windows of the vodka lady's car, all but obscured my view of the countryside. After the dull tankers sledging through the grey sea of Fife, and little towns with unpretty terraces called 'Forthview', what feels like a high coaching road runs through soft hills, between farms and timber. As the sun came out, occasional respectable ladies in plump jodhpurs and cheerful complexions exercised three-quarter-bred hunters. Cupar, with many spires, appeared at the bottom of a long

winding drop in the looping road: it looks at first like a large
Swiss valley town, and is pleasant to walk through: a street called
Bonnygate; tractors in the traffic; small, trim, sweet-faced yet
severe women; firm neo-classical architecture; estate agents called
Pagan Osborne Grace and Calders; a talkative traffic warden who
didn't come 'from anywhere near here: I'm a stranger, I'm from
Kirkcaldy.' The town's flow is dominated by a T-junction, which
on the left heaves the traveller towards long streets and churches,
and to the right makes way for a winged monument and the
countryside again.

Johnson and Boswell drank tea at Cupar, and so did I. At the
table I read Johnson's terse account: 'passed through Kinghorn,
Kirkaldy, and Cowpar, places not unlike the small or straggling
market-towns in those parts of England where commerce and
manufactures have not yet produced opulence'; and Boswell's:
'We stopped at Cupar, and drank tea. We talked of Parliament;
and I said, I supposed a very few of the members knew much of
what was going on, as indeed very few gentlemen know much
of their own private affairs.

> JOHNSON: Why, sir, if a man is not of a sluggish mind, he may
> be his own steward. If he will look into his affairs, he will soon
> learn. So it is as to publick affairs. There must always be a certain
> number of men of business in parliament.

Johnson the Tory pressed on to opine that 'Influence must ever
be in proportion to property,' dismissing Boswell's fears that 'the
common people may be oppressed.' Then they left Cupar; 'We
had a dreary drive,' Boswell continues, 'in a dusky night, to
St Andrews, where we arrived late. We found a good supper at
Glass's inn, and Dr Johnson revived agreeably.'

So did I, but not at St Andrew's. Measuring the time against
the distance on foot, I took a local bus, undramatic and swaying
on its springs, full of silent people, through farmland and woods.
In St Andrews, where I intended to spend the same amount of
time sightseeing as they did (about thirty-six hours), I caught
another bus in darkness and rain, and made a nine-mile digression
to Crail to stay one night with friends. They live an exhilarating

two-mile walk from the town, in a long house made of joined consecutive farm cottages by the sea; he an Irish professor and man of letters, A.N. Jeffares, a Wexford man, the biographer of Yeats and encourager of later poets; Johnson would have relished also the company of his Belgian-born wife and her gift of perhaps second sight, at least first-class insight.

Derry Jeffares comes from the Anglican, or Church of Ireland tradition, collectively included with all 'Protestants', and too often mistaken as pro-English. Yeats said of them, 'We are no petty people.' They are now, numerically speaking, reduced shamefully in one of the least openly discussed strands of Irish history. Identified with the landlord class, and therefore subject to the long memory of the 'native' Irish, that is to say, the Catholics, nationalist or republican, they were forced into decline in the new post-Treaty nation of the Risen People. Some were burned out of their houses; the remainder, although they held their wealth and influence comprehensively – it has only begun to slip in the last decade or so – were eroded by breeding. With not enough 'Protestant' mates to make a marriage market, they inevitably began to marry Catholics and therefore gave in to the 'All the children must be brought up Catholics' rule. By such methods, violent or insidious, Ireland dulled a significant colour in its weave, the stock of Swift, Shaw, Wilde, Yeats, Jeffares the scholar and analyst of them all – and Johnson's friend, Oliver ('Noll') Goldsmith, who inevitably came up in conversation over supper. In his *History of Anglo-Irish Literature*, Professor Jeffares summarised Noll: 'He could write with ease, elegantly yet unaffectedly, wearing his knowledge lightly . . .'

Goldsmith was born on 10 November 1728, the fifth child of a clergyman in Pallas or Pallasmore, County Longford. In his infancy the family moved to the next county, to Lissoy, 'the most pleasing horizon in nature', a landscape whose gentleness must have contributed formatively to Goldsmith's sweet nature. Life did not take the hint from the countryside's pleasantness: Goldsmith caught smallpox at the age of nine, and it pitted his face and may have stunted his growth: he never grew above five feet five inches, even though excessively burly in the frame.

His life for the next thirty years constitutes a chronicle of misfortune brought on largely by his own waywardness, in which he had massive capacity. Useless at school, except in flashes, he got into Trinity College, Dublin only as a sizar, that is, on the University's charity, and while there became notable among the other students chiefly for 'no specimens of genius . . . but only squalid poverty, and its concomitants, idleness and despondence'. He lounged at the College gates; wrote ballads at five shillings a sheet, and had the pleasure of hearing them on the night voices of street-singers; got arrested and denounced for his part in student riots; and was systematically thrashed by his tutor. Determined, it seemed, to deny anyone the glimpse of any possible talent for anything, anywhere in his whole composition, although he claimed to 'turn an ode of Horace into English better than any of them', he pawned his books, quit Trinity, then returned in a worse condition than before with very little sustenance from impoverished relatives – his mother was now widowed – and he kept afloat through one means: he claimed to have been blessed with 'a knack at hoping'.

With a Bachelor of Arts degree – the ink on the parchment must have reeked of his tutor's grudge – Goldsmith immediately consigned himself to a life of doing nothing in his native countryside, where he passed two years in fishing, telling yarns, and gathering ballads to sing. Anxious relatives persuaded him to try for Holy Orders, but he upscuttled that prospect by wearing trousers of shaggy bright scarlet for his interview with the Bishop. He tutored listlessly, then took a fit that he should try out America, got (he said) as far as the boat but (he said) they sailed without him, and after this insufficiently explained six weeks' absence from home, turned up at his mother's weary door on a nag called Fiddleback. The desperate family then funded him for legal studies in London; he only reached Dublin – and was relieved of his cash at a gambler's table.

Thus to Edinburgh, to study medicine, at which he persisted for eighteen months (Boswell was only twelve and therefore not yet in orbit when Goldsmith came to Scotland). From Edinburgh, Noll, in another of his travel fits, decided he would head for Paris – and somehow ended up in Leiden, one of Holland's most significant universities of the day. There he heard the name of

Baron Holberg, a Danish writer and humorist whose hard early years gave Goldsmith cause for identification, and in the same way as Holberg had taken off on a tour through Europe living on his wits and his singing voice, Goldsmith followed suit – stimulated largely by the notion that when Holberg eventually returned to Denmark he achieved great success and respectability. Goldsmith accordingly busked his way from Leiden to Padua, hearing, *en route*, Voltaire in Paris (or it may have been in Switzerland, he seems to have been unclear on this point). He stayed in Padua for ten months, hoping that some of the city's great reputation for medical learning would rub off on him, and he returned to England in February 1756, penniless as usual.

Samuel Richardson, the celebrated author of the novels *Pamela* and *Clarissa*, gave Noll a job as a printer's proof-reader in Fleet Street, in a house at Salisbury Court. Thereafter, he never wandered too far, or for very long, from those, his first literary haunts, the shores of Grub Street, where he saw the publishing process for the first time, and observed the heady transformation from manuscript to book.

Johnson got to know him before Boswell. Goldsmith, after years of hackwork, for which he earned little money and not much respect, began slowly to make a literary reputation, a strong feat-of-arms in the city of Richardson, Smollett, Garrick, Burke and Johnson. His *Chinese Letters* in the *Public Ledger*, ninety-eight disquisitions on life in England purporting to come from a visiting Chinese philosopher, became the most popular reading in London, and Goldsmith grew mildly famous. From life among the beggars in Axe Lane, and among the washerwomen in a tiny close behind the Old Bailey, where the clotheslines flapped against his dingy windows, he acquired good rooms off Fleet Street and, with some coins at last to jingle together, began to entertain.

On 31 May 1761, Johnson, accompanied by his own and Goldsmith's friend, Bishop Percy, accepted Goldsmith's invitation to dinner and even wore a new wig and suit for the occasion. This sartorial fact, however, seems not to have come from respect. 'I hear,' said Johnson, 'that Goldsmith who is a very great sloven, justifies his disregard of cleanliness and decency by quoting my practice, and I am desirous this night to show him a better example.' From that evening forth, the men loved each other, and continued to do so in many not uncritical ways; not even Boswell's jealous interventions could disrupt their friendship.

Had he not so competitively disliked Goldsmith, I could have liked Jamie more – but with the hypocrisy so traditional in the profession of criticism, he put forward his feelings as artistic opinion, when he was really tackling the man not the ball. Anyway, Goldsmith offered an easy target: he walked like a chimpanzee, a cumbersome man, with sore eyes, a protruding forehead and upper lip, a sharply receding chin like a reversed cliff, and a complexion red and pitted from the childhood smallpox. He had a nervous twitch which made it difficult for him to cross the room without pausing and then taking a violent leap. Johnson, though, felt tenderly towards him, and this, along with Goldsmith's success as a poet, essayist, dramatist and novelist, occasioned Boswell's envious judgements: 'His mind resembled a fertile but thin soil. There was a quick, but not a strong vegetation, of whatever chanced to be thrown upon it. No deep root could be struck.'

Sam, though, understood Noll beautifully, and commented to Fanny Burney that Goldsmith 'would have been a great man if he had known the real value of his own internal resources'. Johnson was unwittingly describing an Irish disease; Goldsmith fogged his own talent with the desire to be liked. Boswell reports this fact, by way of Joshua Reynolds's shrewd observation that Noll's outrageous social postures, his foolish, boastful prances, were designed to make people think less of him, and therefore not envy him if he did achieve literary fame: 'Goldsmith's incessant desire of being conspicuous in company, was the occasion of his sometimes appearing to such disadvantage as one should hardly have supposed possible in a man of his genius . . .' But Noll was only trying to claw a little back from his habitually disadvantaged life.

If Boswell himself does not make adverse comment on Goldsmith, he hurls the barbs of others, including Johnson, who, although he loved Goldsmith, often found much to rebuke in him. Every compliment Johnson paid Goldsmith was, when reported by Boswell, tempered with a derogation, slight or serious. 'Dr Goldsmith is one of the first men [i.e., leading] we now have as an author, and he is a very worthy man too. He has been loose in his principles, but he is coming right.'

Nevertheless, Boswell's envy fails his purpose; Goldsmith emerges at a high level in Johnson's opinion. 'Dr Goldsmith's new play, *She Stoops to Conquer*, being mentioned; Johnson: "I know of no comedy for many years that has so much exhilarated an audience, that has answered so much the great end of comedy – making an audience merry."' Goldsmith, said Johnson, 'was a man, who, whatever he wrote, did it better than any other man could do. He deserved a place in Westminster Abbey, and every year he lived, would have deserved it better.'

Once, probably at one of the many rooms they used for meetings in Soho – the Turk's Head in Gerrard Street, or a little farther along Soho, on the first floor of Jack's Coffee House at 33 Dean Street on the corner of Bateman Street – Goldsmith got his own back on all their jibes with his typically gentle wit, born of the need to cope with such general physical discomposition. He persuaded Johnson and the others that his awkward facial appearance was due to the fact that he, unlike them, chewed with his *upper* jaw. For days they grimaced in hopeful, puzzled emulation.

Early in 1774 Noll sickened. In debt again, and severely depressed, he complained of tiredness and general malaise. On 25 March, he took to his bed, with crushing headaches. By Good Friday the newspapers were announcing that he lay 'dangerously ill and his Physicians have not the smallest Hopes of his Recovery'. At a quarter to five on the morning of Easter Monday, 4 April 1774, he died. He was buried on the north side of the Temple, and nearly a century later a slab was erected near where his grave was believed to be. In the epitaph for Poets' Corner at Westminster Abbey, Dr Johnson concluded that Noll 'touched nothing that he did not adorn'.

Johnson and Boswell spent their time in St Andrews as follows. On the night of Wednesday, 18 August 1773, their first night out of Edinburgh, they took supper at Glass's Inn, which stood at what is now number 5 South Street. Afterwards they walked lantern-lit to St Leonard's College, then recently dissolved, now a girls' school, where they stayed in 'very comfortable and genteel accommodation' as guests of Robert Watson, an historian and professor of Rhetoric and Logic, who had just bought St Leonard's as a piece of real estate. Next morning, Thursday, after breakfast they visited the ruins of St Andrews Cathedral, strolled in the cloisters where 'there was a solemn echo', and then walked the few hundred yards, within sight of the sea, to the old castle. Eight academics entertained them to lunch in an inn, after which they visited the Church of the Holy Trinity on South Street, otherwise known as the Town Kirk; then to St Salvador's College, whose chapel Johnson called 'the neatest place of worship he had seen' (so Boswell says: Johnson does not mention it). In the streets of the town, they observed, to Boswell's disapproval, a plump clergyman, and looked at the sign of James Hood who advertised his premises as both a smithy and a school of fencing. At the inn where they had lunched, they later took tea in the company of more academics, and returned to Professor Watson's for supper.

Johnson's presumption of trying to feel the texture of the past had, as an idea, a good, hard core to it. To the cerebral excitement of Scottish politics he could add another arena offering vigorous possibilities – religion. In St Andrews he made clear his views on Scotland's church developments two centuries earlier. From his standpoint as a devout Christian, a composer of prayers, and a loyal member of the Church of England, the post-Reformation religious developments in Scotland incited him to argument and comment. A wall needed demolishing to make it safe: Johnson argued for it to be left standing in the hope that 'it may fall on some of the posterity of John Knox'. Throughout the Tour, although he worshipped wherever he found an 'English' church, he remained highly alert to differences of religious opinion: only by the skin of his great, uneven teeth (and those of several other people) were mighty rows avoided.

St Andrews, of all the places they visited in Scotland, must have promised the most to Johnson's specific interests, with its combination of violent political history, religious controversy and tradition of learning. He was disappointed, as he walked around 'a city which only history shows to have once flourished.' His description of his stay there runs to exactly three pages of factual prose with editorial comment, and is dominated by negative terms: 'ancient magnificence'; 'decayed'; 'gloomy depopulation'; 'reduced'; 'dissolved'; 'the uneasy remembrance of an university declining, a college alienated and a church profaned and hastening to the ground'; 'calamity'; 'pining in decay and struggling for life'; 'mournful images and ineffectual wishes'; Johnson found in St Andrews a huge spiritual *anathema* – the ruined cathedral of a once great national church brought down by the Reformation. And possibly as a consequence, the level of intellectual impoverishment stood, to his mind, at a point below his ideal university standard.

Boswell, in twice as many words, took a more upbeat view from the beginning, when 'we rose much refreshed', and was delighted (as, he insists, was Johnson) to find in Professor Watson, their host, 'a well-informed man, of very amiable manners'. Boswell's account of their St Andrews stay takes the form of reported conversation punctuated or stimulated by their perambulations. At breakfast, cooked by Dr Watson's daughter, they had an energetic conversation, initiated by the Professor's observation that, as proven by the drop in Glasgow university's student population 'since trade increased', education and commerce were incompatible. Johnson disagreed, and argued that learning had become a trade in itself, which pitched them forward into a discussion of patronage.

> BOSWELL: It is a shame that authors are not now better patronized.
> JOHNSON: No, sir . . . With patronage, what flattery! What falsehood! While a man is *in equilibrio*, he throws truth among the multitude, and lets them take it as they please: in patronage, he must say what pleases his patron, and it is an equal chance whether that be truth or falsehood.
> WATSON: But is not the case now, that, instead of flattering one person, we flatter the age?
> JOHNSON: No, sir, the world always lets a man tell what he thinks, his own way.

Next, still at Professor Watson's breakfast-table, they talked 'of change of manners' – in this case, drinking, smoking, dress habits and the domestic use of a house's rooms. Again Boswell quotes

Johnson at length: the Great Bear believed that his generation had begun to drink less 'owing to the change from ale to wine. 'I remember,' he said, 'when all the *decent* people in Lichfield got drunk every night, and were not the worse thought of. Ale was cheap, so you pressed strongly. When a man must bring a bottle of wine, he is not in such haste. Smoking has gone out. To be sure, it is a shocking thing, blowing smoke out of our mouths into other people's mouths, eyes, and noses, and having the same thing done to us.' He perceived that smoking had a value, and could not, he said, understand 'why a thing which requires so little exertion, and yet preserves the mind from total vacuity, should have gone out. Every man has something by which he calms himself: beating with his feet, or so.' Here, Boswell interjected in his text, 'Dr Johnson used to practise this himself very much.' He certainly did: he often had to be stopped from hammering the floor with his feet – one castle owner drily assured him, 'Dr Johnson, I believe the floor is very firm.'

In his next sentence, Johnson continues, 'I remember when people in England changed a shirt only once a week: a Pandour, [a constable or border guard, and in this case an armed Croatian servant] when he gets a shirt, greases it to make it last. Formerly, good tradesmen had no fire but in the kitchen; never in the parlour, except on Sunday. My father, who was a magistrate of Lichfield, lived thus. They never began to have a fire in the parlour, but on leaving off business, or some great revolution of their life.'

All of Johnson's words in that particular conversation at Dr Watson's house did have something to do with 'change of manners', the term Boswell employed to introduce the topics – but did he write down *verbatim* what Johnson said, and did he do it there and then? Which would mean that Boswell sat around with a notebook and pen, and a supply of ink, scribbling down every word literally? This must be unlikely: he can only have recalled it all later, and sat in his chamber putting it down, and then editing it when he assembled it, and then presumably editing it again at final manuscript stage, then at proof stage – which means, does it not, that we receive a thoroughly filtered Samuel Johnson? No matter how we look at Johnson's words as they reach us via Boswell, they have been rigorously attended. At the same time, it becomes noticeable that, as the journey progresses Boswell's reports of Johnson feel more assured.

I had begun to find that the Johnson we read in his own account frequently booms in a different key from the Johnson in Boswell: unfortunately, their books about their time in Scotland are so different even in subject matter, that a good comparison – which might lead me near to the true Johnson – is impossible. There is, however a means of getting closer to the actual daily, ordinary Johnsonian voice – the man's own letters. These display a grumpier, uneasier, yet kindlier man than the hard-minded enquirer of the formal writing, or the lordly sage Boswell gives us. So – we have at our disposal three Johnsons, and his visit to St Andrews affords a splendid opportunity to compare the public and private man, as one incident appears both in Johnson's book and in his letters to Mrs Thrale – though not in Boswell.

It occurred when, after breakfast, they went walking in the ruins of the cathedral. First, Johnson's formal account, from his *Journey*:

> We came to two vaults over which had formerly stood the house of the sub-prior. One of the vaults was inhabited by an old woman, who claimed the right of abode there, as the widow of a man whose ancestors had possessed the same gloomy mansion for no less than four generations. The right, however it began, was considered as established by legal prescription, and the old woman lives undisturbed. She thinks however that she has a claim to something more than sufferance; for as her husband's name was Bruce, she is allied to royalty, and told Mr Boswell that when there were persons of quality in the place she was distinguished by some notice; that indeed she is now neglected, but she spins a thread, has the company of her cat, and is troublesome to nobody.

Now, the epistolary version, in which Johnson tells Mrs Thrale that

> Two of the vaults or cellars of the Subprior are yet entire. In one of them lives an old Woman who claims an hereditary residence in it, boasting that her husband was the sixth tenant of this gloomy mansion in a lineal descent, and claiming by her marriage with this Lord of the cavern, an alliance with the Bruces. Mr Boswel [*sic*]

stayed a while to interrogate her, because he understood her language. She told him, that she and her Cat lived together; that she had two sons somewhere, who might perhaps be dead; that when there were quality in the town, notice was taken of her; and that now she was neglected, but did not trouble them. Her habitation contained all that she had, her turf for fire was laid in one place, and her balls of coaldust in another, but her bed seemed to be clean. Boswel asked her if she ever heard any noises, but she could tell him of nothing supernatural, though she sometimes wandered in the night among the graves and ruins, only she had some notice by dreams of the death of her relations.

Such a difference between Johnson's two accounts: one written by a man with a literary reputation, the other the letter of a friend, full of human interest and understanding of the kind of news the recipient might enjoy. Until they fell out, after her remarriage to another when widowed, he was very fond of Mrs Thrale, the Welsh wife of a Southwark brewer with a house in Streatham; Boswell describes her as 'a lady of lively talents, improved by education'. She stood hardly five feet tall; Johnson called her 'plump, short and brisk' and the relationship he had with her polished his affectionate side. They loved each other convivially; she looked after his health and wellbeing, and his many stays in the Thrale household gave him peace of mind and sunny calm. He rewarded her with his presence, famous conversation, and an obvious and unthreatening regard. She called him 'Dear, good man', and nothing seemed outside the Pale of their talk – food, reputations, poetry, marriage, clothes. 'On her appearing before him in a dark-coloured gown', Boswell reports Johnson's remark; 'You little creatures should never wear those sort of clothes, however; they are unsuitable in every way. What! have not all insects gay colours?'

St Andrew the apostle was crucified diagonally, hence the shape of the saltire cross of Scotland, the white of a human spreadeagled on the blue background of a Greek sky. If it is true that St Rule brought the bones of St Andrew from Patras in Greece to this coast of Fife and founded a settlement here, then the poor man had a chilly time of it in his monkish robes. Asceticism being defined by harsh contrast with easy living, he succeeded fully; Patras, where Byron landed in Greece, enjoys bright warm sun for much of the year, and in St Andrews, winter and summer, a cold breeze whips in off the sea that swishes just outside these sandstone ruins. People with names of Doig, Scott, Chambers had burial grounds here; other corpses include a wife who dropped dead from dancing on her wedding day; the post-Reformation citizens of St Andrews made a large investment in death and their graves bear the carved emblems of mortality – hour-glass, scythe, trumpet, open book.

When Johnson published his *Journey to the Western Islands of Scotland*, critics ticked him off for omitting the chapel of St Rule. Boswell defended him by blaming others for not having told them of it, and appealed for a worthwhile guidebook: 'In every place, where there is any thing worthy of observation, there should be a short printed directory for strangers, such as we find in all the towns of Italy, and in some of the towns of England.' Rubbish, Boswell. You cannot blame the shortage of eighteenth-century guidebooks. The chapel of St Rule is impossible to miss, square and tall as a Florentine tower, slightly less elegant, burlier – and right beside the cathedral.

Something went wrong somewhere in St Andrews's history. From the top of St Rule's it looks like a town that tried to become an Oxford or Cambridge, and failed, though in many ways a charming place. Johnson would undoubtedly have attributed such short measure to John Knox – and in effect, did; 'The change of religion in Scotland, eager and vehement as it was, raised an epidemical enthusiasm, compounded of sullen scrupulousness and warlike ferocity . . .' Boswell 'happened to ask where John Knox was buried. Dr Johnson burst out, "I hope in the highway. I have been looking at his reformations."'

The ancients raised holy places towards the skies: those small churches on Greek mountain-tops brought the priests nearer the floor of Heaven. With typical local practicality the builders of this tower intended St Rule also as a landmark, for pilgrims who, whatever the traditional penury of such pious laity, needed to be housed and fed, and had to pay for such services. If the wind blows from the north-east, it becomes unwise to stand on the summit of

St Rule's, even though barricades prevent one from falling accident-
ally or deliberately. A few hundred yards away, two Leuchars-
based fighter planes pivoted with unpleasant noise in the sunshine
a mile offshore – and confirmed the height of the tower: it seemed
that I was looking down on their wings from above.

Curiously, St Andrews makes little enough of the sea, which
beats almost along the eastern pavements. The town has fought
for its discreet aura, supported now by the grimy fortitude of
Victorian architecture. In the rest of their forenoon, the famous
pair went to see the ruins of the castle on 'the margins of the
water'; it was built, Johnson observed, 'with more attention to
security than pleasure'. The murder of Cardinal Beaton there in
1546 was duly noted by both writers, but with little attention
other than another Johnsonian shaft aimed at Knox: 'He [Beaton]
was murdered by the ruffians of reformation.' Note that
'reformation' receives the same size of 'r' as 'ruffians': how conveniently Johnson cited scripture for his own purpose: Beaton was
a forger, a philanderer and a burner of rivals, and they kept his
body in a chest of salt.

Next, the wanderers visited Principal Murison, who showed
them his library. His pride in it slipped into inordinacy: apparently
unfamiliar with such glories as The Queens College library in
Oxford, he assured Johnson, 'You have not such a one in England.' If I have traced it accurately, Murison presided over what
is now the Psychology Library at Saint Mary's College. Original
beauty may still be seen in the tall old bookcases, the sweet light
oaken colours and the elegantly vaulted, slightly stuccoed ceiling
of ineluctable St Andrews grey, picked out a little in white. But
– new practicality masks an old and pretty aesthetic: the room is
filled with function chairs of horrid blue; individual neon strip-
lighting and metal dividers at each study space; crude tables cut
into window niches; blue-green metal-and-fabric screens lined up
for use; the tall window at the end rendered sightless; flooring of
dreadful brown – this was the large room found by Johnson to
be 'elegant and luminous'.

No fewer than eight gentlemen entertained the pair to lunch. Boswell's snobbish talents for currying multiple favours joined forces

with his capacity to keep records: to biography's everlasting advantage, he names people where he can – even if he does it with the same essential aplomb as a local newspaper gets its photographs captioned accurately (and its patrons' names into print). 'Present: Murison, Shaw, Cooke, Hill, Haddo, Watson, Flint, Brown.' They talked of sorrow and ran into a little competitive *frisson*. Johnson's holding-forth irritated Murison whose interpretation of a remark by St Paul was challenged, Boswell says refuted, by Johnson. Murison 'tried to be smart' and raised his glass: 'Long may you lecture.'

After lunch they visited the Church of the Holy Trinity: I found it locked, and failed to raise the Rev. Armour. Here the pair viewed Archbishop Sharp's monument: it commemorates the prelate hauled from his coach and assassinated by a dozen Covenanters. Nowhere in their accounts of St Andrews did either writer pick up on an aspect of Holy Trinity Church – its reflection of male chauvinism. As well as once having been a prison for dissolute women, Holy Trinity contained the Bishop's Branks, a contraption to imprison the head, with a metal gag, reputed to have been invented against talkative women. The revered Archbishop Sharp had it applied to one, Isobel Lindsay, who heckled his sermons. For Johnson not to have made some observation seems like a missed opportunity – Sam, remember, was the man who said, after Boswell had reported seeing a woman preach at a Quaker Meeting-House, 'Sir, a woman's preaching is like a dog walking on its hinder legs. It is not done well; but you are surprised to find it done at all'; and, in connected mode, 'Supposing a wife to be of a studious or argumentative turn – it would be very troublesome.'

Reached through lanes, and due north of the town kirk, the travellers strolled across to St Salvator's College – walled, sedate and still attractive. A plaque at the gate reads, 'The initials on the pavement nearby mark the spot where Patrick Hamilton, member of the University, was burned at the stake on 29 February 1528, at the age of 24. On the Continent he had been greatly influenced by Martin Luther and on his return to St Andrews he began to teach Lutheran doctrines. Having been tried and found guilty of heresy, he was condemned to death, thus becoming the first martyr of the Scottish reformation.' In the wall above, a face peers from the stone, not formally carved, a natural configuration produced by time and weather: the necessary blood-lore of religion claims that this is Patrick Hamilton's face, etched there by the paranormal force of his martyrdom. He is remembered more prosaically in a Victorian obelisk, the Martyr's Monument, near the junction of Golf Place and The Scores, not far from the Royal & Ancient Golf Club – where Johnson and Boswell did not, it seems, seek to play eighteen holes; although they could have done: the R & A had been in existence for a couple of decades before Johnson's visit. The burghers of St Andrews also roasted to death – more slowly, it seems, than they did Patrick Hamilton – another martyr, one Paul Craw, into whose mouth they also stuffed a brass ball, symbolically obstructing any Protestant utterances, while actually stifling his screams.

Beneath the tranquillity and discourse of this town lurks a filthy and bigoted history, with both sides hacking and burning any who dared challenge a contrary creed. If I can smell the embers today – some trace of hot martyrological coal seems to glow around every corner – did Johnson and Boswell, two centuries nearer such events, feel the heat from the flames? Religion's popularity must have something to do with natural paradox – faith, morals and piety licensing inhumanity, savagery and prejudice. The history of St Andrews makes it feel like some kind of forcing-house for intolerance, all disagreement punished with egregious nastiness. Accused sorceresses, for example, were thrown into Witch Lake, a pool near the rocks east of the golf course: if they sank, they were hailed as innocent, and absolved posthumously; if they swam, they were recaptured and burnt at the stake.

Next morning they visited Colonel Nairne's garden and grotto, now Queen Mary House, where Johnson saw a fine plane tree. No matter what the evidence, Johnson could never be impressed unless he agreed to it, and thereby he had a prejudice happily confirmed; Colonel Nairne assured him of the rareness of such trees in this part of Scotland – the county had only one other such. Reporting this, Boswell covers for Johnson by saying that when

Johnson spoke of trees – his laments for their absence from Scotland drew opprobrium when his book appeared – he meant those large ones of England. Curious that Boswell defended Johnson so often, especially as Johnson had made a large part of his reputation out of being able to speak for himself. In this case, both may be forgiven their postures: the tree of Colonel Nairne grew large enough to hold a platform in its branches, in which later generations held tea-parties.

Queen Mary House has a notice on it outlining restrictions on visits during term time, therefore permitting entry only on a day by which I would have left St Andrews, and so I never found out whether the grotto and garden remain as fine as Colonel Nairne felt them to be. More interesting here than the good gentleman's horticulture, was the young Frenchman, Pierre de Chatelard, who displayed a (not unknown) *penchant* for royal bedrooms. He first declared his passion for Mary, Queen of Scots, when he leaped out from behind her four-poster canopy at Holyrood – and he did it again at Burntisland in 1562. Not at Queen Mary House, however: his journey to St Andrews was a closely-guarded one and when they hanged him here in February 1563, he shouted, '*Adieu*, the most beautiful and cruel princess.' At least he got the 'adieu' part right.

The travellers had arrived on Wednesday night; they left St Andrews at Friday noon. Not including observations, remarks and shafts, Boswell reports five conversations of substance in the thirty-six hours. Few had the general sparkle of those in Edinburgh, although there was one good joke: Boswell told Johnson of a man he knew who 'actually forgot his own name. Johnson: That was a morbid oblivion.' The first exchanges took place at that opening breakfast in St Leonards – trade in Glasgow, patronage, ale-drinkers in Lichfield and other fashions, domestic practices and money. Conversation number two happened over their dinner with the professors, where Johnson – countering Professor Murison, who found all sorrow bad – declared it inherent in humanity. That night at supper and the following morning at breakfast they discussed, with no great passion or insight, the power of memory and the efficacy of prayer.

The most extensively reported discourse took place on the

Thursday afternoon, when Boswell and Johnson returned to their lunchtime inn to take tea, again in academical company.

'We talked,' writes Boswell, 'of composition, which was a favourite topick of Dr Watson's, who first distinguished himself by lectures on rhetorick.' The debate centred on Johnson's tenet, by which he advised 'every young man beginning to compose, to do it as fast as he can, to get a habit of having his mind to start promptly; it is so much more difficult to improve in speed than in accuracy'. Watson contested this on grounds of possible slovenliness; Johnson parried by insisting that 'a man knows when his composition is inaccurate, and when he thinks fit he'll correct it. But if a man is accustomed to compose slowly, and with difficulty, upon all occasions, there is danger that he may not compose at all, as we do not like that which is not done easily.'

On being told of a man slow at composing sermons, Johnson then gave some examples of his own formidably rapid work-rate: a sermon begun after lunch, sent off that night; at one sitting, forty-eight pages of his biography of the wild poet Richard Savage, a feat of mental stamina made the more remarkable in that it was Johnson's first work of any stature; and, said Johnson, 'I have also written six sheets in a day of translation from the French.' Boswell, ever alert with the profound gloss, summarised, 'We have all observed how one man dresses himself slowly, another fast' – trust Jamie to draw an analogy from his experience of more *louche* energies.

Whatever the dilapidation Johnson found in St Andrews, as did many subsequent observers, they say that the place wins people over, that students who wept at being sent there for three years, then wept to leave. Now the town has spread from that core of streets and ruins so forlorn in August 1773: the university has recovered a good deal from the condition indicated in Johnson's valedictory remark: 'to see it pining in decay and struggling for life, fills the mind with mournful images and ineffectual wishes.' The town's boundaries have expanded in all of the three permitted directions: seashore and harbour remain unchanging. St Andrews gives an impression of muted energy, flames that flicker rather than roar.

*   *   *

Their journey to Arbroath, *Aberbrothic* in Johnson's spelling, took them through Leuchars and Dundee, of which Johnson's public account said 'nothing remarkable': privately, in a letter to Mrs Thrale, he said Dundee was 'a dirty, despicable town'. The pace at which they travelled now crystallised: even if walking consistently at Mr Pickwick's good old English rate of four miles an hour, I should never be able to cover the journey in comparable tempo, although I did not begin to clarify this assessment until late that afternoon, and by then I had the stimulus of extraordinary weather to freshen my considerations.

Only one road runs out to Leuchars, the busy A91, from which, a few miles out of St Andrews, travellers for the north turn right at Guardbridge and way up ahead, beyond Leuchars, join the A92 to the banks of the River Tay at Dundee. Beyond the suburbs of St Andrews, down a slope heading north-west, by the golf course, I walked in awkward circumstances. Along here, the A91 has no footpaths – instead, a tussocked, pitted wide verge makes life hugely uncomfortable for walkers, yet provides essential refuge from every vehicle heading towards the town behind. A truck approaches: I jump into the grass: it passes by – I bound out again to the hard road, the soaking rucksack oppressing me more tenaciously than Quasimodo's hump. So, within a hundred yards of the town's outskirts, I am trying to maintain my self-imposed pace, while leaping in and out of this lumpy, ankle-threatening margin.

By now it had long been raining: this was experienced rain, not callow drift or mist, this was rain with a purpose, with malice aforethought, premeditated rain; it heaved down in slapping, wide, soaking slants, with intent to commit a felony; it had ambition, determination and effectiveness, this was gunslinger rain. Like a bear's paw, a lorry's wing-mirror nearly swiped my head off, and the wide haven of a pavement opened up. The rain eased for a moment, drawing its breath awaiting reinforcements – which arrived in a big, dark bulge of cloud. Over Guardbridge, by the paper mills, towards Leuchars, the cloud heeled over on its side and emptied itself like an old bath.

To the right the road forks off to a Royal Air Force base, a vast, violent toyshop: trucks and buggies flick to and from the haughty killer planes lounging primed on the tarmac. Ahead, in Leuchars, the obedient outskirts of which personify forces architecture – regimentation to the eaves – the travellers halted. 'Observing,' says Boswell, 'a church with an old tower, we stopped to look at it.'

They prevailed upon the minister, 'a very civil old man', to tell them such history as he could. I found an equally civil, much younger, man, the Rev. Mr Cassells, whose wife with much good grace permitted me to stand steaming in their hallway, dripping water from every follicle, and then even invited me into the drawing-room. Clergymen's houses encounter all sorts of inappropriatenesses plunging across their doorsteps.

Leuchars means 'a marshy place' or, according to the parish redactions of Mrs Cassells, 'a stream flowing though marshy ground'. The traditional economy of the hinterland and the village includes, principally, farming, and a history of weaving sailcloth for Dundee: the people ate fish and mussels. Boswell and Johnson were told that the church's tower was 'supposed to have stood eight hundred years'. Round and Norman, pleasantly out of twitch with its surroundings, it received considerable mending in 1745, and may have become rather like the man who had the same hatchet for forty years, three new heads and four new handles. The parish celebrated eight centuries of worship in 1987: the Moderator came, and the pageantry included a reconstructed Johnson and Boswell. A green-covered booklet, in which 'The Minister, Kirk Session and Congregation welcome you to St Athernase Church', traces the origins of the parish to a St Bunoc or Bunan, of 900 A.D., and firms up a couple of hundred years later on the first granting of *Ecclesia de Lochres* 'to the Priory of St Andrews, by Ness, son of William, some time between 1183 and 1187'. Crusaders called de Quinci enter the picture, and a thirteenth-century bishop dedicated the church to an Irish saint – the original Athernase was Ethernesc, a man with a stammer, thought to be a contemporary of Iona's Columba. Bruces were here, one of whom died on Flodden field at the age of ninety-eight, when it might be reasonably thought sensible men of that maturity should be at home in their beds. A local lady, daughter of the Earl of Fife, was arrested for subversive activities and kept in a cage suspended from a turret in Berwick for several years: Johnson would probably have approved.

The Rev. Cassells ministers to approximately a hundred and twenty souls of a Sunday, in three churches. His predecessors at Leuchars include Alexander Henderson, who, imposed on an unwilling congregation by the landlord or 'heritor', had to climb in through the window. No such fever seems to hang in the air here now: the atmosphere was as peaceful and quiet as a church in a field in France. I am told by Edinburgh people that farther north, and especially west, religion heats up as if in inverse proportion to the Arctic Circle's proximity: perhaps the top of the world is nearer to God.

How heavy can rain get? Leuchars to Dundee is about ten miles. To make Montrose by nightfall and therefore remain broadly within their scale of time, I would have to be in Arbroath by four; I gave in, and took a bus. Failure already – but in mitigation, even the notes in my wallet were wet when I took one out to buy a doughnut near the bus stop in Dundee at which I caught another bus to Arbroath.

The passage in Johnson's *Journey* covering the road from St Andrews to Montrose never mentions Leuchars. It is along here in his writing that he particularly begins to concern himself with the lack of trees, and he also addresses the undiverting emptiness of the roads, on which the traveller 'seldom sees himself either encountered or overtaken'.

Johnson bases his complaints at the lack of inforestation on economic grounds – 'That before the Union the Scots had little trade and little money, is no valid apology; for plantation is the least expensive of all methods of improvement.' In Colonel Nairne's grotto at St Andrews, Professor Shaw remarked admiringly to Boswell, 'This is a wonderful man: he is master of every subject he handles.' Should forestry be included in this competence?

'From the bank of the Tweed to St Andrews,' Johnson writes, 'I had never seen a single tree, which I did not believe to have grown up far within the present century.' Accustomed to love of a lusher English countryside, he abhorred the nakedness of Scottish landscape, and had to wait until much later in his journey for the satisfaction of a little timber. His observations are borne out by other, more-or-less contemporary observations. Many travellers of the day went to Scotland preconditioned to find it barren. Goldsmith, while at Edinburgh, called it a 'dismal landscape'; although Defoe, entering Dunbar in the 1720s, began to observe that 'Scotland was not so naturally barren, as some people represent it . . . and you hardly see a gentleman's house, as you pass the Lothians towards Edinburgh, but they are distinguished by groves and walks of fir-trees about them; which, though in most places they are yet but young, yet they show us, that in a few years, Scotland will not need to send to Norway for timber and deal, but will have sufficient of her own, and perhaps, be able to furnish England too with considerable quantities.'

Obviously not quickly enough for Johnson: does psychology by now have a word for a man obsessed with trees? A timberphile? He once said to Boswell that were he a rich man he would plant trees extensively. In Scotland, however, he returns to the subject of trees over and over again, to such a degree that he has been given credit for having induced the Scots – most notably some of those with whom he stayed – to invest in planting.

Waiting for a bus, any bus, I stood under, perhaps, the child of one of Johnson's arboriphile results, a spreading beech. That night my sodden notebook read, 'Undulating farms, many woods, no footpath, road-sign to Tayport, road-sign to Kinshaldy Beach. Schoolgirls being teased by bus conductor. Old man with exceptionally and deliciously cross face ticks off schoolgirls for making too much noise. Conductor, safely out of old man's line of vision, hunches shoulders in gleeful silent collusion with nudging girls. Clean-edged fringe of trees where large coppice swerves down into field. Long-billed birds in the wooded field above the Tay. Oil platforms out in the water, huge tanks. European feel to Dundee's skyline.'

Running beside the Tay, the road from Dundee to Arbroath begins with a long, boulevard-ish flavour. Beyond the signposts for Carnoustie, it becomes a road for one of Sir Walter Scott's novels – a lone tree here and there, open spaces, dipping hollows, high hillsides for the highwayman to sit astride his horse, silhouetted against a moonlit sky on a night of hard, high winds. On this stretch, Boswell and Johnson argued about Roman Catholicism and its doctrine of transubstantiation – to Boswell 'an awful subject' – and Johnson believed that 'This is My Body' had a figurative rather than a literal meaning. Boswell does not enlarge much, except to tell us precisely where the big man stood: on the side of the Scriptures, rather than with Boswell's timid support of the Church's 'ancient and continued tradition upon this point. Johnson: Tradition, Sir, has no place where the Scriptures are plain; and tradition cannot persuade a man into a belief of transubstantiation.'

For a further short paragraph, Boswell mutters on about the Church of England maintaining 'a mysterious belief in more than a mere commemoration of the death of Christ, by partaking of the elements of bread and wine'; then he relievedly moves to the question of 'whether a lawyer might honestly engage with the first side that offers him a fee', an ongoing debate between the pair. They did not mention rain; nor lunch: yet it took them from noon to eleven at night to get from St Andrews to Montrose, a distance of forty or so modern miles. Judging from Johnson's enthusiasm – even if Boswell only mentions the place in passing – a chunk of that time was taken up with inspecting Arbroath.

CHAPTER IV

'The greatest man in England, except Lord Mansfield'

THEY HAD STOPPED IN ARBROATH, to view the Abbey. 'I should scarcely have regretted my journey,' claimed Johnson, 'had it afforded nothing more than the sight of Aberbrothick.' The cobbled forecourt has been defiled with intimidating NO PARKING notices, a mote in the eye of the Abbey's red calm. Inside, peace reigns, even in driving rain.

Johnson found it full of weeds; today it is tailored and fitted. A close lawn laps the feet of the giant church's ancient heights, and some of the long-departed community's living quarters are as smoothly preserved as an abbot's jowls. All such buildings resemble huge ships, the gaping walls like spars awaiting rigging. Arbroath's south transept even looks as if it has smelt the wind under which it will sail; it is a tall, bare, one-shouldered hulk with a single blank eye at the high gable top where a rose window used to be. The guidebook, which speaks of lancets, arcades and cusps, says the locals call the eyeless window, with tautological logic, 'the round O'. Flemish illuminations in the abbot's house, now a museum, recall the teeming peasantry of Avercamp and Breughel paintings.

On Christmas Eve, 1950, nationalists stole the Stone of Scone from Westminster Abbey and laid it in the grounds of Arbroath Abbey. In their protest they sought to restore some political coals to Newcastle: the Declaration of Arbroath in 1320 committed the lay and ecclesiastical nobles of Scotland to support Robert Bruce, who stood against proud Edward's army, and sent him homeward to think again.

Always touch the walls of an old abbey – for the currents of ancient idea coming through from learned men, and for the systems that housed them. Arbroath's walls offer a well-groomed feel, powdered silk, which must have as much to do with the history of the place as with Historic Scotland's care. The Abbey was dedicated to the dead Thomas à Becket by William the Lion, King of Scotland, in thanks for the Canterbury saint's supernatural rescue of William from enemies at Alnwick. The air in these places must be invisibly thick with the old sounds of monks, and their thoughts, and their cloistered politics. Arbroath was founded in 1178 by an order descended from Abbot Bernard who left Poitiers for Tiron; monks from this Benedictine reform group of Tironensians established Kelso down on the Borders, and two friars came thence to Arbroath.

Did those scribes care for their hands, tend their fingers, in the way classical musicians are reputed to? If so, would that have been vanity to the point of sin – or merely preserving the Lord's gift? Did they get excited when a new supply of *lapis lazuli* came in from Afghanistan? Who among them caught the badgers and squirrels from which they made their fine paint brushes? Did the women of the locality – and/or the imagination – constitute a perennial problem? Perhaps only if you did not have power: Beaton from St Andrews came to Arbroath in 1524: the Abbey contributed to the lifestyle and wellbeing of his mistress, a fecund Miss Ogilvy, and their seven bastards.

The restorers have thoughtfully provided viewing platforms from which to contemplate the fabric of Arbroath, and search for such things as a volute capital, or a corbel; the guide-book mentions an 'aumbry in the west wall': it must mean 'ambry', a small cupboard, or closet. In the life-givingness of words, Architecture and Building possess the loveliest vocabularies: chamfer, aedicule, caryatid, quoin, hammerbeam, oriel, newel, mandorla, garth – a music unto itself. The Arbroath guidebook's glossary has some of these – '*Clearstorey*: the range of windows in the upper part of a building; *Frater*: a monastic refectory or dining hall [alas not taken from the Latin for 'brother', but from a French reduction of 'refreshment']; *Gablet*: a decorative design in the form of a small gable, often above a window; *Pend*: a vaulted passageway [several pends in St Andrews]; *Slype*: a passage; *Triforium*: the arcaded gallery between the main arcade and clearstorey; *Tympanum*: the enclosed space within the head of an arched doorway [does that mean it has a space behind like a drumhead – an open space inviting impressions to be made upon it?]'

And always listen to old walls. Creatures may live within – small birds, ticking beetles, crickets: no cheeping, nor any active sounds here, just the passive sound of silence. All is not lost – old walls appeal to four of the five senses, taste alone being inadvisable. Their antique regularity, the sense that the insides of those outer courses were last touched by human hand eight hundred years ago, reads like a time-travelling adventure story. They smell of dry dampness, not a readily marketable perfume in the salons of Europe, but an affirming odour, not of sanctity, nor of history – more of the earth, of the quarries from which they were hewn, to be shaped by men who could cut stone as other monks cut the cloth for their grey robes.

Touch, definitely, brings the most rewards: these walls handle like human beings, inviting those with a weakness for the elegiac to enjoy them, and continue rubbing a hand along them. Johnson wrote to Mrs Thrale that however ruined he found it, the Abbey's 'fabrick was once of great extent, and stupendous magnificence'. He may have meant the general composition of what had been the whole great building: who is to say that he did not also intend the look, smell, feel and silence of these stones?

It becomes easy to picture himself and Boswell here, their servant outside holding the horse's head, while Johnson's taxi, his post-chaise, waited: 'The arch of one of the gates is entire, and another only so far dilapidated as to diversify the appearance'; Sam himself with his famous stick prodding in the weeds, gauging the cut of the stone as he might examine the shoulders of a friend's new frock-coat, measuring distances, tracing nave, crossing, choir, transept – inhaling meaning and implication, and converting it into judgment and knowledge.

How noble these pillars, and how good for the imagination. Sometimes, people in ancient places, in flashes of paranormal imagination, see once again the Forum in Pompeii as it must have been a few days before Mount Etna's eruption; or – was it Freud's or Jung's story? – musicians in a Rhenish *Schloss*, playing clavichords for a duke and his family. 'Its ruins,' said Johnson of Arbroath, 'afford ample testimony of its ancient magnificence.'

The twelfth abbot, according to the guidebook, was the subject of complaints to the Pope, that he had treated his flock, 'not like a gentle shepherd, but like a ravening wolf, harrying it "with the stings of affliction, and the bites of persecution", bestowing its property upon his kinsfolk and driving from the monastery those who dared to oppose him'.

How it rained in Arbroath; trying to see through curtains of falling water makes a nonsense of note-taking. Yet, Boswell must have written on the hoof, and in fat detail – a diligence requiring either unstoppable ambition, and an almost morbid discipline – or both.

The *Life of Johnson* makes plain how Boswell had been staking out the ground since their early acquaintance, making notes immediately after each meeting of what he himself was eventually to 'consider the peculiar value' of the *Life*, 'that is, the quantity it contains of Johnson's conversation'. In September 1764, eighteen months after they first met, Boswell told Johnson in a letter from Saxony, 'It shall be my study to do what I can to render your life happy; and, if you die before me, I shall endeavour to do honour to your memory.' He grew less oblique – as in May 1768, five years before the Hebrides tour. Boswell finding Johnson 'in the kindest and most agreeable frame of mind' asked him 'explicitly whether it would be improper to publish his letters after his death. His answer was, "Nay, Sir, when I am dead, you may do as you will."'

The celebrated *modus operandi* was more or less specified by Johnson himself. There is an entry in the *Life* for Tuesday, 31 March 1772, recounting a conversation the pair had in Boswell's lodgings at Conduit Street in London, having lunched with General Paoli, an Italian military statesman, another of Boswell's scalps, to whom he had introduced Johnson. Boswell does not say which of them raised the question of biography, and somewhat out of context he leads into a comment from Johnson: '"Nobody can write the life of a man, but those who have eat and drunk and lived in social intercourse with him." I said, that if it was not troublesome and presuming too much, I would request him to tell me all the little circumstances of his life; what schools he attended, when he came to Oxford, when he came to London, &c., &c., He did not disapprove of my curiosity as to these particulars; but said, "They'll come out by degrees as we talk together."'

A year later, on Tuesday, 13 April 1773, Boswell 'again solicited him to communicate to me the particulars of his early life. He said, "You shall have them all for twopence. I hope you will know a great deal more of me before you write my Life."' So, by the time they went to Scotland, Boswell had visibly engaged with the project, which accounts for the everyday discipline he displayed in writing his *Journal of a Tour to the Hebrides*.

At eleven o'clock that Friday night they arrived in Montrose. The travellers regarded their inn, The Ship (long eroded), as no more than a functional staging-post, an ill-mannered house, too, run by William Driver – an Englishman, as Boswell pointed out to Johnson with some glee. Johnson's account discusses the hostelry's unsavouriness by contrast with the generally strong composure of the town, which he found 'well built, airy and clean', but at the inn 'did not find a reception such as we thought proportionate to the commercial opulence of the place'. Some dirty-finger business again took place with the sugar in the lemonade, as had happened in Boyd's at Edinburgh.

The pair then sat and talked desultorily. For 'proposing to carry lemons with us to Sky [*sic*] that he might be sure to have his lemonade', Johnson ticked off Boswell – on two counts: that he, Sam, did not wish to be viewed as someone who could not do without his preferences; and that it was 'very bad manners to carry provisions to any man's house, as if he could not entertain you. To an inferior it is oppressive; to a superior it is insolent.' They discussed two histories of music recently advertised, and Boswell believed each would suffer from the other. Johnson contradicted this, believing the comparisons would talk both books into greater prominence. The intrusive Boswell then took another liberty – that of pointing out to Johnson 'that he very often sat quite silent for a long time, even when in company with only a single friend', at which Johnson reminded Boswell of an acquaintance who had once observed, 'Sir, you are like a ghost: you never speak till you are spoken to.'

Boswell's biographical method pulls a double bind: he irritates while he rewards. On the one hand, his invasiveness of Johnson triggers an immediate cringe: on the other, were not Boswell so crass so frequently, his readers could not get so close to Johnson. Modern biographers suffer many accusations: that they trawl too widely and deeply; that they pick over entrails insensitively, confirming Dr Arbuthnot's definition of biography as 'the new terror of death'; that they invade their subject's most intimate quarters and lay all bare, regardless, it is said, of relevance or the feelings of surviving kin. Boswell conducted his invasiveness while Johnson was still alive, and even though the result seems not overtly lurid, I doubt whether many areas of Johnson remained uncombed. In general, Boswell's *Life of Johnson* provides an immortal Pepysian and aromatic sweep of eighteenth-century literary society, recounted in Boswell's lovely candour and flawedness. The essential triumph comes from the assembly of details, and the most valuable of these is revealed where contradictoriness is introduced, at which point the picture of Johnson always grows clearer. Thus, at Montrose, Boswell took a sharp likeness, in which we see the other side of the opinionated, often pompous, astonishingly patronising Johnson, the man with a statement on everything, the clumping, farting, knob-faced denouncer; Johnson was also a thoughtful man of good manners and pensiveness, a quiet, reflective, astute man who had been knocked around. When he arrived in London from Lichfield, Johnson had to use his strapping muscles and burliness: he became a porter in Covent Garden in order to subsist. Now, the elderly man who endured a waiter's dirty fingers in his lemonade at Montrose could hardly have been more famous or respected, and there he sits in a dirty inn, happy to enjoy a little quiet, and quite at ease to do so, even in the company of one of the most garrulous men in the realm whose nature abhorred a conversational vacuum; Johnson even expressed a simple delight in being thought as silent as a ghost.

A further gloss on this quieter side of his character appears during Johnson's own reflection in (rather than upon) Montrose – where he comments that he has by now had an opportunity to compare Scotland's beggars with others he has seen. He makes two points: one, that they are as numerous proportionately in Edinburgh as in London, but in Scottish towns more plentiful than in comparable English locations; and two, on the whole he finds them more quiet, and modest. He wonders if this be a drawback, perhaps, to their ultimate aim? 'Though their behaviour may strike with more force the heart of a stranger, they are certainly in danger of missing the attention of their countrymen.'

Next morning, the pair took the air of Montrose; they saw the church, since replaced with another; the town hall had 'a handsome fabrick with a portico', wrote Johnson (it still has), while Boswell noted that it had a 'good dancing-room, and other rooms for tea-drinking'. Today, it houses municipal authorities, and at ten o'clock last night a bell rang continuously from that direction – 'The curfew,' said the hotel porter this summer morning in 1991. A neat museum houses military uniforms of the Johnsonian period alongside a park as tailored as Scottish prudence. Johnson went into an apothecary's with a prescription he filled out for himself; on account of the Latin, and perhaps on account of his title, the chemist's counter-hand took Dr Johnson for a medical man. For all his invasive tendencies, Boswell does not tell us why Johnson needed medicine.

The journey from Montrose to Laurencekirk, ten and a half miles, takes three hours and a quarter on foot, on the undulating and awkward A937. Hugh MacDiarmid, who lived at Montrose, and edited the local newspaper while enjoying a fruitful period of his literary life, described Montrose as 'a very attractive small burgh with a wide agricultural hinterland', and these fields now began to materialise. Distant, forested hills to the left and smaller hills on the right contributed their surges to the surface of the countryside, and these undulations across the land ran under the roadway like energy cables, sapping the strength from the legs. Johnson found the terrain 'still naked' but bountiful, with land so utterly ploughed that he wondered where the grass grew to feed the plough-horses.

Before they headed onwards, Boswell wrote a note at their unappetising inn.

Montrose, 21 August

My dear Lord,

Thus far am I come with Mr Samuel Johnson. We must be at
Aberdeen tonight. I know you do not admire him so much as I
do; but I cannot be in this country without making a bow at your
old place, as I do not know if I may again have an opportunity of
seeing Monboddo. Besides, Mr Johnson says, he would go two
miles out of his way to see Lord Monboddo. I have sent forward
my servant, that we may know if your lordship be at home.

I am ever, my dear lord,
Most sincerely yours,
James Boswell

Monboddo was one of eighteenth-century Britain's quirks. A
judge and landlord, he throve on amateur metaphysics and early
anthropology, purveying monkey theories almost a century ahead
of Darwin. A tinch less rigorous, though: Monboddo believed
that monkeys became men when the practice of sitting down
eventually eroded their tails. An etymologist too: in a study called
Origin and Progress of Language, which appeared in six volumes
between 1773 and 1792, Monboddo dismissed Johnson's most
singular achievement in the same field, saying Johnson 'had compiled a dictionary of a barbarous language, a work which a
man of real genius, rather than undertake, would choose to die
of hunger'.

Johnson held a not dissimilar reciprocal opinion, comparing
Monboddo to another of his own bugbears, Rousseau. Four years
earlier he told Boswell that the difference between the two was
that whereas Rousseau talked nonsense and knew he did – because
he talked it so well – Monboddo, who talked an inferior brand,
did not know he was talking nonsense. In other words, for a man
to talk lowgrade nonsense, at any time, much less constantly, and
never know he was doing it . . . ? What, thus, may we infer
exactly from Johnson's remark that he would go two miles out
of his way to meet Monboddo? Only two?

Laurencekirk has another of those long, long streets; home for
four years and by then long gone, of Thomas Ruddiman the gram-
marian, mentioned by Boswell and admired by Johnson. They
called on the minister in Laurencekirk, who at first refused to

respond to the announcement of their arrival, until Boswell sent in his name. Then the minister deigned to appear and defended himself by saying he had once come out to a stranger who called, but the man proved to be 'a little worth person'.

Lord Monboddo's eccentric grandeur has disappeared. A speculative developer rearranged the ancient house, and in the grounds built several modern houses, so that the original configuration of the mansion's direct surroundings has almost been obscured. Over the cream pebble-dash and olive grey windows of the great house, some turrets may yet be seen beneath what I take to be the original small roof-slates; and a plaque high on the wall – '1635 RE' with what looks like 'ID'; and a couple of lions guarding the door. No reply from the down-a-step hall door: the new owners have raised a fine hedge of thick honeysuckle; an enormous monkeypuzzle dominates the immediate skyline. 'Monboddo,' says Boswell, 'is a wretched place, wild and naked, with a poor old house; though if I recollect right, [he did] there are two turrets which mark an old baron's residence.' *En route* across this bare land, Johnson recited Macbeth's speech on meeting the witches. 'Say from whence you owe this strange intelligence? or why upon this blasted heath you stop our way with such prophetic greeting?' His Lordship Monboddo, wearing a little round hat and a farmer's suit, met them at the gate.

The area surrounding Monboddo must have contained an aerodrome at some stage, perhaps during wartime, as evidenced in a few remaining Nissen huts, now filled with old packing cases and pallets, and undistinguished, domestic timber artefacts of all sorts. Although the landscape did not disappoint me nearly as severely as it did Johnson – subsequent farmers have grown many trees, and in the distance a great house still touches the sky – Monboddo may no longer be considered a classical Scottish fortified house. Nigel Tranter, in volume four (published 1966) of his series *The Fortified House in Scotland*, claims that Monboddo merits attention, even if 'decayed' and 'in a bad state structurally'. Since Tranter's description, the renovator has removed any possibility of seeing, for instance, a gaunt and wild building like the House of Shaws in *Kidnapped*, where David Balfour almost met his death at the hands of his scheming uncle. Tranter found something like six hundred of these fortified houses across Scotland, and attributes their presence to a combination of national character and links with France. When tall, angled, high-gabled and firm, they have perfected the art of looming, and some of their gateways are arched with stone, and some of their tower windows might still have a Mary, Queen of Scots, or a tartan Lady of Shalott roaming soulfully behind their small winking panes, or a Rapunzel leaning out into the sunshine. They symbolise 'Adventure-Scotland', with that certain Gothic-ness of Stevenson again, and Scott even more. What imagination anywhere could not respond to the image of strangers galloping hard on a moonswept night towards such high turrets? Not so in Monboddo today.

When Greek met Greek here, they talked of a Greek, Homer – and of other things, farming, and Virgil, and cider-making, and emigration, and manners, and biography, and learning. The conversation flowed with the current of many Johnsonian exchanges – a topic raised, a little amplification and a final exegesis, leading to a brief conclusion, in which Johnson habitually dangled one of his bright flashes of learning, catching the sun. His capacity for controversy in such social encounters had gained Johnson a great deal of his divinity in English letters, but in Scotland, with the good manners of a visitor necessarily prevailing, such intercourse invariably proved pleasant, Lord Monboddo's house typically thus. Neither man liked the other, but they had strewn eggs in their own pathways towards each other and they walked on them all afternoon.

Except at the beginning, when the eccentric lord immediately clashed with Johnson, even though Johnson says that the magnetism of Lord Monboddo's conversation 'easily drew us out of our way, and the entertainment which we received would have been a sufficient recompense for a much greater deviation'. Monboddo opened the game with his belief that our ancestors were greater than ourselves. Johnson disagreed: 'No, no my lord. We are as strong as they and a great deal wiser,' which, as Boswell points out, 'was an assault upon one of Lord Monboddo's capital dogmas, and I was afraid there would have been a violent altercation in the very close, before we got into the house'. Fortunately Monboddo's 'ancient *politesse*' stirred itself, and thereby was social catastrophe averted. Johnson thereafter responded to his host's familial hospitality with courtesy and agreeableness.

This is how the afternoon proceeded. Monboddo led them in, saying that since he was dressed like a farmer, they should have with him a farmer's family dinner. Remarking that he would not have forgiven Boswell had he not brought Johnson to Monboddo, he showed the travellers a stalk of corn, his *laetas segetes*, his abundant crop, and remarked that Virgil, to judge from his writings, seemed an equally practical and enthusiastic farmer. Whereupon Johnson observed that it did not necessarily follow 'that a man who has written a good poem on an art, has practised it', citing excellently instructive verses on cider by a man never known to have made any. Boswell raised the topic of emigration: Johnson distinguished between its value to 'a man of mere animal life' and 'a man of any intellectual enjoyment': the former content to wait for the earth to produce, the latter unlikely to wish barbarism upon himself and his descendants.

In the next exchange – or, rather, Boswell's footnote to it – comes another part of the answer to that literary-sleuth question of Boswell's physical *modus operandi*. Today he would have had a tape recorder: did he, like Dickens, at least have shorthand, a not unknown writerly aid since Cicero's time? In London he sat beside Johnson in their various venues; now he rode beside him in the post-chaise taking them up through eastern Scotland; next he would canter along beside him to the Western Isles. Did he pause to note the whole lot, or did he have extraordinary recall, writing in his room late at night or next morning, or did he get the bones down on paper, and afterwards flesh out the rest with Johnson's consultations? Given the unevenness and venereal adventure in Boswell's private life, any recollection in tranquillity would, in general, seem likely to be patchy. Nowhere so far in my limited knowledge of the pair has evidence of shorthand materialised – although at law he may have had some awareness of the skill. But surely too many conversations are recorded in the *Life* for Boswell to have checked them all in literal detail? Roadside reading at Monboddo in pleasant susnhine begins to provide answers to these questions.

'He and my lord spoke highly of Homer. Johnson: "He had all

the learning of his age. The shield of Achilles shews a nation in war, a nation in peace: harvest sport, nay stealing." '

At this point Boswell inserts an asterisk, and his footnote begins, 'My note of this is much too short. *Brevis esse laboro, obscurus fio.*' ('I labour to be brief, I make myself unclear.') Declaring that he wishes to offer to the public 'the very *Journal* which Dr Johnson read', he says he will not 'expand the text in any considerable degree, though I may occasionally supply a word to complete the sense as I fill up the blanks of abbreviation in the writing'.

So that is how he did it: *as I fill up the blanks of abbreviation in the writing* – with 'wd', and 'wl', and 'sd', and 'J', and 'Ld M', and 'ystdy', and 'Abrdn', and 'Mntrse', and 'Ednbro', or some such? It casts a new light (well – a farthing candle) on Boswell's recordings of Johnson's aphorisms: 'Whn a mn is tired of Lndn he is trd of lfe.' And what about that remark – 'the very *Journal* which Dr Johnson read'? Surely he meant that Johnson read it all the time, as Boswell wrote it? Or, since Johnson was dead when the *Journal* was published, did he mean that Johnson read the later stages of the manuscript as Boswell worked his way through it?

Other questions – did he have a quill pen, and therefore a supply of ink? Did he have lead and a slate? Later we learn that he used a pencil: Faber in Germany were already making graphite rods. All this leads to another question (thesis students, please note) – the relationship, if any, between the physical form and intellectual product of a writer's trade. The American novelist Thomas Wolfe wrote standing at a tall refrigerator – a chair and table being too cramped for the big mountain man – and he dropped unnumbered sheets, each with a few scrawled words, into a cardboard box at his feet. Churchill also stood, at a tall writing desk. Edgar Wallace dictated at speed. James Joyce wore a dentist's white jacket in the hope that the reflected light would make the words brighter to his poor hurting eyes. John Betjeman scribbled verses on the backs of envelopes and read them aloud in his car. Nigel Tranter writes his novels on small cards while out walking. Roald Dahl sat in a garden shed with an array of pencils and erasers on a board across his knees. Vladimir Nabokov squeezed tiny writing on small record or filing cards. Alan Ayckbourn leaves his new play until the last terrible moments when the cast has been assembled and the theatre booked and the tickets sold.

No matter how Boswell did it physically – and later it will transpire that he wrote some of it in a notebook Johnson gave him; no matter how he proceeded editorially, whether through a combination of this abbreviated writing, then checking afterwards what was said, and finally choosing – or agreeing – how much of Johnson's commentary and observation he should release, Boswell achieved something at least as important as a legally accurate record – he created, above everything, the *feel* of a full account. The conversation at Monboddo that afternoon exemplifies it; they considered how Homer never describes his characters, but permits them to develop themselves.

> MONBODDO: The history of manners is the most valuable. I never set a high value on any other history.
> JOHNSON: Nor I; and therefore I esteem biography, as giving us what comes near to ourselves, and what we can turn to use.
> BOSWELL: But in the course of general history, we find manners. In wars, we see the dispositions of people, their degrees of humanity, and other particulars.
> JOHNSON: Yes; but then you must take all the facts to get this; and it is but a little you get.
> MONBODDO: And it is that little which makes history valuable.

Such were the exchanges that Boswell, with his (by our standards) imperfect means of record, noted down – and even had time to comment that the two men had begun to 'agree like brothers'.

They next moaned about the decrease of learning in England, with Monboddo complaining of, in Scotland, not learning's mere decrease, but its extinction. Johnson attributed such decline in England to the fact that the bishops were now using other, more political rather than intellectual, methods of gaining preferment. Johnson then 'examined young Arthur, Lord Monboddo's son, in Latin. He answered very well.' Monboddo and Johnson debated 'whether the Savage or the London Shopkeeper had the best existence': unamazingly, no firm conclusion was reached, apart from Boswell's recurring delight at how well the encounter went between the two men.

Johnson went to the lavatory – at least, that is presumably what Boswell means when he says, 'having retired for a short time' – and Boswell and Monboddo engaged cordially with each other. Johnson returned, and as the ladies left the table, Johnson, a man who 'insisted that politeness was of great consequence in society', stood. 'Depend upon it,' he said, 'the want of it [politeness] never fails to produce something disagreeable.' Boswell concludes the account of their visit by satisfying a little further his search for concord between Johnson and Monboddo – each had a black servant. Johnson, having established that Monboddo's servant, Gory, had been baptised – and even confirmed by the Bishop of Durham – gave the man a shilling.

At this point Boswell records having experienced a qualm regarding Johnson's continuance of the journey, because the previous night Johnson had said, 'If we must ride much, we shall not go, and there's an end on't.' Seeing him in good spirits now, Boswell teased him for his earlier hestitancy, called him 'a delicate Londoner . . . a macaroni', and Johnson defended himself with an unserious disingenuousness by saying he had only feared not finding a horse able enough to carry him.

Boswell employs over a thousand words to describe the Monboddo visit, which began around mid-day, and ended when they had to leave for Aberdeen which they did not reach until late that night. Johnson flits over it all in a sentence, and in his letters to Mrs Thrale he came forth only a little more, alluding only to the success of the visit, and to the debate as to whether the savage or the shopkeeper had the best life. 'Our opinions were, I think, maintained on both sides without full conviction; Monboddo declared boldly for the savage, and I perhaps for that reason sided with the Citizen.' This accords with a remark Johnson made to Boswell as they drove towards Aberdeen: 'I might have taken the side of the savage equally, had anybody else taken the side of the shopkeeper.'

Not a savage nor a shopkeeper to be seen on this windy, sunny afternoon, great clouds pillowing across the sky. Across the scrubby ground past the Nissen huts runs a main road, with a bus service to Stonehaven on the A94, where it would again pick up the A92. Warm scents rose from a honeysuckle hedge at Mon-boddo, the much-changed home of a man who, according to Sir Walter Scott, went out at night with a candle to inspect his turnips growing in the fields; who, hating to sit behind a horse's backside, would not travel in a carriage and therefore – he was in his eighties – rode to London on horseback; who took a cold bath every day and damaged his children's health by insisting they did the same; and who, when in residence at Edinburgh, gave dinner parties at which his wine-flagons were wreathed in garlands of roses.

'We came somewhat late to Aberdeen,' wrote Johnson, 'and found the inn so full, that we had some difficulty in obtaining admission, till Mr Boswell made himself known. His name overpowered all objection, and we found a very good house and civil treatment.' Mr Thrale had written to Johnson care of Boswell at Aberdeen; probably a refreshing fact to Sam who in his final illness observed to his servant, 'An odd thought strikes me – we shall receive no letters in the grave.' Handing over the envelope from Mr Thrale, the waiter at the New Inn recognised Boswell's name and likeness to his father: Lord Auchinleck stayed there on circuit. Thus, Boswell and Johnson found a room at the crowded New Inn, which no longer exists: the corner where it stood, and which it once shared with the city jail, is now occupied comprehensively by a bank. They stayed in Aberdeen from the night of Saturday, 21 August, to the morning of Tuesday the 24th, venturing forth from the New Inn to see and be seen, to be entertained and, in Johnson's case, to be honoured by the body municipal.

'As Scotland is little known to the greater part of those who may read these observations, it is not superfluous to relate that under the name Aberdeen are comprised two towns standing about a mile distant from each other, but governed, I think, by the same magistrates.' Johnson was human too: in writing to Mrs Thrale he contradicted this point and stated more correctly that both towns had separate civil and academic identities. There are still two towns – in effect, however, the new Aberdeen has all but completely superseded Old Aberdeen, which now exists only in the way many international cities have a Latin Quarter or a Chinatown, only somewhat smaller and – as becomes all Aberdonians and most east-coast Scots – very discreet. Johnson's report otherwise remains applicable, with Old Aberdeen the 'ancient episcopal city', possessing 'the appearance of a town in decay', and New Aberdeen the location of bustling commerce: 'the houses are large and lofty, and the streets spacious and clean. They build almost wholly with the granite used in the new pavement of the streets of London . . . It is beautiful and must be very lasting.'

Insofar as their Scottish adventure was concerned, Boswell the diarist and biographer, and Johnson the man of letters and lexicographer, had become travel writers. Aberdeen, whatever its staging-post status in their plans, received the same attention as their eventual western destinations, and Johnson approached it with the attitude he later brought to the Highlands and the west, with Boswell, for his part, consistent in the manner and style of his own reportage – observing Johnson as he observed Scotland. These arrangements would not have differed had they been in the Fens, or watching Scandinavia's hot springs: Johnson went to inspect the landscape he described: Boswell took his landscape, the lumpy Dr Johnson, with him.

Johnson thereby validated the journey in his reports, and, true enquirer that he was, did not accordingly neglect to report on such a major place as Aberdeen. Even if it were not a leading objective of his tour, his natural intelligent curiosity, and his conscientiousness on behalf of his readers overcame any notional hierarchy of information. Scotland he had gone to see, and Scotland they would receive from his eyes and words.

Thus, the Aberdeen report in his book, however he anticipated his Hebridean travels, is the largest so far, with St Andrews a close second: his longest passages are naturally reserved for Skye and the islands. In so measuring him, another consideration must be taken into account. Johnson was a proportionate man: his language and thought had balance in them, as had his own spirit. It is possible to argue that he wrote in the proportion to which each location claimed or received his spans of time and attention – and as he spent more than twice the length of time out on the islands as he did getting there, the greater part of his book addresses the west.

*   *   *

For Sunday, 22 August, Boswell once more makes available their timetable and (almost unrelievedly academic) personnel record. Professor Thomas Gordon joined them for breakfast at the New Inn, after which they went to a Service at the 'English chapel', that is to say, the Episcopalian, that is to say, the Anglican church in Scotland. The congregation was 'respectable', the organist, a Mr Tait, 'admirable'. After service they strolled down to the waterside, where they talked about stockings and the weaving of plaid; 'What particular parts of commerce are chiefly exercised by the merchants of Aberdeen, I have not inquired,' wrote Johnson. 'The manufacture which forces itself upon a stranger's eye is that of knit-stockings, on which the women of the lower class are visibly employed.' Turn to Boswell for the gloss – that it was 'Cromwell's soldiers taught the Aberdeen people to make shoes and stockings, and to plant cabbages.' At which information Johnson laughed.

One of Boswell's invaluable moments occurs here. From time to time in the *Life*, he describes Johnson's voice as manly, or deep, or sonorous, or loud. Others have chosen to describe not so much the sound, as the use – to harangue, to interrupt, to hold the floor, to declaim. Johnson, as he did at Montrose, also employed much silence, and many who had come to one social occasion or another expecting to hear the grand disquisitioner, found him disappointingly reticent and withdrawn, even if making little antic noises to himself. Perhaps in those preceding silences he took himself through some sort of editing process, preparatory to making an entrance in which not a word would be wasted. When he chose to speak, he used his voice to argue fiercely and with great precision, and now, on a Sunday morning ramble in Aberdeen, Boswell suddenly became aware, 'to an extraordinary degree, of Dr Johnson's excellent English pronunciation. I cannot account for its striking me more now than any other day, but it was as if new to me; and I listened to every sentence he spoke as if to a musical composition.' Given that Boswell does not record any singularly new form of felicity in Johnson's speech, perhaps he was struck with the contrast between Johnson's mode of speech and the Doric accents of Aberdeen.

Strolling, they pondered public education versus private schooling; Johnson wondered why boys from England had been sent as far as Aberdeen to be educated, with 'so many good schools in England', and they went back to the New Inn, to be joined there by Sir Alexander Gordon, an old friend of Johnson's, who had sent a card in advance, and through Boswell we join their conversation as it drifts back to the stocking-making.

Sir Alexander, Professor of Medicine at the King's College, revealed that in peacetime Aberdeen exported a hundred thousand pounds' worth of stockings a year, and in wartime a hundred and seventy thousand. When Johnson enquired the cause of the difference, Sir Alexander claimed that there was 'more occasion for them in war', but Professor Thomas Gordon (no relation, Boswell?) said, 'Because the Germans, who are our great rivals in the manufacture of stockings, are otherwise employed in time of war.'

JOHNSON: Sir, you have given a very good solution.

Johnson ate 'several plate-fulls of Scotch broth, with barley and peas in it, and seemed very fond of the dish'. When Boswell, hearing his praise of it, said, perhaps enquiringly, 'You never ate it before,' Johnson replied that he had not but did not care how soon he ate it again. (In a long letter to Hester Thrale on 30 September, written from Ostig on Skye, he remarked with a different emphasis: 'Barley broath [sic] is a constant dish, and is made well in every house. A stranger, if he is prudent, will secure his share for it is not certain that he will be able to eat any thing else.')

In the afternoon they all had tea with the 'lively, cheerful, sensible' wife of an Episcopalian minister – Mrs Riddoch, Boswell's cousin, the former Miss Dallas: her husband was unwell and stayed in his sick room. Johnson met Mrs Riddoch's little niece, Stuart Dallas, and, with his voice deliberately booming and hollow, told her he was a giant, that he slept in a cave, 'and had a bed in the rock, and she should have a bed cut opposite it'.

Throughout their journey several topics remained alive between them, to be returned to again and again, not so much as if the first discourse had not resolved matters – more as if they remained as life issues, or questions of the day. These included – in broad, and in aspects – politics, religion, and, one of Johnson's favourite subjects, the law. On the night he came to Edinburgh, sitting up with Boswell in James's Court until two o'clock in the morning, they talked of a recent case in which a murder, committed twenty years before, became a legal talking-point when the judges of Scotland allowed, as a plea, the length of time elapsed. Johnson returned to this case now in Aberdeen, saying that even though he understood how difficult it would be to ensure accurate evidence, it still did not make it right that a murderer should go unpunished. Then, as he frequently did, he took a moral line, based on what he saw as natural law, and said he would not blame, and might even assist, the victim's relatives in such a case, should they wish to exact retribution and then hide. Then, Boswell and Johnson returned to the New Inn and sat quietly all evening, and (it being Sunday presumably) discussed Christ and Christianity. 'Never,' writes Boswell, 'did I see him in a better frame; calm, gentle, wise, holy' – with Johnson opining that the essence of the Crucifixion lay in showing to the world that even the Son of God suffered on account of sin, and in doing so, displayed how heinous a thing sin must be.

On the evidence of the many religious interpolations reported by Boswell, Johnson could have been a divine, a mystic. His faith comprised curiously disparate elements – the rough, frightened, humility of the countryman; the thoughtful worshipper; the vigorous enquirer; and even though not a micro-molecule of disrespect ever enters his attitude towards his Deity, his natural radical-ness stood so near at hand one can almost feel its heat. It never broke out above the surface: he feared heresy and blasphemy too much.

On Monday, more academics swam in Johnson's travelling aquarium: Principal Campbell, Professor Ross and a Dr Gerard, who had 'come six miles from the country on purpose'. First of all, they viewed the Marischal College, and at one o'clock went to the Town House, or Town Hall, where the magistrates waited to honour their distinguished visitor.

The place of this ceremony has also disappeared, but a contemporary record describes a fine, high-ceilinged, large-windowed room, hung with candle sconces and more than one crystal candelabrum. Johnson took enormous pleasure in the honour, and reported it in both his book and, more touchingly, in his correspondence with Mrs Thrale: 'I had the honour of attending the Lord Provost of Aberdeen, and was presented with the freedom of the city, not in a gold box but in good Latin. Let me pay Scotland just one praise. There was no officer gaping for a fee; this could have been said of no city on the English side of the Tweed.' He mentions this 'fee' in his book, too; he may not have relished the idea of paid officials cadging tips.

Part of the honour in Aberdeen included the conferee's right to wear his citation, or burgess-ticket, all day in his hat. When the parchment had been read aloud – *Samuel Johnson, L.L.D. receptus et admissus fuit in municipes et fratres guildae prefat burgi de Aberedeen* – it was then sealed, rolled like a diploma and fastened to Johnson's hat with a red ribbon. 'I wore my patent of freedom,' he told Mrs Thrale, 'in my hat from the New town to the Old, about a mile.'

Boswell amplifies in a way which casts a slightly different glow on the affair: he comments on how striking it was to hear all the aldermen of Aberdeen drinking Johnson's health with much exclamation of the great man's name. Neither Boswell nor Johnson would have been so damningly ungracious as to suggest (as other Scottish cities accused), that in the interests of free drink Aberdeen's city fathers were promiscuous with their honours.

After the walk to Old Aberdeen, Boswell and Johnson ate lunch. The following seven people sat around the table – both Gordons, that is, Professor Thomas and the host Sir Alexander; Provost Jopp, he of the conferring; Professor Ross and Professor Dunbar; Boswell and Johnson. After they had eaten, Dr Gerard arrived, as did Professor Leslie and Professor MacLeod. It all seems to have lacked sparkle; Johnson told Mrs Thrale, 'Boswell was very angry that the Aberdeen professors would not talk,' while Boswell says they were afraid to, and as a consequence he and Johnson found themselves 'barren' – having already spent a morning in which they had scant conversation with anyone. For whatever reason, they all now sat in some dumbness at Sir Alexander Gordon's table, and it is the only meal so far recorded by Boswell in which he has no conversation to report, nor argument, nor words of Johnson.

Dr Gerard, from six miles out, he who had come in specially, did try to sling something in. He told Johnson that Warburton (the combative English divine and man of letters, whose generally controversial national presence made him a common topic of Johnsonian conversation) had a close relationship with an unnamed 'eminent printer'. Johnson, never under an obligation to generate social ease, dismissed that by saying 'The intimacy is such as one of the professors here may have with one of the carpenters who is repairing the college,' Johnson's point being that the printer, having printed some of Warburton's works, might perhaps have bought the copyright in one or two of them. Dr Gerard fought back, by saying that he had seen a letter from Warburton to the printer, complaining that one half of Scotland's clergy were fanatics, and the other half were infidels, but Johnson still gainsaid him; Warburton, he believed, wrote as he spoke – without thinking; 'Sir, the very worst way of being intimate, is by scribbling.'

Other than this exchange, and a desultory extension of it, in which Boswell tried to get his Bear to perform by raising the quality of genius as a conversational topic, lunch and its aftermath proceeded to a dull conclusion. Unlike Edinburgh, Aberdeen did not groom the fur of *Ursa Major*.

After lunch they walked in Sir Alexander's garden 'and saw his little grotto, which is hung with pieces of poetry written in a fair hand'. Johnson complained of having been rendered exhausted by Sir Alexander's over-zealous efforts to entertain him. They visited two booksellers' shops, looking for a volume of poems by the Aberdonian Latin poet, Arthur Johnson, who had been Principal of the Marischal College. They called on the unwell clergyman Mr Riddoch, and again finding the conversation wanting – the poor man was unable to tell Johnson how much a university education cost at Aberdeen – the couple resisted all invitations to supper. Back at their inn, they sat quietly reflecting how little Aberdeen had offered them in terms of conversational or intellectual stimulation – or, as Boswell reported Johnson's remark, 'that the Aberdonians had not started a single *mawkin* [the Scottish word for hare] for us to pursue'.

Fingers across the map to retrace their journey – from the New Inn they went to the English chapel, walked to the shore, saw the Marischal College, were welcomed at the Town House, viewed Old Aberdeen, looked at the Old College, visited the King's College where Sir Alexander Gordon was professor of Medicine, and visited two bookshops. Not a challenging or penetrating tour of enquiry, especially as the population of Aberdeen at the time must have been not less than twenty thousand.

In Johnson's report, the education offered by the city takes precedence over any popular descriptions or concerns, beginning with an interest in the fact that Hector Boece or Boethius became the first President of the King's College, in 1494, at the instigation of Bishop William Elphinstone, effectively the founder of Aberdeen University – whose tomb may still be seen. Johnson admired Boece, not for his historical accuracy, but for his prose and intellectual style, 'formed with great diligence upon ancient models, and wholly uninfected with monastic barbarity'. He excuses Boece's historical inventions – on account of which his Latin History of Scotland and others have been long dismissed, and now have only curiosity value – by saying that Boece wrote in an age when all men, owing to lack of true knowledge, were credulous, and, dazzled with the light of discovery after such long dark ages, could not see distinctly.

Johnson also enjoyed catching sight of ancient texts in Aberdeen – a Hebrew manuscript 'of exquisite penmanship', and 'a Latin translation of Aristotle's *Politicks* by Leonardus Aretinus, written in the Roman character with nicety and beauty, which, as the art of printing has made them no longer necessary, are not now to be found'.

He also interested himself in the administration of this seat of learning, the colours of the students' gowns – scarlet; and the professors' – black. The eating and sleeping arrangements of the students, whether in college or abroad about the town, caught his attention; the length of the courses; the kind of degree available, and all the curricular paraphernalia of learning. He had addressed such matters in Edinburgh, St Andrews, and would in Glasgow, with an awareness that he was reporting Scotland for an English audience as he might have reported Bavaria or Sweden. Johnson therefore knew in advance the principal social and economic demography of his readership – the professional and/or wealthy classes in and around London.

Aberdeen has a feeling of true foreign-ness, a different flavour – Scottish, undoubtedly, and therefore brisk and organised, but not without a feel of Norse and beyond. The quayside had as many ferries lined up as a Greek port, big-snouted vessels bound for Orkney or the Shetland islands, and perhaps distant Ophir. It feels more like Trieste, though, than Piraeus: the sounds of the voices in the streets murmured similarly of exotica. In Trieste a number of nations converge – Albanian and Yugoslavian, as well as Italian and Venetian; here the Scandinavians and the Calvinists and the hard Canadian men of the oil lift the city's atmosphere out of a local *milieu*.

All things sparkle in bright light: a dowdy creature will gleam in a ballroom. The stone they used to build Aberdeen may be built for endurance rather than seduction, but when it catches the sun it offers a lively spirit as well as a safe haven. Much of the Aberdeen they saw is now no more. The strongest and oldest main parts of the current Granite City suggest Victorian wealth, not-very-old money – long Union Street, and Albyn Place and Albyn Terrace, Queens Gardens, Prince Arthur Street: behind these façades live a class who, a century and more ago, would have populated the novels of an Aberdonian Trollope or Thackeray. The firmness of the houses has not changed; a few may have become offices, or been sub-divided into what must surely be splendid apartments, but the depth of the society persists. Stout merchant and professional cash built these statements of position and status all over these islands. If one may suspend conscience, and forget the conditions and costs of labour which allowed them to create this wealth, then these streets – as they do in London and Edinburgh, and still to be seen in Dublin – define the comfort of the eighteenth- and nineteenth-century middle classes. With haughtily reassuring windows, tall, regular, gleaming, discreet, and vivid brass bellpulls, and deep steps of extraordinary cleanliness, a poor man might walk here as a Dickensian child put its face to a windowpane.

Turn left at the end of Union Street for the Marischal College, a tall and wide building of white-grey stone, with many windows and pinned down by several bus-stops. Other than at Oxford and Cambridge, educational buildings seem generally to have become disappointing. Their great preserved facades give way to the necessities of low-budget modern living – poor furniture, inhibited taste, as at St Andrews, and a disappointing lack of the glories of old lecture theatres. The Marischal College has an attractive staircase, and that curious atmosphere of university colleges – a busy air, yet with few people in evidence. A person, perhaps a porter, said there was not a lot to see at the Marischal College. Any College treasures, any old manuscripts for example? He said, no, nothing like that, all gone, that occasionally the place held exhibitions of Mankind and so-forth and they were quite interesting. Any portraits of interest? No, no. Any beautiful rooms? That would be a matter of opinion; he had a newspaper which he kept looking at, and shaking out. How many students attended the Marischal College? Quite a lot, but they come and they go. Anybody to whom one could talk about the place? Depends on what you want to find out. Any record of Dr Johnson's visit? He doubted that. Well, maybe somebody would know. But he's away. 'We often get tourists here,' he said.

Well – Boswell and Johnson found Aberdeen a place where conversation had not proved stimulating. Then, like a host who becomes most animated when his guests are leaving, this leader of the campaign against garrulousness gave me succinct directions to Old Aberdeen.

Johnson's 'about a mile' takes twenty minutes on foot, quite a downhill journey, and, if Old Aberdeen be small, it is also pleasing. Colleges on one side, sweet-cheeked houses on the other, and ahead an old municipal building; the architecture of the larger properties, though varied, is still Sir Walter Scott-gothic. The stretch called College Bounds becomes High Street, crosses the busy St Machar's Drive and forks: to the right, Don Street, to the left, the discreet Chanonry. Both rows converge upon St Machar's Cathedral, and then wander their separate ways through Seaton Park to the River Don, and eventually the Brig o' Balgownie – although Johnson does not seem to have walked that far.

He did visit the King's College and Boswell name-dropped regarding the chapel, wherein lies the fifteenth-century Bishop Elphinstone, 'of whom I shall have occasion to write,' declared Bozzy, 'in my history of James IV of Scotland, the patron of my family': Auchinleck was granted to the Boswells in return for favours rendered. The delightful chapel had no other callers; the afternoon light turned the stained-glass windows to kaleidoscopes, and outside, the westering sun gilded the tiles and eyebrows of the roofs and high old buildings. A wedding had begun at St Machar's – gowned shenanigans and excitements, the cars, and the relatives, and the best feet forward. Brides do not tremble, they fuss; bridesmaids even more so, and men stand about sheepishly, collies waiting for a whistle telling them what to do.

How was Johnson at Aberdeen? Bored, and humane, and gentle with the little Dallas girl, to whom he said he was a giant. His capacity for addressing children impressed all who saw it. When the Thrale children played games he participated – racing them barefoot, or pleased to be cast as the elephant in their zoo of animals. He retained many child qualities of his own, including a liking for an excellent roll downhill, witnessed by one of his friends, a Mr Langton, who had walked with Johnson to the top of a very steep height. 'When we understood what he meant to do, we endeavoured to dissuade him; but he was resolute, saying he had not had a roll for a long time; and taking out of his pockets whatever might be in them – keys, pencil, purse, or pen-knife – and laying himself parallel with the edge of the hill, he actually descended turning himself over and over till he came to the bottom.'

At night, the streets of the Granite City proved astonishingly full. Crowds of people roistered along, chattering and sometimes cheering, of all ages and types. A waitress in the hotel said they all remembered the day of the big Piper Alpha rig disaster 'in the same way that we remembered where we were when Kennedy was shot'. The police, patrolling numerously, said this midnight populousness was not uncommon in Aberdeen, but was perhaps unique in Scottish cities. No such nightlife or streetlights here in August 1773; moments in Boswell's *Life* fix a fleeting glimpse:

'When he walked, it was like the struggling gait of one in fetters' – even in Aberdeen? Even with a diploma pinned to his hat, its red ribbon-seal fluttering in the breeze? This large man, 'whose countenance was the cast of an ancient statue', says the concluding passage of the *Life*, tolerated unstimulatedly the hospitality of the silent professors, and wandered through Old Aberdeen looking for a book of poetry, then back to his inn.

The ear being the truest witness, Boswell's remark about Johnson's voice is very arresting. It introduces the thought that in his speech as well as in his writing, Johnson understood that the essence of art lies in the perfect marriage of form and content, therefore, Boswell may have reached for an accuracy beyond sycophancy. If Johnson did speak as he wrote – economically, pithily and with a gift of great accuracy – Boswell's Aberdeen observation means that he also sounded beautifully.

But again the questions – was Boswell telling the truth about Johnson, or was he presenting him in the best possible light? Did this biographical relationship grow out of Johnson himself? Who was manipulating whom? Boswell had by now made it plain over a number of years that he wished to write Johnson's *Life*. Ought we to think less of Johnson for agreeing because he knew full well that he could influence Boswell? Another question: did Boswell write so glowingly of Johnson in Scotland in order to obtain Johnson's biographical blessing? When Johnson, as we know he did, dipped into Boswell's Hebrides *Journal*, its tone cannot have put him off the notion of Boswell writing a *Life*. In a footnote to an observation made in Mull, Boswell writes, 'It is no small satisfaction to me to reflect, that Dr Johnson read this, and, after being apprised of my intention, communicated to me, at subsequent periods, many particulars of his life, which probably could not otherwise have been preserved.' Johnson, however, fully aware of the likely number of biographers he might attract before and after his death, found here a biography in which he could have a say, thus not only securing his immortality, but controlling it.

They left Aberdeen at eight o'clock on the morning of Tuesday, 24 August, and, climbing to high ground above the city, headed north-east along the coast through insignificant country – 'naked', observed Johnson, 'of all vegetable decoration'. Coastal erosion, the advance of the sands, had interested him insofar as it had destroyed the estate of a landowner who then chose to relinquish the property rather than pay the requisite taxes. At Ellon, where the modern road forks right over the bridge on the A92, and a pretty walk runs along by the river Ythan, the landlady of an inn where they breakfasted wished she had remembered to show to this great doctor (of whom they had heard) a child of hers with a chronic lump in his throat. Useless for Boswell to point out that notwithstanding the title 'Doctor', physick did not belong in Johnson's otherwise comprehensive repertoire, and here it was that the landlord made a distinction which so pleased Johnson: 'They say he is the greatest man in England, except Lord Mansfield.' Without the qualification, Johnson felt the remark would have been devoid of enjoyable meaning. He understood the depth of the compliment: the landlord had compared him favourably with that greatest of heroes, a local boy made good (so long, of course, as he makes good far away). Mansfield, from Perth, progressed through the law to a political career of unusual prominence at Westminster.

Some miles beyond Ellon, the A92 bifurcates: the right-hand fork becomes the A952 which eventually leads to Peterhead and its gaol by the sea. Boswell and Johnson took this road to Cruden Bay, in order to fulfil an invitation put in train by a lady they had met at worship in Aberdeen on Sunday morning. Lord and Lady Errol owned Slains Castle, a wide pile on the land's edge: the pair arrived as the dinner bell rang at three in the afternoon.

This timing gives some idea of how long their travelling habitually took: still in a post-chaise, and allowing an hour, say, for breakfast, they required seven hours or so to travel a distance of about twenty-eight miles. The variations within that calculation are not extreme – perhaps an extra half-hour at breakfast; perhaps they did not leave Aberdeen precisely (Boswell says 'about eight in the morning'), perhaps the road wound around to make thirty miles. Even with the wind of generosity at their back, why did they travel at a man's walking pace? It seems likely that the condition of the roads had begun to grow uneven after Aberdeen: today, upon leaving the main road, the castle, now ruined, may only be approached on pockmarked and muddy lanes, and if these approximate to the surfaces upon which Johnson had to travel once he entered a remoter Scotland, his pace may be understood and excused, and his courage further applauded.

Whether viewed from the high road, or across the low fences and stone ditches and grassy banks of the surrounding farms, the ruin of Slains looks familiar. Not so much in appearance as in mood, a fact which could owe to the Gothic-ness of another literary association. This is where Bram Stoker reputedly completed his novel *Dracula*, which was published in 1897. His lore says that Abraham Stoker, a graduate of Trinity College, Dublin, had given faithful service as general *amanuensis* to Sir Henry Irving, the fearsome Victorian actor-manager – for whom Stoker had given up his civil service career. When Stoker approached him with a play intended for his master, Irving, taking no thought of the devotion shown by his *factotum*, reacted along a scale from dismissiveness to contempt. Whereupon Stoker, gifted with Dublin's malice, wrote instead a novel – about a bloodsucking, ennobled gentleman whose business was carried on at night, in or around grand dramatic buildings. If the cap fitted Irving, presumably he could wear it.

Slains may be approached in two ways: comfortably by means of a long quiet climbing lane from the trees on the edge of Cruden, or more adventurously, once alighted from the bus on the upper road, between stone walls, along that wide lane of sticky brown clay, perilously full of holes. As I walked by, someone's car stuck there and would not move, and a neighbouring farmer, irritably habituated to such incident, hauled it to the road with his tractor.

Just inside the entrance proper, the sea slices a vicious swathe inland, describing almost a half-circle. Boswell says, 'We walked round the house till stopped by a cut made by the influx of the sea. The house is quite built upon the shore; the windows look upon the main ocean, and the King of Denmark is Lord Errol's nearest neighbour on the north-east.' Note – the *King* of Denmark, not a farmer, or a Danish crofter: Boswell the consistent upward aspirant.

Confusion may arise regarding Slains, where two castles exist.

One, a little farther up the coast, is called 'Old Slains' and was built several centuries earlier: it is now ruined far beyond the one in which Boswell and Johnson stayed. Old Slains stands even more perilously close to the North Sea cliffs, and in high weather the waves climb and spray the windows of the people who live in the houses under the shadow of Old Slains's remaining high wall. A cannon or two have been placed around a modern Scandinavian-type house, more for ornament than effectiveness.

At that eighteenth-century mid-afternoon table in 'new' Slains, sat Lady Errol, Charles Boyd – Lord Errol's brother whom the visitors first mistook to be the earl – and some of the Errol children with their tutor and governess. Acquaintance was renewed between Mr Boyd and Dr Johnson: they had met 'at Cumming the Quaker's' (whose principles Johnson once called upon to illuminate an argument with Boswell. Tom Cumming, on account of his religious denomination, said he would not fight in the 1745 Rebellion, but would drive an ammunition cart: Johnson's point had to do with the difference between religious texts meant to be taken literally, and those intended for general guidance.) After lunch, Lady Errol paraded all her children – six girls, two boys.

Johnson soon wished to leave, and pressed Boswell, who, of his very nature, did not want to go until he had met the Earl. Lady Errol intervened through her brother-in-law, informing Johnson, in the hyperbole of hospitality, that she would never allow him to enter Slains again if he left now, and, with the daylight of the long summer evening available, she provided her coachman so that the travellers could view a couple of local geological curiosities, the Buller of Buchan and the rock of Dunbui.

When his *Journal of a Tour to the Hebrides* appeared, Boswell's reflections caused him some trouble, including threats of actual bodily harm from people he mentioned. As all third parties do, we may delight in his indiscretions – but Charles Boyd did not, nor did any Scots of allied sympathies. 'Mr Boyd was engaged, in 1745—6, on the same side with many unfortunate mistaken noblemen and gentlemen' – meaning he was among those on the Stuart side at Culloden and elsewhere.

Nor did Boswell the North Briton confine himself to political toadying to London, as he swung from compliments to conveyed slights: '[Mr Boyd] entertained us with great civility. He had a pompousness or formal plenitude in his conversation, which I did not dislike. Dr Johnson said "there was too much elaboration in his talk."' Mr Boyd had escaped to France after the '45, had married a French wife, who now lived with him in Aberdeen, and he tried his best to cure the local people using the knowledge he had gained from some medical text-books he found in a house on the island of Arran while on the run.

The wind coming off the North Sea along here can skin your lips, even on a day when the sun appears to be shining. Some of the fields surrounding Slains castle had unkempt crops in them, awaiting tending, prior to lifting. The sea's cut into Slains's yard is as deep and threatening as a wound, and on the far side, only a little sward exists between the front of the castle and the cliff standing over the water. Inside, the ruin is elaborate, a warren of old rooms and passages. The house's former importance can be measured according to its size, exquisite, courageous location, and the remains of huge fireplaces. 'From the windows,' wrote Johnson, 'the eye wanders over the sea that separates Scotland from Norway, and when the winds beat with violence must enjoy all the terrifick grandeur of the tempestuous ocean. I would not for my amusement wish for a storm; but as storms, whether wished or not, will sometimes happen, I may say, without violation of humanity, that I should willingly look out upon them from Slanes [sic] castle.'

This is a formidable ruin. From here, Norse longboats were sighted, ever before a castle was raised: fishing-boats must have perished within earshot; the sunlight on the water (to paraphrase Louis MacNeice's poem) hardened and grew cold. It is possible to see the weather from a long way off, but as the people at Old Slains know, the weather then arrives at such speed over the surface of the North Sea that seeing it approach seems hardly sufficient warning. Bram Stoker may have been a genial enough fellow externally, but he knew how to find a place which would match the chill in the soul of his novel.

*　　　*　　　*

When they drove out from the castle, Johnson found little in Dunbui's yellow rock to engage his attention, other than the remarkable fact that the Guillemot, known locally as the Coot, while as small as a duck, lays eggs as large as those of a goose. The Buller of Buchan had more appeal, and he summarised it with glittering accuracy: 'It has the appearance of a vast well bordered with a wall.' Here, the sea has eroded a cavity, which could only be refilled with a deep plug of rock, a column pegged into the hole. Johnson wrote, 'The edge of the Buller is not wide, and to those that walk round, appears very narrow.' Johnson braved the walk. 'He that ventures to look downward sees, that if his foot should slip, he must fall from this dreadful elevation upon stones on one side, or into water on the other. We however went round, and were glad when the circuit was completed.' Boswell felt discomfort, albeit at the sight of Johnson striding irregularly along.

Johnson then insisted on descending to the shore and boating into the basin itself, which was entered by means of vigorous rowing to the very entrance, then, oars shipped, by gliding the rest of the way, as the extended oars would not squeeze through the opening – although they might today, after two centuries of further erosion. Mr Boyd told them that the name 'Buller' derived from the French *bouloir*, reduced by local folk to 'the Pot', in which cauldron Dr Johnson now gambolled with a certain heartiness, speculating upon the depth of the caves, and their uses for smugglers and pirates, or shelters for boatmen: Mr Boyd also told them of people from Peterhead holding picnics in one of the caverns.

They returned to the castle for tea and coffee in the drawing-room. Mr Boyd had patients waiting, a fact I do not quite understand, since he had just told Boswell and Johnson the story of one of Lord Errol's tenants. Too far from Aberdeen for convenient medicine, the Earl, in order to have his own surgeon, had the son of one of his tenants thus educated. Came a day when the man revealed that he had kept an exact account of all the money laid out on him, and could now, in his unexpectedly good situation in life, pay every penny back to his benefactor. 'The earl,' reports

Boswell, 'was pleased with the generous gratitude and genteel offer of the man; but refused it.'

By the bow-window Johnson, probably inspired by the potential fury of the sea, recited Horace's ode *Iam satis terris*. I wish Boswell had thought fit to quote as much as Johnson uttered, if only to observe Johnson's intimate, word-perfect familiarity with Horace, and whether he also added a translation. How far did he go? The entire fifty-two lines? Or only down as far as the moment when the Tiber is hurled back violently from the Etruscan shore? The glimpse of Johnson reflecting on the position of Slains Castle in relation to the perilous sea, displays a man with a capacity for the learned *mot juste*, surely a gift which Johnson polished, having discovered how he might impress with it.

With Mr Boyd ministering, and Lady Errol attending to her children, Boswell and Johnson passed the time – it will have been close to, or even after, seven o'clock by now – chatting quietly, admiring the sea view, inspecting the pictures, including a portrait of Lord Errol by their 'amiable and elegant friend', of whom Johnson observed, concluding some complimentary remarks, 'Sir Joshua Reynolds is the most invulnerable man I know; the man with whom if you should quarrel, you would find the most difficulty how to abuse.'

Being in a noble house, they discussed inheritance of land by means of 'entails', the settling of land upon members of a family in a predetermined order to prevent any one owner or inheritor bequeathing it outside the family. Three years later, this question would much trouble Boswell. When his father raised the question of who should inherit the estate after him, and whether he should choose 'heirs general', that is to say, include females in the vexed question – in an earlier generation, four sisters had been passed over in favour of a Boswell nephew – Boswell consulted Johnson repeatedly, before the matter was resolved to Boswell's general satisfaction. (He subsequently became an excellent landlord at Auchinleck.)

It also troubled Peggie Boswell, and arose in those memorable letters between herself and Johnson.

16 May 1776: Madam – You must not think me uncivil in omitting to answer the letter with which you favoured me some time ago.

I imagined it to have been written without Mr Boswell's knowledge, and therefore supposed the answer to require, what I could
not find, a private conveyance. The difference with Lord Auchinleck is now over; and since young Alexander has appeared, I hope
no more difficulties will arise among you; for I sincerely wish you
all happy. Do not teach the young ones to dislike me, as you dislike
me yourself; but let me at least have Veronica's kindness, because
she is my acquaintance . . . Pray take care of [James], and tame
him. The only thing in which I have the honour to agree with you
is, in loving him; and while we are so much of a mind in a matter
of so much importance, our other quarrels will, I hope, produce
no great bitterness.

Johnson declared himself in favour of such prescribed succession:
'His opinion was that so much land should be entailed as that
families should never fall into contempt, and as much left free as
to give them all the advantages in case of any emergency.' In this
cake-and-eat-it arrangement, no one possessor could sell off the
estate, yet in Johnson's view, the landowner should have enough
over and above the inheritance to bargain with, should he need
to raise cash by sale or mortgage, but never so much as to dis-
inherit his succeeding generations.

Works by Hogarth hung in the gallery at Slains: the library
contained 'a valuable numerous collection', and Boswell renders
one of his usual excellent off-the-cuff services to our understanding of eighteenth-century domestic arrangements: 'The noble
owner has built of brick, along the square on the inside, a gallery,
both on the first and second story, the house being no higher; so
that he has always a dry walk, and the rooms, to which formerly
there was no approach but through each other, have now all separate entries from the gallery.'

The noble owner returned around nine o'clock, and renewed
his acquaintance with Dr Johnson, with whom he had once dined
in London. Here, Boswell raises again the widest of smiles, at the
sight of his heart, pulsating with snobbery, on his sleeve: 'I was
exceedingly pleased with Lord Errol. His dignified person and
agreeable countenance, with the most unaffected affability gave
me high satisfaction. From perhaps a weakness, or, as I rather
hope, more fancy and warmth of feeling than is quite reasonable,

my mind is ever impressed with admiration for persons of high birth, and I could, with the most perfect honesty, expatiate on Lord Errol's good qualities; but he stands in no need of my praise.' (Just as well in all the circumstances.)

Time to leave Slains. Even a warm sun could not mellow the North Sea breeze, and falling stones here and there warned against following the outlines of the gallery too closely. On that night, Tuesday, 24 August 1773, they talked of murderers being hanged – Lord Errol must have had a fund of such stories: he was the Lord High Constable of Scotland; then they drank port, and were seen to their rooms by their host himself. Boswell had a fire in his 'most elegant' room overlooking the sea, but he did not sleep well because the sea made its wild noises, and the pillows were stuffed with the feathers of 'some sea-fowl, which had to me a disagreeable smell'. He also called to mind the noble Earl's father, Lord Kilmarnock, beheaded in London for his part in the '45; the son who hosted Boswell and Johnson broke with the family's rebellious tradition and sided with the King and London. On the field at Culloden, the last of the Boyd clan horse had been disarrayed and the strength reduced to footsoldiering. The old earl had raised his army on account of a personal admiration for Bonnie Prince Charlie, and Kilmarnock's Horse Grenadiers rode south with the Jacobites on their foray to Derby. One of his two sons who served in the British Army fought on Culloden Moor with the Royal Scots Fusiliers. Kilmarnock was held in reserve, but, as the day collapsed, he rode forward into the Stuart Second Line, which soon became a bedraggled ribbon neither in the van nor the rear. The Earl lost his men in the mist and the smoke, and mistakenly appealed to those near him – not only Cumberland's soldiers, but Scots Fusiliers, who took him prisoner. The old man had lost his hat, and wept tears of shame at his forced surrender. In one of Culloden's many poignant legends, a tall and impressive Fusilier officer came forward and, bowing low, offered the Earl his own hat; it was, of course, his own son, James, the noble Lord Errol who entertained Boswell and Johnson.

A Gothic castle on the edge of the cold waters, on treeless cliffs where boats founder, where villages vanish ghostlily in shifting sands, and a reef where once a year appear the ragged bodies of all ever wrecked thereon – it begets legend. How it suited Bram Stoker for his Transylvania. The red stone gleamed in the sun; the white birds floated on the thermals, wheeling in silent inspection; on the rocks below, other birds screamed now and then. Reconstruction in Victorian times may have rendered the building even more forbidding. Wolves may not howl here in the moonlight, as they did in the journal of Jonathan Harker, but I have no difficulty in seeing Slains as he saw Count Dracula's castle in Bukovina, the tall black windows from which not a glimmer of light came, and the jagged battlements glimpsed when the moon came out from behind the fitful clouds.

Stoker had a poorly childhood in Dublin, and he grew up in the city of Sheridan Le Fanu who took opium and drank green tea, and wrote a truly dreadful tale about a lamia by name of Carmilla, who, as lamias often do, set out to suck the blood from a virginal girl called Laura. It interests me not a little that Sheridan Le Fanu should have found in Dublin sufficient inspiration to write the story of a horrendous shark-like sorceress: Carmilla's real name was, with appropriate euphony, Countess Karnstein, and when her grave was excavated, her body was found to float in many inches of blood. Anything else would have been inappropriate.

Before he wrote *Dracula*, Stoker, by then a civil servant, published a rather different book: *Duties of Clerks of Petty Sessions in Ireland*, and in the year of its publication, 1878, began his business association with Irving. Whatever influence Le Fanu's works may have had on Stoker, the young Dublin boy must have known that in the prevalent Celtic legends the graves open all over the Irish countryside on All Souls' Night and the dead walk across the fields – and Irving's performances and demeanour sealed the future of his fictional imagination. Stoker watched Irving on stage night after night. Contemporary accounts recorded Irving's capacity for the eerie. Prone to throwing the stage into complete darkness, he then allowed a single candle, or dancing firelight, to illuminate his face, while the stage manager cast a white calcium beam on the actor's head. Max Beerbohm described Irving as having 'an incomparable power for eeriness, for stirring a dim sense of mystery; and not less masterly was he in invoking a dim sense of horror'.

Having seen all of this, Stoker, they say, told Irving he wished not only to administer Irving's theatrical affairs, but to write for the great man. Hence the laughter, hence the wounded feelings, hence the novel about a man who works in darkness and lives off the lifeblood of others. A guest of the Errols at Slains, Stoker later retired to Whinnyfold, southwards a little along the coast.

The original 'new' castle began here at the end of the sixteenth century; developments a century later added the bow window in which Johnson stood looking out at Norway, and repeating the words of his ancient star, Horace – in the same room as Boswell wished for an introduction to the King of Denmark. Its outline may still be traced despite the extensive Victorianisation of 1836, which clad the original structure with granite facings and extended upwards and sideways. From 1925, when the roof was taken away, ruin took over and spread throughout.

It was just past mid-day, and noon does not dim the ruin's eeriness. The journey immediately ahead held little of interest from the Johnson and Boswell point of view, and nothing much, therefore, to look forward to until the Forres of Macbeth's witches. Along the road, another glimpse of the Buller of Buchan: they claim that in stormy weather the waves crash over the top of the Buller, a full two hundred feet. Now the slanting sun struck deep into the Buller's shark-angled mouth, and a tongue of almost Mediterranean blue slavered at the rocks far below.

CHAPTER V

'All was rudeness, silence and solitude'

JOHNSON FOUND THE LAND after Slains 'neither unculti-
vated nor unfruitful: but it was all still arable. Of flocks or
herds there was no appearance.' Playing his new-found tune,
he wrote, 'I had now travelled two hundred miles in Scotland
and seen only one tree not younger than myself.' Many lands in
Scotland may then have lain more fallow than they should; however, new, post-Culloden initiatives led to ever greater cultivation
in this quiet territory north-west of Slains towards Inverness.

'We dined this day,' writes Johnson, 'at the house of Mr Frazer
of Streichton, who shewed us in his grounds some stones yet
standing of a druidical circle, and what I began to think more
worthy of notice, some forest trees of full growth.' Boswell has
a different spelling – 'Strichen', and so it is today: and he gives a
direction to the place: 'we went four miles out of our road, after
passing Old Deer, and went thither.' Which means that from
Slains they took some old route perhaps across the Moss of
Cruden, then crossed where the A92 runs now, and from the
modern A950, or a comparable road, went up to Strichen through
the Forest of Deer: today's byroads may have been old lanes or
drovers' trails.

Strichen, so orderly and serene, was a 'planned village', established to lure tradesmanship and manufacturers to Lord Strichen's
estate. Newspaper advertisements hailed the convenience and
amenities of the place; specifications were laid down as to the
length and style of houses. The imposed regularity of the architecture gives the village its still pleasant air, an unexpected oasis of
prosperous history, almost a tiny Edinburgh among the trees.
Odd that Johnson did not take note of Strichen, whose develop-

ment was in full swing when he called there for his Wednesday lunch. That a village should be created, rather than grow from an organic root, such as a river ford, or a crossing of forest paths, would surely have drawn a *mot* from him.

In the early eighteenth century, rural management in Scotland had begun to change. The estate owners tightened their systems, with a view to greater productivity – new breeds, crops, implements and methods. They founded two germane organisations in the 1720s – the *Honourable Society of Improvers in the Knowledge of Agriculture*, and the *Board of Trustees for Fisheries and Manufactures in Scotland*. So the 'planned village' emerged – designed to keep people within the realm of the estate but not necessarily dependent on it. Estate owners had begun to find the grazing of animals more profitable per acre than the tenanting of farmers. In theory, the planned village would absorb the people displaced by the new, more commercial economics of farming; the population would be kept in the countryside, thereby impeding an early flight from the land. Instead of tenanting, the locals would become the focus of rural manufacturing. Village foundation was to be yet another example of developing the total resources of the estate, and in such enterprises the landowner was supposed to display concern for his former tenants newly displaced.

The broadest classification of this development fell into three categories of village – estate, textile and fishing. Estate villages provided houses for tradesmen, foresters, and other estate workers; they would be paid wages rather than be allowed to take their own living from estate lands, no more grazing of their own sheep and cattle. Textile villages (the most numerous) and factory villages were founded on water-power sites. Flax mills and handweavers – also useful generally because they helped at the harvest and other farm-intensive moments – came to these villages which were advertised as having little plots of land, enough to sustain a cow, and enough peat to keep a family fireplace burning, and enough life in general to support those married, or intending to marry.

The advertisement placed by Lord Strichen in an Aberdeenshire newspaper in November 1763 offered stone to build with; lime for the land; 'a weekly market and four great fairs annually; the situation is within six miles of nine fish towns and would be a most convenient receptacle for all persons concerned in the linen manufactureys, and there is already plenty of yarn spun in the country . . .'

When Johnson and Boswell visited Strichen, Mr Fraser had a wealthy and palatial mansion. Its Victorian replacement, with long drives and a portico of columns, has fallen into disuse. The druidical temple which Johnson saw would have proved extremely difficult for me to find, were it not for the presence in Strichen of one of the most useful guiding systems on earth – a group of local schoolboys idling on their bicycles. One boy had been taken there by his grandfather, and he knew the way exactly.

The formal directions of a local guide book say, 'Turn off A981 Fraserburgh/New Deer Road 1.3 km S of Strichen and fork right in 250m. Park on track to cottage and pass along right hand side of house and uphill for 400m.' Technically speaking, this will certainly lead to the semi-recumbent stone circle of Strichen in the district of Banff and Buchan – but the dry guidebook makes no mention of a long, glorious stone wall, part of an old kitchen garden boundary; in the distance loomed the huge ruined house of the Frasers. The gardens are gone; herds of cattle grazed in the forecourt.

Erected in the third or second century B.C., the circle now sits in its original position once again. Not long after Johnson saw it, a tenant farmer demolished it, wishing, perhaps, to use the stones for his own building, like the Greeks who lived near Delphi, or the old villagers of Avebury – but the landowner, presumably the same Mr Fraser, had him rebuild it. The farmer cannot have known of ancient alignments, and his reconstruction did not accord with the circle's original orientation on the southern moon. In due course, another demolition took place, and then in the late 1970s, archaeologists on an excavation returned the stones to their original precise locations.

On the cold hill, a fence now surrounds the circle, and it interferes not at all with the mood or countenance of the rocks. They march in a track of the moon, and one flat stone, shaped like a tall and very thin rhinoceros, lies between two uprights. Strichen circle is a smaller, domestic version of the great stone rings. A few men at a time could have manipulated each of these stones into position, yet the collective force of the place feels not reduced accordingly. This owes as much to the location of the ring, as to the size of the stones: given the view across the countryside, with nearby lower hills, and distant smooth green fields, a full moon over Strichen will have conveyed powerful mystery.

Neither Boswell nor Johnson recorded much here. It may be that depredations had occurred before they got to Strichen; Boswell, who had visited fifteen years earlier, clearly expected more from the druidical circle, although whether to impress Johnson further, or to avoid being thought an inaccurate provider of anticipations, is difficult to tell, as he does not expand beyond saying, '. . . But I had augmented it in my mind; for all that remains is two stones set up on end, with a long one laid upon them, as was usual, and one stone at a little distance from them. That stone was the capital one of the circle which surrounded what now remains.'

Strichen lies a little way down from the left shoulder of Scotland along which they travelled to reach Inverness. After they left the druids' circle at Strichen, Boswell and Johnson exchanged a number of observations, the first of which had been an expression of compassion for Mr Fraser. Boswell here lets fly with a breathtaking assumption that country folk had a lonely, miserable time: 'I had a most disagreeable [that is to say distressing] notion of the life of a country gentleman,' and he left Mr Fraser, he said, 'as one leaves a prisoner in a jail'. Johnson, who should have known better, believed Boswell right in assuming such folk unhappy, 'for that they had not enough to keep their minds in motion'. They seem to have disregarded one immediately evident aspect of Mr Fraser's life; it being Fair Day at Strichen he had guests at lunch, one of whom had at least been sufficiently energetic to have attended a lecture Dr Johnson gave at Lichfield.

To enliven their dull stretch to Banff, Boswell had started a conversational entertainment, into which Johnson entered merrily – that their famous Literary Club in London should take over St Andrews university, and thereby rebuild the city. Founded in

1764, the Club was not (as is often assumed) Johnson's brain-child: Boswell's *Life* makes it clear that the idea came from Joshua Reynolds; and once a week they met at seven in the evening, in the Turk's Head, a Soho hostelry. The original dozen members, who included Goldsmith and Edmund Burke, grew to thirty-five members by 1773, and, according to Boswell's footnote, had moved premises more than once – but always to a place where liquor could be had. They also changed their rules of gathering, confining themselves to a fortnightly meeting during Parliament's sessions. The membership comprised lords, writers, debaters, academics, men of opinion and strong mind, some bishops, dukes and gentlemen. Garrick joined, and Adam Smith, thereby ensuring that Johnson did not always have the discourse his own way.

Now, on the chaise to Banff, Boswell planned with Johnson that they would regenerate the University of St Andrews according to the abilities or conceits of the Club members, each of whom would be granted a Faculty or two. Garrick would teach public speaking; 'Goldsmith, poetry and ancient history . . . Reynolds, painting, and the arts which have beauty for their object.' Johnson at first declared 'I'll trust theology to nobody but myself,' then gave way a little to Bishop Percy, but held on to logic, metaphysics and scholastic divinity. This was not a conversation they could safely have had within earshot of any educated Scot.

After Strichen, Banff, where verification of their visit takes little time; a plaque on a wall reads: 'Site of the Black Bull Inn visited by Johnson and Boswell, 1773'. Although Johnson twice found the hillocky little town lacking – 'At night we came to Bamff [*sic*], where I remember nothing that particularly claimed my attention'; and 'Finding nothing to detain us at Bamff, we set out in the morning' – he yet managed to write a short exercise in observation of Scottish small borough architecture. Intrigued by the means of domestic entrance – 'often by a flight of steps, which reaches up to the second story, the floor which is level with the ground being entered only by stairs descending within the house' – he compares their dwellings with the architecture of England, and inevitably, when he draws such comparisons, a little bee flies into his bonnet.

In Banff, he sounded off about windows. He did not like that leaded panes rarely featured here; nor that, instead of hinges, they had a sash-and-pulley arrangement, meaning the windows did not easily stay open. Ever a man for taking the particular to exhibit the general, this allowed him a global crack at the Scots: he claimed that they were not interested in doing anything unless it had natural awkwardness in it: 'What cannot be done without some uncommon trouble or particular expedient, will not often be done at all. The incommodiousness of Scotch windows keeps them very closely shut . . . even in houses well built and elegantly furnished, a stranger may be sometimes forgiven if he allows himself to wish for fresher air.' Too sniffy and cursory for today's friendly Banff with its many tractors and willing hospitality: the hotel being closed, the lady behind the counter in the newsagents offered to make me Dr Johnson's pleasure, a cup of tea.

Johnson and Boswell both pay little attention to this leg of the journey, and skip quickly on. At breakfast next morning in Cullen the Great Bear met Arbroath smokies. When served with 'dried haddocks broiled', Boswell reports, 'Dr Johnson was disgusted at the sight of them, so they were removed.' From Cullen, where they got a fresh chaise 'and very good horses', to Elgin is a distance of about twenty-five miles, through whiskified Speyside. It rained upon them at Elgin and Johnson again ran into culinary difficulty with a lunch he could not eat at the Red Lion inn. He complained, not at length: 'This was the first time, and except one, the last, that I found any reason to complain of a Scotish [sic] table, and such disappointments, I suppose, must be expected in every country, where there is no great frequence of travellers.' Boswell echoed briefly; 'We fared but ill at our inn here.'

When Johnson's *Journey* appeared, sensitivities combusted spontaneously in Scotland. His negative comments, however accurate, were converted into slights, compounded by Johnson's nationality and famous stature. Reactions divided typically – between outright rebuttal, angry repudiation of the invader, and reasoned explanation. Elgin became a good example of the reaction to Johnson in Scotland. Regarding the Red Lion lunch, the town searched its soul, and more than a century later was still justifying the inedible meal. It seems that the landlord of the Red Lion, called Leslie, and held up as an elegant fellow, instigated enquiries as to how such food came to be served to Johnson, and the following explanation emerged.

One of the inn's habitués, a commercial traveller named Thomas Paufer, bore an uncanny resemblance to Johnson. This Paufer preferred drinking to eating, and spent his slim budget proportionately. The staff of the Red Lion became habituated to Paufer's arrangements; accordingly they mistakenly served Johnson the kind of secondary food doled out to drunken Paufer. That is their story.

The faithful in Scotland called Elgin Cathedral 'The Lanthorn of the North', drawing them to the peace and Christian power of the place, and its light still shines through the ruined windows and stone crosses: moss, whether on old garden walls, or as here, in ancient grounds, encourages reflection. Johnson pondered the ruin of the building: 'The church of Elgin had, in the intestine tumults of the barbarous ages, been laid waste by the irruption of a highland chief, whom the bishop had offended.' Two centuries later, a second dilapidation occurred, when the roof leads were stripped to make coinage for military upkeep. In later times, castles and great houses in Ireland, the possession of absentee landlords, suffered likewise when local plunderers exploited the international need for lead in the manufacture of munitions. Elgin's roof-leads, with those of Aberdeen Cathedral, went to the bottom of the sea when the ship foundered on a voyage to Holland, and Johnson invited every reader to 'rejoice that this cargo of sacrilege was lost'.

Notwithstanding the former grandeur of the Cathedral, Johnson wrote no more than a page on Elgin, concluding with an attractive clue to a traveller in his wake: 'In the chief street of Elgin, the houses jut over the lowest story, like the old buildings of timber in London, but with greater prominence: so that there is sometimes a walk for a considerable length under a cloister, or portico.' Although, long before Johnson, Daniel Defoe found Elgin 'a very agreeable place to live in' – those gentry not wishing to venture as far as Edinburgh or London came in from the Highlands for the winter – Elgin's time came later: a half-century after our heroes' visit, it became a little classical Victorian market town whose streets and suburbs echoed Edinburgh's New Town in elegance and spaciousness.

Boswell dismisses Elgin in a couple of paragraphs, partly though boredom, partly embarrassment at Johnson's bad meal there; but again – the invaluable gloss on Johnson's version – Boswell liked the jutting arcades, which he called 'piazzas'; he approved of 'such structures in a town, on account of their con-veniency in wet weather', and then reports Johnson's dislike of them on account of the way in which they made 'the under story of a house very dark, which greatly over-balances the conveniency, when it is considered how small a part of the year it rains'.

In the grounds of the Elgin Cathedral, I mentioned to a passing man, a local, with whom I had fallen into conversation, 'Dr John-son had a meal here, that was so bad he couldn't eat it.'

'When was that?' he asked.

'In August 1773.'

'Ach,' he said. 'He could have had the same yesterday.'

On the road from Elgin to Forres, about twelve miles long, Johnson quoted:

> How far is't called to Fores? [*sic*] What are these,
> So wither'd, and so wild in their attire?
> That look not like the inhabitants o' the earth,
> And yet are on't?

Boswell says that Johnson's recitation – 'he repeated a good deal more of *Macbeth*' – was 'grand and affecting', after which Johnson, in a parody of the witches, aimed a pleasant dart at Boswell. 'I had purchased some land called Dalblair; and, as in Scotland it is customary to distinguish landed men by the name of their estates, I had thus two titles, Dalblair and Young Auchinleck. So, my friend in imitation of "All hail Macbeth! hail to thee Thane of Cawdor!" condescended to amuse himself with uttering "All hail Dalblair! hail to thee, Laird of Auchinleck!"'

Johnson treats the same Thursday afternoon as follows: 'We

135

All hail Dalblair.' hail to thee Laird of Auchinleck.'

went forwards the same day to Fores, the town to which Macbeth
was travelling, when he met the weird sisters on his way. This
to an Englishman is classic ground. Our imaginations were heated,
and our thoughts recalled to their old amusements.'

Shakespeare transfixed Johnson all his life. When he was nine
he read *Hamlet*, no doubt a copy from his father's bookshop, and,
as he told Mrs Thrale later, when he came to the ghost scene he
left the kitchen fireside and stood reading at the street door in
Lichfield in order to 'have people about'. Fanny Burney said to
Johnson that Shakespeare 'could never have seen a Caliban', and
Johnson told her that having seen a man Shakespeare knew how
to vary one; 'A man who would draw a monstrous cow, must
first know what a cow commonly is; or how can he tell that to
give her an ass's head or an elephant's tusk will make her monstrous?' On his deathbed, he quoted to his physician Macbeth's
own words to the doctor attending Lady Macbeth for her 'thick-
coming fancies';

Canst thou not minister to a mind diseas'd,
Pluck from the memory a rooted sorrow,
Raze out the written troubles of the brain,
And with some sweet oblivious antidote
Cleanse the stuff'd bosom of that perilous stuff
Which weighs upon the heart?

Johnson never loved uncritically. 'Shakespeare,' he told Boswell in 1769, 'never has six lines together without a fault.' He had studied the plays exhaustively, and published in 1765 a new edition whose Preface has been called the most famous Shakespearean essay ever written. To equip the definitions in his Dictionary, one third or so of nearly a hundred and twenty thousand quotations come from Shakespeare – many, it seems, chosen as much for their philosophical or moral point as for their usage value. Of the plays, *Macbeth* appears to have received his greatest attention, and, in 1745, while still in his thirties and making his literary way, he produced his 'Miscellaneous Observations on the Tragedy of *Macbeth*', which begins: 'In order to make a true estimate of the abilities and merit of a writer it is always necessary to examine the genius of his age and the opinions of his contemporaries.'

It is an astonishing essay, full of large generosity to the reader, delivered by way of glosses and fearlessly-held, warmly-offered opinions. It contains no pretentiousness, has scarcely dated, and throws out many lessons – not least Johnson's writerly good manners: if he uses a Greek tag he gives the translation.

The Preface fetches information from other ages and brings it forward, and hands it to us, cleansed and ready for consumption, and presented in a style that makes it clear Johnson wished to be read. Through it all runs the most noble assumption – that no human need be daunted by the stature even of a genius such as Shakespeare, that his wisdoms and magics are for us all and that Johnson himself is an eager and willing guide. If, in Nabokov's assertion, a writer may be a storyteller, a teacher, or an enchanter, and a great writer all three – Dr Johnson, even in this academic territory, long rendered prosaic and often inaccessible by other writers, was already a great writer at the age of thirty-five.

To read *Macbeth* with Johnson's 'Miscellaneous Observations' open alongside is a great pleasure. Example: 'The arguments by which Lady Macbeth persuades her husband to commit the murder afford a proof of Shakespeare's knowledge of human nature. She urges the excellence and dignity of courage, a glittering idea which has dazzled mankind from age to age and animated sometimes the housebreaker and sometimes the conqueror.' To this gloss on the idea that even a thief should have to screw his courage to the sticking-place, Johnson adds the argument that if all else he had written were lost, Shakespeare should have become immortal for the way in which he shows Macbeth 'distinguishing true from false fortitude in a line and a half':

> I dare do all that may become a man;
> Who dares do more is none.

In Johnson's footsteps, these roads across Scotland's shoulder become Shakespeare country.

The travellers each commented only on the 'admirable' inn where they stayed overnight in Forres. 'At Fores,' writes Johnson, 'we found good accommodation, but nothing worthy of particular remark, and next morning entered upon the road on which Macbeth heard the fatal prediction; but we travelled on not interrupted by promises of kingdoms.' Sueno's Stone, or 'King Duncan's Monument', as Boswell calls it, stands on the edge of the bypass. Once thought to commemorate a Viking encounter, but now believed to be a Class III Pictish monument, centuries older, Sueno's Stone has panels and friezes of headless corpses, horsemen, battles or skulls. I saw nothing of them: the eight-yard-high obelisk was swathed in wooden bandages, as impenetrable as Scott's Monument had been in Edinburgh.

Beyond Forres, in the open countryside, stands Brodie Castle, now a National Trust property, a tall sixteenth-century building on a long-inhabited site, direct from the frames of a Disney film of Rob Roy or Alan Breck. Groves of trees, carefully planted, give shelter: Brodies of Brodie date back nine centuries. Turn right off the road to Nairn, by the castle, then past woods by a duck-thronged mere, turn to the west, that is, left, off the lane into a similarly tight by-road and, around a corner, stands Macbeth's Hillock.

Macbeth fought King Duncan in 1040, and killed him, perhaps near Elgin, not far from Lossie Forest. Presumably Shakespeare researched his play in Holinshed's histories – but how could he have known of the eeriness of atmosphere available all around here? The folk of these towns and villages took their convicted witches, stood them in pitch-filled barrels and set them afire: in Forres stands a witches' stone, site of such burnings – in thunder, lightning, or in rain?

At Macbeth's Hillock, the grue rises a little cold on the nape of the neck. A round, gradual, shallow cone, the Hillock has, at first sight, no context: it stands in the middle of a field, growing scrabby grass, an egregious lone breast. Unlike the 'fairy forts' in Ireland, it bears no evidence of fortification, and seems not to have been inhabited. From its easily-reached little summit not much of a view – therefore, it cannot have been a hill-fort: in the tradition of Maiden Castle, or the great Heuneberg in Danubian Germany, this is not even a bungalow. Yet, to the north, a couple of hundred yards away, lie a series of long, barrow-like earthworks. Maybe they are recent, agricultural bulldozings – or, in this gathering dusk, antiquities, entirely consistent in shape, length and intensity with ancient burial places from Poland to Galway, early European shapes. Which would mean that Shakespeare had Macbeth meet the witches in as moody a place as a writer could conceive – an ancient cemetery.

Locally this area is known as the 'hard muir', with the term 'Macbeth's Hillock' thought to be a Victorian fancy. Might a dig at Macbeth's Hillock, in concert with textual sleuthing, yield exotic fruit – the skeletons, perhaps, of three witches in one coffin, with a shrivelled newt or toad nearby? Whatever the reticence of archaeologists on the matter – perhaps they fear being thought fanciful by their academic colleagues – excavations have begun to confirm the details in legends and myths. The 'Celtic Tutankhamun' in Stuttgart Museum, a chieftain from the fifth century B.C., was decked out head to foot in the kind of gold hero-gods wear in Celtic myth. In Shakespeare too, the art mirrors the life. Sir Peter Hall, researching a new production of *The Merchant of Venice*, discovered in the archives that the Bard's father was prosecuted twice for usury.

*   *   *

'At Nairn we may fix the verge of the Highlands, for here I first saw peat fires and heard the Erse language.' To reach this point Johnson has taken up a third of his *Journey to the Western Islands*, and one can now sense the lift of excitement in him, a man about to broach the exotic. So unlike the attitude of his equally famous French contemporary: nine years earlier, Boswell 'mentioned our design to Voltaire. He looked at me, as if I had talked of going to the North Pole.'

Johnson said of the royal burgh of Nairn, 'If once it flourished, [it] is now in a state of miserable decay.' It has evidently come on since then. I intended to stay longer than their short breakfast stop – because this is the town of David Thomson, who spent part of his childhood here; his late adolescence and young manhood in Ireland; his maturity as a writer and BBC radio producer.

The fascination of writing is the attempt to render personal experience into objective beauty and understanding, how to take the fleeting run of life and suspend it, turn it to something tangible, capable of being perused, of being learnt from by others, beginning with the passionate subjective, ending in the dispassionate objective. Discovering Johnson raises the issue of whether this is best done in fiction, where the imagination would seem to have freer rein, or in non-fiction, a more finite, circumscribed form. In Samuel Johnson and David Thomson, Nairn created a happy conjunction of two men who turned the factual stuff of their lives into beauty: not by great timeless plot, nor by intricate, archetypal and immortally-spoken characterisation, as Shakespeare did, but by felicity of spirit and language.

Thomson, born in India in 1914, had Scottish parents, and until 1929 spent fourteen years of summer holidays and many other times in his grandmother's family home, Newton, now a hotel, on the edge of Nairn. He grew to be a knobby-faced, large-headed, academic-looking man, loving and thoughtful, who overcame great difficulties in his inner life – depressions and other emotional waylayings – to produce a small body of exquisite and delicate work in print and on radio. The focus of his concerns seem to have lain close to tradition, and although what he wrote may be called natural history and social history, such definitions trammel him. When he wrote about seals, as in *The People of the Sea*; and when he discussed the personality of the hare; and when, in books such as *Woodbrook* and *Nairn in Darkness and Light*, he traced the fading and departing of old ways – he might have been writing poems or novels. He was an artist who viewed the passing of wider tradition as part of his own, and the century's, ageing process.

I met him once, in the late 1980s, a year or so before his death, in a pub in Camden Town: he was a quick, if ageing, inquisitive and half-bolting creature: more for his thick spectacles than his literary associations, other drinkers in the pub called him 'The Professor'. In an obituary, Seamus Heaney wrote, 'There was about him a delicate wildness, and he often thought that the hare, about which he had gathered so many entrancing stories, was his proper, total animal. Shy, vivid and capable of swift epiphanies.'

In common with Johnson, Thomson had poor eyes. Their first soreness and troubles led him to Nairn. After a robust game of rugby football in London – although his sight had never been excellent – his family sent him to his grandmother's up here to give him some rest.

The Newton Hotel is quite easily found, and from Thomson's book I had anticipated its view of the sea, if not quite the shaggy russet Highland cattle grazing in front of the Victorian house. Before that, I recognised the building under the trees, *de luxe* bedroom suites now, but still the same structure, on the left-hand side of the drive, just before the sweep around to the hotel steps: 'The stables which formed part of the rectangle of low buildings out of which that archway to the henyard led, had long been disused but somebody swept them now and then, dusted the curved metal hay racks, wiped manger and woodwork and shone the brass tethering rings so brightly than whenever we pushed a door open and looked into the dusky twilight we were welcomed by a small round gleam of light.'

Light was where he found it: in my room I open *Nairn in Darkness and Light* at random: windows, lamps, doorways, the sky, night, fire. And things that mean, or attract, light – flowers, clouds, uniforms with shiny buttons, horse-harness, railway stations, the waves on the shore, the kettle dancing on the stove. And things that shut out light: small boxrooms, closed doors; 'when I snuffed out my bedside candle'; a local history of appalling sandstorms; unfriendly adults of grim, dour mien, with tight acerbic mouths, the 'grey granite' stare of a harsh grandmother: he says, 'I cannot remember ever hearing her use my Christian name in the vocative.'

A colour brochure I picked up in the hall speaks of the '27 acres of secluded grounds with magnificent views over the Moray Firth and the Ross-shire hills beyond . . . imposing combination of Georgian and Scottish Baronial architecture . . . four course *table d'hôte* menu of very high class plus an *à la carte* menu including a range of steaks charcoal grilled . . .': no mention of David Thomson. I also found a modest typed item: 'Newton or Easter Newton, as it was sometimes designated, was a possession of a branch of the Roses of Kilravock, having been rebuilt in about 1650 . . .' A bit more promising, it traces the possessors of Newton – Colonels, and Lords, and then the Thomson connection, but this I glean only from *Nairn in Darkness and Light*: 'In 1887 Newton was acquired by R.B. Finlay, Q.C.': this must be Uncle Robert who said 'a lengthy grace in Latin, perfectly enunciated': clearly the same Mr Finlay who was 'a generous friend to the Golf Club, the new clubhouse, as well as the Newton ground being given to the club in free occupancy'. The hotel leaflet ends a few paragraphs on: 'The Newton has had many celebrities who have stayed with us over the years, including the late Harold Macmillan and Charlie Chaplin . . .' No mention still of dear David Thomson: the world of publicity does not quickly recognise celebrities (and celebrants) of the inner life. The hotel is a large, rambling building and I strain my ears to hear the laughter and running feet of the young Thomson, the boy version of the man with the thick glasses and the white cantilever-domed head.

Nairn in Darkness and Light gives us Thomson set in his own history, a man observing his personal continuity in the context of his ancestral surroundings. He quotes from local antiquarians and contemporary records; 'Alexander Brodie of Brodie, the Laird of the lands adjoining the Barony of Culbin, kept a detailed diary throughout the years from 1651 until 1680, when he died. His public interests were religion, politics and law'; leading to 'In 1640, on Thursday December the 28th, this Alexander Brodie was one of a party which included my ancestor, the Laird of Innes, that came to the grand old cathedral of Elgin and destroyed every object in it.'

When I first read *Nairn* (it was published in 1987) I had not been contemplating Johnson: now, in the late sunlight coming through my bedroom window, I rushed to him and Boswell. No, not enough of a clue as to whether these were the same depredations Johnson had deplored: Elgin had suffered marauders more than once. A pity: I should have been delighted if the two writers, Johnson and Thomson, could achieve a time-machine meeting over the vandalising of Elgin Cathedral. In fact, had Johnson been made aware, in any sort of detail, of the destructiveness of Thomson's ancestor, he would have written much more heatedly: Thomson's account continues, 'They tore down and ripped medieval paintings, smashed the screen which was beautifully carved, probably gilded like most ancient screens, and adorned in patterns of blue, red and green. The screen and the ornamental woodwork of pulpit, font lid and choir stalls they chopped up for firewood. All this they did to please God, who had since the foundation of the Christian Church, been plagued by the gaudy contrivances of man.'

In the 1930s, at the age of eighteen, David Thomson went to tutor the children of an Irish 'Great House', Woodbrook, on the road between Carrick-on-Shannon and Boyle, in County Leitrim. All those lands have water, either acknowledged as lakes, or in winter pools throughout the poor, snipe-grass farmland; how lovely the light must have been to his eyes. Down the road from Woodbrook lay a little affinity. In Kilronan churchyard lies the blind harper who, it is said, wrote the music for the tune that became 'The Star-Spangled Banner' – Turlough O'Carolan, led across Ireland on a white horse by his servant, and sleeping with his harp in the bed so as not to let the instrument's wood warp in damp rooms.

In Leitrim, David Thomson began twin love affairs that took his life along a particular direction – with Phoebe Kirkwood, his young charge; and with Ireland, later the focus of many of his broadcasts. He arrived when the life of the Anglican gentry such as the Kirkwoods was changing forever, as the newly independent nation called in all its old slights and insults, and willingly saw off 'the Protestants'. In a miniature echo of Tsarist Russia, those of the Ascendancy who were dwindling, Goldsmith's children, and Swift's, were permitted to carry on fading; those more vigorous were not made to feel welcome in the new Ireland of 'the Risen People'.

Secondly, at the time when the flight from the land became a cultural European fact, a time evoked in rural England by Laurie Lee in *Cider with Rosie*, David Thomson witnessed the same poignant development in Ireland, but with undertones of old scores and the curious mixture of religion and politics that has taken so long to biodegrade. The Kirkwoods had to sell their horses, had to endure the slow oncoming tread of gentility in all its shabbiness, to watch the encroaching, ever-drawing-near of the Irish natives who had long been in the tenure and service of the Great House, and now never would be again. It matters not that these natives were the people who had the original rights, and Thomson's own humanity would never let his reader forget that fact; all he lamented, as he always did, was the passing of an old way, especially when the future replacing it felt less sound.

The book he gleaned from all of this, *Woodbrook*, his masterpiece, draws a beautiful parallel between personal destiny and ineluctable social forces. As David watches events that can never take place again, such as the Woodbrook dance, and observes the cloaked distress of the family at their growing impecuniousness, he falls deeper and deeper in love with Phoebe, his Venus rising up through adolescence into womanhood. All ends in tragedy: David's tragedy, the Kirkwoods' tragedy, above all Phoebe's, and by implication, tragic loss of all the old Irish ways.

Nairn, as a holiday resort, has the name 'the Rye of the North', and along the shore and near the golf clubs – one of them built on that land donated by David Thomson's great-uncle – people park caravans hoping for mildness from the Moray Firth. The 'small hard town' as Thomson called it, whatever his loving reminiscences of its Fishertown or nearby magic streams, has, alas, no

Johnsonian or Boswellian relevance, and therefore no reason – this time anyway – to linger.

They did visit Cawdor Castle, which lies about six miles south-south-west of Nairn, reached by the B9090 and linking with the B9101 to the village of Cawdor. Unexpectedly peaceful gardens with *Delphinium* called *Johnson's Blue*, some mauve-white and cobalt *Campanula*; peonies; poppies; trefoils in brilliant mauve; scents of lavender and musk rose; four phallic cypress bushes, two of acid-green-yellow, two of dark green; on the tower, eyeless turrets each with a little pennanted wind-vane, the wind is from the west and the flag flies, brilliant yellow predominating, a ship with sails filled, a cross in black and red, and an antlered deer's head; in the bright, southern lee of the castle's core, long buildings roofed with tiny slates, stepped corners; the comfort of a loosely-enclosed, highly aromatic rose-garden; a peony walk, a wall of *Euphorbia*; in the reaches of the garden, oasal recesses, stone steps leading up to stone seats; a bee visited along thick heavy honey-suckle; rectangular stone troughs, abundant and velvet with flowering plants; old walls placid with centuries of absorbed heat from the sun; a holly tree: did Cawdor once contain all the seven sacred trees from the Celtic grove? Somewhere, they told me in Nairn, is a hawthorn tree carbon-dated 1372 which I must find, because Boswell mentions it; the 'hawthorn-tree, which rises like a wooden pillar through the rooms of the castle; for, by a strange conceit, the walls have been built around it'. I count again the different growths: *Hosta, Euryngum, Thalictrum,* giddy lupin, *Astilbe,* goldenrod.

'The draw-bridge is still to be seen,' wrote Johnson, 'but the moat is now dry. The tower is very ancient: its walls are of great thickness, arched on the top with stone, and surrounded with battlements.' Sir Dracula Irving, Bram Stoker's boss, copied the entrance façade for a production of *Macbeth*. The Thane of Cawdor's family name is Campbell, and they own other estates in south Wales, at Bosherston, where ponds with a curiously cool water temperature from the underground springs, breed lovely expanses of water lilies. Boswell failed to have them meet the Earl: presumably the 'prosperous gentleman' was examining his water-lilies in Wales when they called. Nevertheless, Boswell enlightened his readers regarding 'The thickness of the walls, the small slaunting windows, and a great iron door at the entrance to the second story as you ascend the stairs, all indicate the rude times in which this castle was erected.' A sage advised a northern Thane to load his donkey with gold; the castle of Cawdor should be built where the animal stopped from fatigue – by a hawthorn-tree, as it happened: hence its preservation.

Sleekness, an attention to detail, and obvious continuing care have made Cawdor a model property. This, regrettably, is not the castle where Lady Macbeth did her sleepwalking. Shakespeare gave the play five castles: Forres; Inverness in which the assassination of Duncan 'were done quickly' with the dagger Macbeth saw before him; Macduff's castle in Fife; the King's palace in England, and Dunsinane where – '*Enter Lady Macbeth with a taper*: Out, out damned spot! out, I say!' In Forres that morning, Johnson and Boswell argued about evil.

Johnson: Moral evil is occasioned by free will, which implies choice between good and evil. With all the evil there is, there is no man but would rather be a free agent, than a mere machine without the evil; and what is best for each individual, must be best for the whole. If a man would rather be the machine, I cannot argue with him. He is a different being from me.

Boswell argues back that 'A man, as a machine, may have agreeable sensations; for instance he may have pleasure in music.' With the usual kindly swat, and again directing his intellectual energy towards moral concerns, Johnson replies, 'No sir, he cannot have pleasure in music, at least no power of producing music; for he who can produce music may let it alone; he who can play upon a fiddle may break it: such a man is not a machine.'

At the end of the avenue, the village of Cawdor looks as kempt as a pinafore. Johnson and Boswell, who both called the village 'Calder', stayed at the manse, now burnt down. Their host, the Rev Kenneth MacAulay, great-uncle of Thomas Babington of that name, had sent a letter explaining that he could not meet them in Nairn: his priestly duties detained him in Cawdor – to which Boswell adds a footnote. When they arrived at the manse, between twelve and one o'clock on the Saturday, the Reverend, according to Mrs MacAulay, had gone to the church distributing tokens – 'little pieces of tin, stamped with the name of the parish'. Each token, a seal of approval awarded by the minister to those of whom he approved morally that week, had to be handed up on Sunday; those without tokens could not receive the sacrament. Boswell adds a tantalising footnote: 'This is a species of priestly power, and sometimes may be abused. I remember a lawsuit brought by a person against his parish minister, for refusing him . . .' Facts, Boswell! What case? The name, the name! Give us dates! Places!

Boswell had two fears for the sociability of their stay at Cawdor: that his eminent companion might quarrel with their host who had revealed a *penchant* for speaking 'slightingly of the lower English clergy', and that 'a whole evening at Calder-manse might be heavy'. Neither materialised. A neighbouring minister joined them, a Mr Grant (his grandson, Captain James Grant, accompanied John Hanning Speke to trace the source of the Nile): 'intelligent and well-bred' sniffs Boswell of Reverend Grant. They talked of hereditary occupations in the Highlands; the rigour of church rules and creeds; they looked at Latin books, and tiptoed around a delicate matter – whether Johnson the Anglican might wish to hear Mr MacAulay say their Presbyterian prayers in the household, which Boswell doubted. The Reverend offered to forgo the proceedings, and Boswell advised Johnson of the 'over-delicate scrupulosity of our host'. Johnson tushed, and so the other clergyman, Mr Grant (being well-bred), said the prayers, evoking a comment from their distinguished visitor who upbraided him just a little for not including the Lord's Prayer.

The stay of Johnson and Boswell at Cawdor manse captures Johnson in a neat capsule. We see his professional disdain: before he arrived he spoke disparagingly of his impending host, doubting that Mr MacAulay had himself authored the history of the island of St Kilda, which bore his name. Johnson's superiority complex goes on show: while there, he used the power of his frown and his supervening wit to silence MacAulay's disregard for the English clergy: 'This is a day of novelties: I have seen old trees in Scotland, and I have heard the English clergy treated with disrespect.'

Intellectual snobbery: he dismissed the bookshelves of the manse upstairs as 'rather a lady's library, with some Latin books in it by chance'. A liberal spirit: he listened courteously and placidly to Presbyterian prayers. And, a definition of the excellent guest, one who keeps promises given during the hospitality: as well as giving the lad his own Sallust, Johnson promised to create the introductions by which young MacAulay could enter university, and he kept his word, although the boy eventually chose not to avail himself of it.

They stayed at Cawdor from Friday lunchtime to Saturday late morning. The village can have changed little, although many of the houses feel Edwardian rather than Georgian, and the new manse is Victorian. On Friday night, the factor of the estate, drinking tea with them, wrote a letter of introduction to nearby Fort George. Their detour to Fort George crossed what is now the main road from Nairn to Inverness, and they arrived some time in the late morning. A gossipy exchange developed between Boswell and a Major Brewse, or Bruce, of the Engineers, regarding the Major's surname.

> BOSWELL: He had dined at a house in London, where there were three Bruces, one of the Irish line, one of the Scottish line, and himself of the English line. He said he was shewn it in the Herald's office spelt fourteen different ways.

At this point, 'Dr Johnson observed that there had been great disputes about the spelling of Shakespear's [*sic*] name: 'At last it was thought it would be settled by looking at the original copy of his will; but, upon examining it, he was found to have written it himself no less than three different ways.'

Touring the fort, commanded by Sir Eyre Coote of the 37th Regiment, an unexpected knowledge surfaced: 'Dr Johnson talked of the proportions of charcoal and salt-petre in making gunpowder, of granulating it and of giving it a gloss' – although he admitted to Boswell afterwards that he had 'talked ostentatiously'. Boswell enjoyed the martial ambience of the fort: 'At three the drum beat for dinner. I, for a little while, fancied myself a military

A typical Edinburgh close.
DR JOHNSON: 'Boswell has very handsome and spacious rooms level with the ground on one side of the house, and on the other four stories high.'

'And we were too proud,' wrote Boswell, 'not to carry him to the Abbey of Holyrood House, that beautiful piece of architecture, but alas! that deserted mansion of royalty.'

Slains Castle, on the coast north of Aberdeen, where Bram Stoker completed *Dracula*. Boswell noted, 'The house is quite built upon the shore; the windows look upon the main ocean, and the King of Denmark is Lord Errol's nearest neighbour on the north-east.'

The Buller of Buchan, near Slains. Johnson walked its perimeter and reported, 'It has the appearance of a vast well bordered with a wall . . . He that ventures to look downward sees, that if his foot should slip, he must fall from this dreadful elevation upon stones on one side, or into water on the other. We however went round, and were glad when the circuit was completed.'

Banff plaque.
JOHNSON: 'At night we came to Bamff [sic], where I remember nothing that particularly claimed my attention.'

Elgin Cathedral, the Lantern of the North.
JOHNSON: 'The church of Elgin had, in the intestine tumults of the barbarous ages, been laid waste by the irruption of a highland chief, whom the bishop had offended.'

Cawdor Castle. 'The draw-bridge is still to be seen,' wrote Johnson, 'but the moat is now dry. The tower is very ancient: its walls are of great thickness, arched on the top with stone, and surrounded with battlements.'

Inverness. They stayed at Mackenzie's Inn, and on Sunday morning went to the English chapel: Mr Tait preached a sermon on 'Love Your Enemies'. They saw the Quay and Macbeth's Castle, had lunch with Mr Keith, the excise collector, and Boswell 'begged permission to . . . run about and pay some short visits to several good people of Inverness'.

Ratagan. 'Upon one of the precipices,' wrote Johnson, 'my horse, weary with the steepness of the rise, staggered a little, and I called in haste to the highlander to hold him. This was the only moment of my journey, in which I thought myself endangered.'

The broch near Glenelg. Johnson considered how the primitive builders might have raised the heavy stones with wooden lifters: 'Savages, in all countries, have patience proportionate to their unskilfulness, and are content to attain their end by very tedious methods.'

The Sound of Sleat at Glenelg, where Johnson, staying overnight
in an inn as sparsely catered as it was unhygienic, reflected,
'Of the provisions the negative catalogue was very copious.'

man, and it pleased me.' If the flavour of his text so far is to be believed, Bozzy was as much a soldiering man as Coleridge, which is saying less than very little.

At dinner a military band played; the governor's wife was 'a very agreeable woman, with an uncommonly mild and sweet tone of voice', and the governor told Johnson and Boswell that 'the Arabs could live for five days without victuals, and subsist for three weeks on nothing else but the blood of their camels, who could lose so much of it as would suffice for that time, without being exhausted.' Discussion moved to matters of the stage, to comparisons of great performers, to criticism of Garrick's pronunciation of certain words in *Hamlet*, and the qualities of Mrs Cibber's expression. The conversation, the 'dinner of two complete courses, variety of wines and the regimental band of musick playing in the square' all enchanted Boswell, and according to him, Johnson too, whom he reports as saying, 'I shall always remember this fort with gratitude.'

Johnson, however, devotes one mere paragraph to a description – or rather a non-description – of their visit. 'Of Fort George I shall not attempt to give any account. I cannot delineate it scientifically, and a loose and popular description is of use only when the imagination is to be amused. There was every where an appearance of the utmost neatness and regularity. But my suffrage is of little value, because this and Fort Augustus are the only garrisons that I ever saw.'

By visiting Fort George, and by going straight from there to Inverness – they said goodbye to the officers between six and seven o'clock – Johnson and Boswell made a revealing choice. They elected to bypass Drummossie Moor, site of the battle of Culloden in 1746, twenty-seven years earlier. Neither mentions the battlefield. It seems impossible that they could not have known where they were; they can only have ignored it deliberately, and therefore perhaps for political reasons of their own. Boswell needed the good opinion of the Establishment as a lizard needs the heat of the sun. Johnson was receiving a pension from the King whose brother was the Duke of Cumberland, the butcher of the day. Yet Boswell and other Johnsonians report that, long before the pension, Johnson wondered aloud 'if holding up his right hand would have secured victory for the Stuarts at Culloden to Prince Charles's army, he was not sure he would have held it up; so little confidence had he in the right claimed by the house of Stuart, and so fearful was he of the consequences of another revolution on the throne of Great Britain'.

Had Johnson walked Drummossie he would have had to contemplate the events there, and the long reverberations of 1746, and the gloatings and celebrations that took place annually in Inverness long afterwards, and since he was chronically and constitutionally unable not to give an opinion, whatever he said would have landed him in difficulty with somebody.

Again, I hear the smack of collusion between Johnson and Boswell in their separate accounts of their Highland jaunt. It may simply be the case that Boswell, seeing that Johnson chose not to mention Culloden, took the same course of action. After all, Boswell's *Life of Johnson* derives from what Johnson said: but do we know what proportion Boswell reported of what Johnson said? And I cannot believe that the two did not exchange at length here, passing the very threshold of such a dominant historic occasion, an event which still burnt into the consciousness of all Scots at the time. In Sir Walter Scott's time – and he was, after all, born twenty-five years after Culloden – Scotland still uttered the name Cumberland 'with an infant hatred'.

Johnson was in his thirties in 1745, and well aware that the Duke of Cumberland mustered his armies on Clapham Common, while London waited and wondered whether the Stuart Pretender would truly drive on south and attack the capital. A year later, in that one heart-wrenching day at Culloden, Scotland capitulated. Yet many subjects throughout the whole island of Britain retained an affection – partly romantic – for the Stuarts. Johnson's writings and conversations indicate a highly politicised man, and nobody, unless an apolitical hermit, could have been uninterested in, unaware of, the Stuart Rebellion of 1745–6, and the Cause behind it.

Furthermore, Boswell reports Johnson's clear sympathy with Jacobitism. In the *Life*, he makes a number of references – to Johnson's high regard for a man he knew to be in hiding in London on account of having borne arms in the '45; to the curious fact that Johnson wrote almost not at all during the year 1745 – though Boswell, a windblown reed at best where politics were concerned, attributes this to preparation for the great Dictionary, rather than to any politically-induced melancholia. He also refers to Johnson's condemnation in 1760 of the fashion for defaming and decrying the House of Stuart; and he reports a violent argument between Johnson and a Whig called Taylor, during which Johnson not only insisted that the Stuarts owned the true right to the throne of England, but that people disliked the Hanoverians (as Johnson himself did) and were so disaffected by them that they had generally lost interest in the monarchy altogether.

Again, observing the conversation of a rainy night in July 1763, Boswell wrote of Johnson's perceivable affections, 'He no doubt had an early attachment to the House of Stuart; but his zeal has cooled as his reason strengthened . . . Yet there is no doubt that at earlier periods he was wont often to exercise both his pleasantry and ingenuity in talking Jacobitism.' This was the same evening on which Johnson wryly said that now the Hanoverian King had given him a pension, he could hardly drink Stuart health with the wine thus bought. 'I think that the pleasures of cursing the House of Hanover, and drinking King James's health, are amply over-balanced by three hundred pounds a year.'

Incontrovertibly, therefore, Johnson had embraced Jacobitism to some degree of sympathy at some stage, and perhaps even quite vehemently, and perhaps for quite a long period of his life – but, as with the formation of many political tastes and stances, the dalliance owed as much to what he disliked (the Hanoverian kings) as to what he espoused and idealised. A traditionalist, he was guided by the natural right of succession and in his view, 'the house of Stuart succeeded to the full right of both the houses of York and Lancaster, whose common source is the undisputed right.' So how can it be that Johnson and Boswell passed this woeful and apocalyptic place, faces averted?

Although the story has been long and widely recounted (John Prebble's heartbreaking book, *Culloden*, brings the event to life), nothing compares with walking the field, seeing the small cairns marking where clansmen fell, measuring the rides of the horse-troops. Wednesday morning, 16 April 1746, rained, it was chilly, and the citizens of Inverness came out from the town to view this spectator sport. The armies saw each other for the first time at just after eleven o'clock. Another heavy shower swept across the marshy ground. The English with their Scottish support had breakfasted well; the Highlanders had left their supplies at Nairn, and were cold and unfed. They had no chance – perhaps they had no chance from the beginning. Right cause, wrong leader: Prince Charles has come to be viewed as a drunken, disorganised fop. Departing Brest on a French frigate on 16 July 1745 he landed on the island of Eriskay saying, 'I am come home.' Alexander MacDondald of Boisdale, the Highland chief who met him on arrival, begged him to go back to Europe. Bonnie Prince Charlie refused, and many of the clans rallied to his support; others ratted and joined the King's forces.

Although the romance has powered many a writer, notably Stevenson, some latter-day Scots take the harder, colder view of the Pretender – such as the novelist and poet Iain Crichton-Smith, who, in his novel *The Dream*, has one of his characters muse, 'He was an evil ghost who had drifted into the Highlands, like some kind of vaporous poison, with his powdered hair and his boyish rapacity for adventure, intoxicated by the new air, the mountains, the lochs, the heather, and by his selfish opportunism he had brought tragedy on the Highlands. And later he was cruel, a wife-beating drunkard, after he had destroyed the Highlands in a storm of hailstones and fire.' Bonnie Prince Charlie was also a Catholic, another of the facts for which he was never forgiven and another contribution to the ambivalence he excites.

Charles and Cumberland were as ill-matched personally – the unrealistic *poseur* versus the eighteen-stone professional soldier – as they were ill-matched militarily. The Duke had powerful artillery and trained soldiers; the Prince had lesser firepower and undisciplined goodwill. Prebble quotes the Chevalier de Johnstone who fought with the Glengarrys: 'What a spectacle of horror! The same Highlanders who had advanced to the charge like lions, with bold and determined countenance, were in an instant seen flying like trembling cowards in the greatest disorder.'

Such blood, and the mud of Culloden, were the last Gaelic colours to fly over Scotland; the clans looked straight into the mouths of Cumberland's cannon and died, and with them expired a way of life – the Stewarts of Appin, and the Maclarens, and the Camerons, and the Atholl Brigade, and behind them Ogilvies, and behind them the Prince himself. The wind was blowing hard at the Highlanders' faces, according to the literature given out at the Culloden Visitors' Centre, and the two armies were in position at one o'clock, approximately four to five hundred yards apart. 'The battle was over in less than an hour,' says the leaflet, and eventually the Prince's message went out, 'Let every man find his own way to safety the best way he can.' Two days later seventeen Highland officers, held prisoner at Culloden House (where the Prince slept the night before the battle), were murdered: Cumberland lost five hundred men: the Jacobites two and a half times as many.

It is a wide field, and a road crosses part of it; there is no shelter here and the ground is still soft, especially in the winter. In the summer, even when the sun is shining, it can still be cold, whether from the weather or the ghosts of the dead. Paraphrasing Tacitus and Byron, the Visitors' Centre has the last word on Bloody Cumberland: 'he created a desert and called it peace.'

All tragedies have cruel footnotes. An unreliable horseman on the Stuart side, witnessing the first charge of the clans on the Cumberland army, believed no troop could withstand such an onslaught, and he rode south to Edinburgh declaring victory, causing the Jacobites of the city to dance and sing. Their position was reversed when the truth circulated; they went into hiding – as did Scots and Catholics in London: not only did the King's supporters crow and celebrate, they also took revenge.

Inverness, a likeable city, is visible from a distance. In this town of bridges, Johnson stayed at Mackenzie's Inn, now a supermarket, and on Sunday morning went to the English chapel, long since gone: it was a coarse little place anyway, and Mr Tait preached a sermon on Love Your Enemies. Boswell felt depressed for a brief time, and homesick: no letters had arrived for him, the cause of a little worry. In Inverness, Johnson held forth on the benefits Scotland had derived from the Union, and after church they saw the Quay and Macbeth's Castle, and had lunch with Mr Keith, the excise collector, whose wife quizzed Johnson about his 'drinking water'. Johnson volunteered some information about the size of the excise duty his friend Thrale the brewer in Streatham had paid the previous year and, says Boswell, 'after this there was little conversation that deserves to be remembered.'

One interesting nugget gleams on this page of Boswell's *Journal of a Tour*. When he and Johnson got back to their inn, Boswell 'begged permission to leave him for a little while, that I might run about and pay some short visits to several good people of Inverness'. Boswell does not divulge any names or addresses: was he in search of sport among the streetwalkers of the north? If he had bumped into anyone worthy of half a mention he would have told us. Johnson said to him, 'You have all the old-fashioned principles, good and bad.' That night, Sunday, Mr Grant, the well-bred reverend gentleman they met at Cawdor manse, joined them, and Mr Keith the excise man, and they ate roasted kid 'which Dr Johnson had never tasted before. He relished it much.'

Maybe they should have collaborated on a book, instead of writing separate accounts. In Johnson's company, you leave Inverness with a full impression of its contemporary military, social and commercial importance. He asserted that the good people of Inverness owed all they had to the previous conquest and occupation by Cromwell. 'Yet what the Romans did to other nations, was in a great degree done by Cromwell to the Scots: he civilized them by conquest, and introduced by useful violence the arts of peace.' Interesting euphemism: 'useful violence' – leading perhaps to the creation of terms such as 'constructive murder' or 'helpful massacre'?

Johnson had travelled hopefully and was about to arrive: the following day he would leave the comparative comfort he had hitherto enjoyed, and head into the wilds, and not in a coach but on horseback. He wondered, in his Inverness passage, whether it was 'peculiar to the Scots to have attained the liberal, without the manual arts, to have excelled in ornamental knowledge, and to have wanted not only the elegancies, but the conveniences of common life'. He goes on to make the point that the Scots possessed advanced tastes and understanding in literature, with a Latin poetry that 'would have done honour to any nation', but then ponders aloud – no wonder he offended them so – why 'men thus ingenious and inquisitive were content to live in total ignorance of the trades by which human wants are supplied, and to supply them by the grossest means. Till the Union made them acquainted with English manners, the culture of their lands was unskilful, and their domestic life unformed; their tables were coarse as the feasts of Eskimeaux, and their houses as filthy as the cottages of Hottentots.' Thus did, and do, travellers in other countries offer huge insult. He continued even more offensively: 'Since they have known that their condition was capable of improvement, their progress in useful knowledge has been rapid and uniform . . . But they must be for ever content to owe to the English that elegance and culture, which, if they had been vigilant and active, perhaps the English might have owed to them.'

In his account of their two-night stopover at Inverness, Boswell left out of his *Journal of a Tour* one enchanting detail. An incident at dinner on Sunday night became part of the Reverend Mr Grant's conversational furniture, a story he told for many years later. Johnson, it seems, began to regale the table concerning some extra-ordinary creature recently discovered in New South Wales, and began to imitate the animal, the kangaroo. Suddenly, he stood upright, held out his hands like paws, then bunched up the tails of his huge brown coat in front of his stomach to convey an impression of the kangaroo's pouch, and began to bounce about the room.

What a pity the kangaroo had been discovered too late for Johnson's Dictionary: Captain Cook makes the first reference to it three years earlier, in his Journal for August 1770. I like to think Johnson would have gloried in the most likeable derivation of the word 'kangaroo', even if lacking evidence for its provenance. The philological folklore claims that the animal was named when an English explorer (Cook himself?) asked an Aboriginal, 'What in Heaven's name is that?' as the exotic animal bounced across his view. To which he allegedly received the reply, 'Kangaroo' – native tongue for 'I don't understand what you are saying.'

*   *   *

When they left Mackenzie's Inn at Inverness early on Monday, 30 August, two Highland guides ran along ahead of them, John Hay and Laughland Vass; Johnson told Mrs Thrale they were 'active, officious, civil and hardy'. Other than a girl he had seen at a spinning-wheel and singing a song in the Gaelic at Nairn, this was Johnson's first true contact with the Scots of the west. The timbre of his text begins to alter just east of Inverness: his explorations were about to begin.

On their right, Loch Ness beamed at them: a glorious day. Johnson reported the lake water, so often gunmetal and brooding, as 'remarkably clear and pleasant, and is imagined by the natives to be medicinal'. This, in itself, ought to quieten speculation about a Loch Ness monster; the water's reputation for healing clearly belongs to ancient traditions, and when a place so powerfully atmospheric generates one legend, it is surely capable of throwing up several more. When he gets to Iona, Johnson will walk for the second time in footsteps he does not yet know about, those of the man who caused the folklore – Columba was here. In 565 he came down from the islands to try and convert a Pictish king. On the way, he met a distressed group of Picts: one of their number had just been eaten alive by a monster in the lake. Columba sent one of his companions into the water, and just as the creature opened its jaws for its second course, Columba with a wave of his hand banished it: Nessie, all humps and coils, fled whining.

Boswell says, 'The scene was as sequestered and agreeably wild as could be desired, and for a time engrossed all our attention.' Johnson's 'low trees' – or their grandchildren – are now grown to great green heights. They ignored a Druid's temple – Johnson said, 'one is quite enough' – and then came to 'a little hut, with an old looking woman at the door of it. I thought, here might be a scene that would amuse Dr Johnson; so I mentioned it to him. "Let's go in," said he.'

Johnson devotes a long paragraph to the old woman's hut as Dr Livingstone might have described an African *kraal*. His word-picture also describes the typical Bronze- and Iron-Age European small dwelling developed from the wooden buildings of the Hallstatt and La Tène periods, from 700 B.C.: 'The wall, which is commonly about six feet high, declines from the perpendicular a little inward. Such rafters as can be procured are then raised for a roof, and covered with heath, which makes a strong and warm thatch . . . No light is admitted but at the entrance, and through a hole in the thatch, which gives vent to the smoke. This hole is not directly over the fire, lest the rain should extinguish it; and the smoke therefore naturally fills the place before it escapes.'

The woman was boiling a goat, one of her herd of sixty, when the riding party arrived; the two Highland guides interpreted her Gaelic. She had an interesting marital structure. Johnson calls her an 'old woman', and true, her husband was eighty years old. But the eldest of her five children was thirteen – therefore Boswell's observation of 'an old looking woman' had a truer ring. She invited them to be seated and offered them a drink.

Their reports of this encounter highlight the difference between Johnson and Boswell as human beings. Johnson's account acknowledges the woman's pastoral existence, and he dignifies her with a detailed report, pointing out that her circumstances were by no means on the lowest and most impoverished social scale. He does his readers the service of conveying to them the life and living of a family they might never encounter, or have had occasion to consider. Boswell struggles, sometimes unsuccessfully, against an instinct to disparage. He calls the hut 'a wretched litle hovel of earth', and makes comparisons only on a social scale, as distinct from Johnson's genuine anthropology. He even manages a lewdness. 'Dr Johnson was curious to know where she slept . . . She answered with a tone of emotion, saying she was afraid we wanted to go to bed with her. This coquetry, or whatever it may be called, of so wretched a being, was truly ludicrous.' Johnson and Boswell later bantered on the matter, each playfully accusing the other of being the one the woman feared – 'the wicked young fellow, the wild dog' or the 'terrible ruffian' fortunately accompanied by 'a civil decent young man'.

As he so often does, Boswell missed the point – or two. How natural for a woman sensible of her humble circumstances not to wish to unveil the total intimacy of her house to passing strangers. Secondly, he ignored folk memory of the English and the noble Scottish and their depredations: *à propos*, a story came to light much later, and recurs in local annals and in the works of many Johnsonian students

In 1746, one of Cumberland's officers on his way back from victory at Culloden had invaded the very same hut and raped a girl (his troopers held her down) then strangled the grandmother to command her silence. The 'old looking' woman whom Boswell and Johnson met took over that house the following year, by which time the crime had been punished. Even though the story reverberated through the Highlands, there is no evidence that either Boswell or Johnson knew the tale – had they done so, Boswell might have been less merry with his lubricious reasons as to why the woman would not show them the bedroom. Indeed, Boswell's insensitivity went further. Against the woman's express wishes, he lit a piece of paper and went into her bedroom anyway, and reported a 'bedstead of wood with heath [heather] upon it by way of a bed; at the foot of which I saw some sort of blankets of covering rolled in a heap'. Johnson did not drink her proffered dram, but Boswell and the two guides did, and when she asked them for snuff, her great luxury, they had none, but gave her money instead.

Boswell's rendering of the Loch Ness day skips ahead to lunch in a pub then their overnight stay with the deputy Governor of Fort Augustus. Johnson's account pauses at the Fall of Fiers, today called Foyers, a little more than halfway down the south-eastern length of the Loch. Opposite a café and shop, a tall, sparse wood leads down to a dramatic view of the Falls, a cataract powerful enough to feed a local hydro-electricity station. Johnson observes that 'the country at the bridge strikes the imagination with all the gloom and grandeur of Siberian solitude.' Not today; two pathways, both of soft going, lead to the Falls – the right-hand one for a good, distant view, the left-hand, less comfortable and over risky stones, for a close-up. Johnson took this latter and soon 'began to wish that our curiosity might have been gratified with less trouble and danger'. All he saw was the ghost of the waterfall: 'we visited the place at an unseasonable time, and found it divested of its dignity and terror.'

*   *   *

I cannot say whether they travelled on this good modern road. More likely, they followed a route now reduced: like Kipling's road through the woods, 'weather and rain have undone it again and now we shall never know there was once a road through the woods.' Full of sky, the landscape gleams with distant water. This road swoops. Past little stands of foxglove in the green foreground before a copse, the floor of the wood swerves sharply down to a fast stream the colour of nickel.

The party lunched on mutton, bacon and eggs, with rum, whisky and wine – Johnson again drank water – in a house called The General's Hut, named for that good strong Irishman, George Wade, to whom the Highlands owe their road system. General Wade built forty bridges up here inside a decade: and he carried the metaphor of his construction over into his administration – under his command, military rule in the wake of an insurrection proved less brutal, more instinctively communal, than the savagery of the butcher Cumberland who followed him.

At dark they arrived in Fort Augustus. They had made the length of Loch Ness in one day, not bad going for an old man on horseback; 'when he rode,' says Boswell at the end of the *Life*, 'he had no command or direction of his horse, but was carried as if in a balloon.' Even if they followed an older, slightly more direct road, it still amounted to a total of about thirty-three miles.

Any Johnsonian interest Fort Augustus once had has disappeared: the travellers tried an inn here, found it 'wretched' and stayed with the deputy governor at the fort, a gentleman of French extraction named Trapaud. A monastery occupies the foundations today, the military buildings having been largely pulled down long ago. At breakfast, having walked the governor's garden, they talked to a couple of officers who had fought the Indians in America, making Johnson wish he lived there so that he could write a book about them. In their separate entries for Fort Augustus, it is the fleeting observation that once again gives such valuable illumination. Johnson displays almost no preoccupation with the place, which he summarises as 'much less than that of St George . . . It was not long ago taken by the Highlanders.' Not the building Johnson stayed in: he slept in a new fort built to replace the one destroyed by the Jacobites. 'But its situation,' continues Johnson, 'seems well chosen for pleasure, if not for strength'; and then in half a sentence he gives us a glimpse of local life and activity: 'It stands at the head of the lake and, by a sloop of sixty tuns, is supplied from Inverness with great convenience' – which description immediately conjures the vessel plying up and down Loch Ness with provisions, armaments, soldiers' wives.

Fort Augustus offers two things worth relishing: that its canal provides a waterway down to Loch Oich and Loch Lochy and into Loch Linnhe and therefore out to sea and to Mull and Manhattan and Newfoundland. Secondly, it conjures the Wild West by virtue of its position as the middle of a line of three forts, Fort William to the south, and Fort George to the north.

They resisted Mr Trapaud's invitation to lunch. According to Boswell, 'Between twelve and one we set out, and travelled eleven miles, through a wild country, till we came to a house in Glenmorison [the modern spelling adds a 't' – Glenmoriston: Johnson calls it Glenmollison] called Anoch, kept by a McQueen.' To hit this road they had to go north a little from Fort Augustus and then swing to the west. Just beyond Fort Augustus a trace of their road may still be found; now impassable, it must have been a fearful route: the climb up to any height of it is ferociously demanding – or else I hit it at the wrong spot. Johnson comments, 'To make this way, the rock has been hewn to a level with labour that might have broken the perseverance of a Roman legion.' Therefore, unless hiking with considerable fortitude, the only way to approximate their journey is to take the normal road up as far as Invermoriston and then continue on its south-western fork, the A887, and in time it becomes the road – or so I presume – Johnson and Boswell travelled, the one cut by General Wade, straight across the rising land and emerging a little over half-way along the present road through Glenmoriston. They then followed a path in the lee of the mountains to Loch Cluanie (near which the upper and lower roads converge) and thence Glen Shiel.

Other than the hope of eagles, there is nothing in these tense high glens, north or south of Fort Augustus, to detain the traveller. Johnson says he saw no animals. I saw a bird of prey, a hen harrier, as intent as an osprey, beating her wings at early evening against a stand of firs, hunting like a cruise missile along the edge of a windbreak. Where Johnson found a country 'totally denuded of its wood' – how he loved the confirmation of his prejudices – forestry now swathes the unpromising terrain. In one of those asides, Johnson with the eye of a painter gives the last glimpse of these high ways in 1773: 'Once we saw a corn field, in which a lady was walking with some gentlemen . . .' Both writers make light of this crossing from Fort Augustus to the middle of Glenmoriston, even though it must have proven their most arduous stage so far – eleven miles of high, hard going, 'cut in traverses,' as Johnson says, 'so that as we went upon a higher stage, we saw the baggage following us below in a contrary direction.'

They came to Anoch in the early afternoon, having to break their journey early, because the opportunities for food and lodging were not evenly distributed between Fort Augustus and Glenelg: Johnson says, 'the only house, where we could be entertained, was not further off than a third of the way'. That night, they had plenty of opportunity for conversation, and here they had one of their most memorable encounters. McQueen, a genuine Highlander, kept the inn (such as it was) at Anoch and he brought Johnson the closest he had yet been to the controversies of the recent Stuart cause.

This cultivated man, McQueen, had fought at Culloden. He spoke accentless English with excellent grammar, proved civil and hospitable and well-read: in his stone-and-wattle premises he possessed a volume of *The Spectator*, a volume of Humphrey Prideaux's *The Old and New Testament Connected in the History of the Jews*, and, judging from Boswell, the man reflected annoyance when Johnson expressed surprise at finding books in his house. Johnson dwells on McQueen's diction, complimenting him upon it and being told in return that the man had 'learned it by grammar', and Johnson goes on to contemplate that such good English must have been acquired while such people served in the armed forces. Evidently it did not occur to him that it could also have been a case of the mastery of English becoming a kind of weapon in the mouths of the dispossessed.

The pair stayed overnight at Anoch, where the McQueens possessed some small acres of turnips and potatoes, a fact which, as with so much of such crofting, mystifies; these fields, very little flesh of earth on the bones of rock, seem only capable of mosses and heathers. On that afternoon of Tuesday, 31 August, McQueen's daughter served them tea; she wore a print linen dress, and had been to Inverness for a year's education in reading, writing, sewing, knotting, lace- and pastry-making. (A decade later, Johnson, on a journey to Oxford, sat in the stage-coach beside a Mrs Beresford and her daughter; the girl was passing the time in knotting, a kind of tatting, in which coloured threads are knitted into decorative knots. Miss Beresford, in a hero-worshipping whisper to Boswell, said of Johnson, 'How he does talk! Every sentence is an essay!' Johnson, who was looking askance at Miss Beresford's occupational therapy, said, 'In the scale of insignificance, I think knotting is to be reckoned next to mere idleness – though I once attempted to learn knotting . . . but I made no progress.')

Neither Boswell nor Johnson states Miss McQueen's precise age, but she seems to have passed sufficiently beyond pubescent embarrassment to converse relaxedly with the great Englishman, and Johnson made her a gift of a book, an act of generosity which later caused not a little controversy. Many of Johnson's readers wished to know what kind of reading Dr Johnson thought suitable for young ladies, and it transpired, to much amusement, that he had given young Miss McQueen an arithmetic. The laughter which this caused proved irritating to Johnson, but usefully stimulated a response which gives a good insight. He resented the implied criticism, and defended himself by saying he merely gave her a book which he happened to have with him, rather than one he felt suitable for such a person. It was not a book that he had packed when leaving London: he had bought it a day or two earlier in Inverness, and to Boswell, years later, he gave, not unmemorably, his reasons for buying it at all: 'Why, Sir, if you are to have but one book with you upon a journey, let it be a book of science. When you have read through a book of entertainment, you know it, and it can do no more for you; but a book of science is inexhaustible.' We have no record of whether Miss McQueen – 'not inelegant in either mien or dress', as Johnson found her: Boswell calls her 'a modest, civil girl, very neatly dressed' – found *Cocker's Arithmetick* equally absorbing. Johnson hoped that his gift would ensure she did not forget him.

Within the inn at Anoch, walled with thick turves of earth, wainscotted with wicker, and by its chimney distinguished from the other two huts nearby, the landlord and his daughter – no mention of a Mrs McQueen – served them a meal of eggs, chicken, sausage and mutton, with rum. Mr McQueen joined them at table, and gave Johnson the kind of local knowledge he loved – the economics, way of life, problems of such an existence. Already, seventy men had emigrated from the glen to America, and McQueen intended to follow them within the year. All the difficulty sprang from high rents; for his own farm, the landlord now paid four times more than he had twenty years ago, and he found this unfair: he would have been happy to go from five pounds a year to ten, but not to twenty. Johnson took McQueen's side and observed acidly that it was the Laird who should be forced to emigrate, at which McQueen respectfully and loyally demurred, knowing that the laird, to quote Boswell, 'could not shift for himself in America'.

A party of soldiers arrived at the inn; the travellers had earlier met them road-building between Fort Augustus and Anoch and in deference to the hospitality they had received from Mr Trapaud, Johnson and Boswell gave the men cash to buy drink – which now they did. Johnson gave them more money, the not inconsiderable sum of a shilling each, for which generosity they hailed him, addressing him as 'My Lord'. The soldiers stayed up all night, brawling their guts out.

The pair of travellers slept in a somewhat makeshift room, where a woman's dress hanging on a rope acted as a partition between two beds. Mrs Boswell had packed sheets in her husband's luggage, and Joseph Ritter laid them on both beds. Boswell feared vermin; Johnson anticipated the chill as if stepping into a cold bath, and tied a coloured handkerchief around his head. In merry companionship both men braved the hardship of the landlord's sleeping arangements and settled for the night, chatting idly and humorously across the partition like schoolboys in a dormitory.

Copiousness of detail excepted, a fundamental difference in the attitude of each traveller again lies deep within and beneath their texts when they write of Anoch and Mr McQueen. Johnson was warm, Boswell uncertain. Johnson responded to this courteous, gentlemanly Highlander; Boswell failed to see beyond the Gael, the Jacobite. After his initial *gaffe* that McQueen should own books, Johnson opened out to a man of culture, a man who understood his own problems and who had thought a way through them to a solution, however sad emigration might prove. Boswell, contrarily – and patronisingly – feared danger. 'Wednesday, 1st September: I awaked very early. I began to imagine that the landlord, being about to emigrate, might murder us to get our money . . .' and claims that Johnson had entertained the same fears, although Johnson never mentions such thoughts. Neither writer gave McQueen the credit of his own history; neither enquired into, or assessed, the status he might have had before the '45 Rebellion, in which he had participated, and by which he had most likely been reduced to keeping this crude but hospitable inn. It may have been a stopping-place for drovers – but he could still do Dr Johnson the honour of making lemonade from fresh lemons. And he still practised sufficiently the ways of the Highland families to send his daughter to Inverness for as good an education as a girl could get within reach at that time.

Next stop, the boat to Skye from Glenelg, and after an early breakfast, they left Anoch at eight o'clock. Mr McQueen walked some miles with them into the mountains. He gave Johnson his economic statistics, a hundred each of sheep and goats; twelve milch cows; twenty-eight dry beef cattle ready to be sold, 'awaiting the drover'. He also cited a local laird's wealth – or lack of it: from a hundred square miles of property, sixty thousand acres, he could raise only four hundred pounds a year, no matter what rent pressure he put on his tenants. In the final conversation he had with them, McQueen told Boswell and Johnson of his adventures in the 1745 Rebellion, when he had been part of Bonnie Prince Charlie's invasion force of England and got as far as Derbyshire, and fought at Culloden.

Boswell sometimes stinks faintly of hypocrisy. No doubt can exist of his Anglophilia, yet he now says that when he heard

McQueen tell the story of the '45, 'I could not refrain from tears,' and qualifies his response by discussing a set of feelings not a million miles from sentimentality; 'The very Highland names, or the sound of a bagpipe, will stir my blood, and fill me with a mixture of melancholy and respect for courage; with pity for an unfortunate and superstitious regard for antiquity, and thoughtless inclination for war; in short, with a crowd of sensations with which sober rationality has nothing to do.'

Two guides: one very tall servant: Boswell and Johnson on horse-back; the quaint party pressed on beneath these lovely forbidding mountains to Glenshiel. Johnson remained relatively unimpressed, even by a glimpse of snow that had persisted to this, the first day of September. His eye measured these impressive heights coolly, relating them always to sea level rather than to their own grandeur, and correcting Boswell's exultation over 'another mountain I called immense: Johnson: "No; it is no more than a considerable protuberance."' Little by little, however, the force of this long glen beneath the austere greyness of the Five Sisters touched Johnson, and he moved his position from that of first considering the political role of such remoteness, and the opportunities it gave for military strategies and subsequent escapes – Glenshiel had been the scene of a battle fifty-four years earlier in which local Highlanders unsuccessfully reinforced a Spanish invasion force – to being lulled by the sight of so many waters, brooks, burns, and silver rivulets, 'which commonly ran with a clear shallow stream over a hard pebbly bottom'.

Now that he had arrived at the wildest part of Britain, he wished to use his adventure in the same spirit as that in which Montaigne wrote his famous *Essais* – as trials of himself, as investigations of the ideas that arose in the non-stop chatter of his mind. At noon, in a narrowing part of the glen, a stretch which offered a little more greenery than the earlier reaches, the Highland guides, knowing of the climb ahead, halted to feed, water and rest the horses. Johnson grasped hold of some solitude and became for an hour or so a noble savage and a member of the armies of medieval romance, communing with nature on the bank of a stream: 'The day was calm, the air soft, and all was rudeness, silence and solitude. Before me, and on either side, were high hills, which by hindering the eye from ranging, forced the mind to find entertainment for itself.' That passage and the two meditative paragraphs which follow, constitute the high point of his adventure in the wilds so far, and the first true narration of the adventures of his mind among remoteness.

When his *Journey* was published two years later, this quiet moment received great acclaim, hailed by one reviewer as 'a fortunate event in the annals of literature . . . we congratulate the public on the event . . .' The critic was reacting to Johnson's capacity for inventive response. Time after time on his Scottish travels he conjured original ideas from his encounters with the unfamiliar. But when the published version is contrasted with his more mundane conclusions, as in his letters to his friends, an element of performance can be seen in the formal account. For example, to Mrs Thrale he described the scene of this famed moment of quietude briefly – 'on a green bank, with a small stream running at my feet, in the midst of savage solitude, with Mountains before me, and on either hand covered with heath' – then commented, 'I looked round me, and wondered that I was not more affected, but the mind is not at all times equally ready to be put in motion.' However, in his *Journey to the Western Islands* he takes a much more elaborate position: 'The imaginations excited by the view of an unknown and untravelled wilderness are not such as arise in the artifical solitiude of parks and gardens, a flattering notion of self-sufficiency, a placid indulgence of voluntary delusions, a secure expansion of the fancy, or a cool concentration of the mental powers.' He contrasted these with the force of the wild where 'man is made unwillingly acquainted with his own weakness, and meditation shows him how little he can sustain, and how little he can perform'.

A puzzle solved itself out here. On several occasions, and in many places, it had surprised me that Johnson made no comment: Strichen, the planned village, in particular, and the Pictish ancestry of Forres. These and other similar resonances seemed to me hand-fashioned for Johnson's interest – but time and again, no comment. Now I knew the reason. When he sat down on his romantic bank by his crystal brook, the thought of turning the journey into a book was born: 'Whether I spent the hour well I know not; for here I first conceived the thought of this narration.'

After their rest, they began the last push to the islands, the most difficult part of their journey yet. At Shiel Bridge, at the head of Loch Duich, the road climbs west up into Ratagan Forest and up through Glen More, emerging out onto a short Jack-and-the-Beanstalk plateau, and then hard and drearily down to Glenelg from whose shore the Isle of Skye across the Sound of Sleat may almost be reached by fingertip. Although Ratagan was beclouded, the sun shone through behind me, putting a shine on the slate-coloured waters below. I knew in advance that I would have to retrace my steps on this road, to get to the Skye boat at the Kyle of Lochalsh, as there is nowadays only a summer ferry to the island from Glenelg. The physical aspect of my journey had collapsed: a heel injury became aggravated, with a cut almost in as far as the bone, and the rest of the tour found me on wheels or afloat more than on foot.

Before Boswell and Johnson began this ascent, which in parts feels almost vertical, they made one more stop – at the hamlet of Auchnasheal or Auknasheals, 'consisting of many huts', wrote Johnson, 'perhaps twenty, built all of dry stone, that is, stones piled up without mortar'. No trace of Auchnasheal exists, although somewhere beneath the moss the stones must still lurk.

The place gave Johnson another whiff of anthropology: here he stood as if in Africa or Arabia, greeting wild natives in their habitat: these Macraes might have been Xhosa tribesmen, or Tuaregs: 'The villagers gathered about us in considerable numbers, I believe without any evil intention, but with a very savage wildness of aspect and manner.'

An extra man, says Boswell, had joined their little party, 'Evan Campbell, servant to Mr Murchison, factor to the Laird of Macleod in Glenelg ran along with us today. He was a very obliging fellow.' Evan Campbell, or John Hay, or Laughland Vass, or perhaps all three Highlander guides, knew that milk could be had from the Macraes of Auchnasheal; the travellers sat down outside a house and were brought wooden dishes – Johnson calls them 'pails' – of milk. Boswell: 'One of them was frothed like a syllabub. I saw a woman preparing it with such a stick as is used for chocolate, and in the same manner.'

For this *largesse* the tourists replied in kind, and in the manner of explorers. They distributed in paper twists small parcels of snuff and tobacco, bought at Fort Augustus for this very purpose at the instigation of Mr Trapaud, and Boswell also gave them their leftover wheaten bread, a substance unknown among the oats and barley eaters of the Highlands. Next, they offered to pay the woman of the house for the milk, and she asked a shilling, at which some of the men goaded her towards more; when she refused to raise her price, Boswell gave her a half-crown (influenced, I feel, not so much by her honest generosity, but by her shapeliness which he described as 'comely almost as the figure of Sappho').

Johnson makes less of his stop among the Macraes than one might have expected. Auchnasheal merits no more than three paragraphs, two short and one long. His letter to Mrs Thrale contained more detail, expressed with greater pungency, and it confirms the 'Dark Continent' feel of his experience: 'The Inhabitants, a very coarse tribe, ignorant of any language but earse [*sic*], gathered so fast about us, that if we had not had Highlanders with us, they might have caused more alarm than pleasure.' However, he does use his recollection of the journey over Ratagan, his eyes filled with mountains, to reflect in the *Journey* generally upon the condition of remoteness as it affects human beings, and thereby touches the core of his reasons for travelling. Accordingly, we are treated to an immediate and excellent example of Johnson's mind at work.

He begins by summarising that for the obvious reasons of inaccessibility and defences, the peoples who reside among mountains are the last to be conquered: he progresses to consider similarly-caused impediments to civilisation: he deduces the part remoteness plays in the preservation of ancient languages.

From his discussion of how such isolated clans as the Macraes, in such hollows of the world as Auchnasheal, repel all boarders, Johnson opens up a discussion of how mankind in this condition regulates itself. Having decided that the rude manners and customs of an outback community 'are rather produced by their situation than derived from their ancestors', he examines first how they regulated themselves traditionally; then, the introduction and enforcement of the country's general body of legislation – for instance, theft of cattle from drovers had long been a problem in the Highlands; now their passage was growing safer. And he moves up the scale from the creation of individual regional statutes, to address the law enforcement problems caused by peculiar geography, to the place of the law in the body politic. At the lower end of his debate he describes how 'in the Highlands it was a law, that if a robber was sheltered from justice, any man of the same clan might be taken in his place'; at the upper end, close to his conclusion, Johnson summarises: 'As government advances towards perfection, provincial judicature is perhaps in every empire gradually abolished.'

In effect, he is tracing the means by which anthropologically quaint units decline. The over-running and Anglicising of the Highlands after Culloden, when even the traditional form of dress was banned, would soon lead to assimilation, and even though 'the inhabitants of mountains form distinct races, and are careful to preserve their genealogies', Johnson concludes without emotion that 'while their rocks seclude them from the rest of mankind, and kept them an unaltered and distinctive race . . . they are now losing their distinction, and hastening to mingle with the general community.'

The passage, some three pages long and called 'The Highlands', is a masterly performance – notwithstanding the implicit condescension that such a wide region could be thus briefly treated. It becomes a great pleasure to read this passage, another justification of those who assured me that *A Journey to the Western Islands of Scotland* remains one of the fundamental works in the literature of travel.

Of climbing Ratagan (which they spelt in different ways: Boswell, 'Ratakin': Johnson, 'Ratiken') in the early afternoon, Johnson confided in Mrs Thrale (to whom he spells it 'Rattiken') 'more difficulty than we had yet experienced', a formidable demur, given the harshness of the ride out from Fort Augustus to Anoch. To begin with, they left it too late – but, measuring the distance from Shiel Bridge way below and behind me, and judging the terrain, even though this modern road has been impressively built, I do not know how they might have bettered their arrangements. They could hardly have camped, and without exact locations for Anoch and Auchnasheal, I cannot say whether they would have improved their lot by aiming for Auchnasheal when leaving Fort Augustus, instead of breaking the journey at Anoch.

In any case, they breasted the height of Ratagan, and now the difficulty began in earnest. Dr Johnson's weight interfered with his equestrian comfort, and 'upon one of the precipices, my horse, weary with the steepness of the rise, staggered a little, and I called in haste to the Highlander to hold him. This was the only moment of my journey, in which I thought myself endangered' – a surprising comment, given what lies ahead. On the steep descent, things deteriorated further. The guides suggested that Johnson, so as not to tire one horse wholly, should alternate between mounts. But when he opted for either of John Hay's horses, they argued: Johnson had to settle for the grey owned by Laughland Vass.

They moved forward, Joseph Ritter bringing up the rear, Hay and Vass either side of Johnson's bridle, the great man clearly frightened. John Hay, seeing Johnson's fear, talked to him all the time as to a child, trying to keep him cheerful, but this measure only excited Boswell's scorn, especially when he heard Hay trying to distract Johnson with the antics of the local goats. 'Here now was a common ignorant Highland clown imagining that he could divert, as one does a child, – *Dr Samuel Johnson!* The ludicrousness, absurdity, and extraordinary contrast between what the fellow fancied, and the reality, was truly comick.' So they rode on through the twilight, the guides either side of Johnson soothing him forward.

At this point, Boswell decided he would hurry on ahead to secure their food and accommodation at Glenelg. To his astonishment, Johnson yelled angrily at him and there broke out the most serious row the pair is reported ever to have had in their long association. They even let the sun go down on their wrath. As Boswell began to move off, Johnson called him back heatedly. Boswell explained, patiently enough to judge from his text, that he merely intended to see that all was well at Glenelg, to which

Johnson replied, 'Do you know, I should as soon have thought of picking a pocket as doing so?' Boswell hit back: 'I am diverted with you, sir,' and Johnson laid him low: 'Doing such a thing makes one lose confidence in him who has done it, as one cannot tell what he may do next.'

Matters did not improve when they got to Glenelg and found an appalling inn – although it did draw from Johnson one of his best remarks of the entire tour. Reflecting that the place lacked milk, bread, eggs, and wine, he observed, 'Of the provisions the negative catalogue was very copious.' Someone sent somebody out to kill two hens; a local gentleman, knowing the lie of the land, sent his servant to the inn with rum and sugar and an apology for not knowing of their arrival in suficient time to put them up, and he had to leave for Inverness at the crack of dawn; Boswell still had some bread despite the amount he had doled out to the Macraes. The landlord of this slate-roofed building cooked them mutton chops which proved inedible, and Johnson's supper, later traced in Boswell's notes, consisted of bread and a lemon.

When they got to the bedroom, further surprises awaited them: 'Out of one of the beds, on which we were to repose, started up, at our entrance, a man black as Cyclops from the forge.' Boswell found the room 'damp and dirty, with bare walls, a variety of bad smells, a coarse black greasy fir table, and forms [benches] of the same kind'. The guides, unable to find livery for the horses, found fresh hay for the beds and the quarrellers, still sullen with each other, retired. Johnson slept on the hay in his huge-pocketed greatcoat; Boswell laid the sheets his wife had packed on top of the hay and, observed Johnson, 'lay in linen like a gentleman'. Eighteen days out of Edinburgh, they perched at the edge of the Hebrides.

CHAPTER VI

'The inquirer is kept in continual suspense'

FOR THE NEXT SEVEN WEEKS they moseyed around the Western Isles, often encountering rough weather: Skye, Raasay, Coll, Mull, Ulva, Inchkenneth and Iona. Of Glenelg they saw little; after breakfast on Thursday, 2 September, having parted company with their guides John Hay and Laughland Vass, they walked down to the shore and were ferried to Skye.

Johnson and Boswell made up their quarrel when they rose, with Johnson saying he would not have turned back, as he had threatened, and headed for Edinburgh. The weather cleared too, and they were rowed diagonally south-west across the Sound of Sleat. Boswell measured the water journey from Glenelg as twelve miles; the boatman called it six miles, confusing old logical Johnson with the assertion that a mile on the land equated to two on the sea. Their hosts for the first few days, the Lord of the Isles, Sir Alexander Macdonald, and his wife Jane, a relative of Boswell's, waited on the shore at Armadale, a small, dirty, sandy horseshoe of a bay, to greet them. A portion of the original stone jetty still stands at Armadale, within sight of the modern ferry port linking Skye to Mallaig on the mainland. Trees on the upland behind the harbour cloak the Macdonald estate. At the pier, shops sell batiks and woollens to the ferry travellers: families with packed cars and roof-racks; men with sheepdogs on the way to trials at Mallaig; bikers on some kind of round robin according to their luggage tags – 'Genève-Edinburgh-Brugge-Genève'. The distant mountains form the backcloth of an opera set.

Skye is called the winged, or flying, island. On the map, or from high in the air, it looks like a proud bird, profiled like a phoenix. On my first visit, several years ago, I saw – and they

THE RECONCILIATION.

are unmistakable – eagles. Near Portree, 'the harbour of the king' – James V, father of Mary, Queen of Scots, once sailed in – I lay on heathland and watched first one, then another, high against the clear blue sky. Such grace: they soar and wheel, the lions of the air. One Skye man told me how, sitting on his lawn one afternoon, he heard a sudden great beating of wings and like passing royalty an eagle swooped low across the trees.

Although not the only outsiders to record the place – Johnson's favourite travel writers Martin Martin and Thomas Pennant made copious observations – the visit of Johnson and Boswell to the isle became a significant part of Skye's history, on account of the extent of their commentaries and the literary distinction they have retained. Johnson considered as many aspects of life here as he could possibly think of, or so it seems: and Boswell recorded Johnson with similar energy. Their experience of the island became comprehensive; they visited the south, then the east, then the north-east, then the north-west, the west and back to the south again. Weather did not deter them; it rained most of the time and they traversed ground that had little or no trace of thoroughfare.

On Skye, Johnson hit his anthropologist's and historian's strides. In the Macdonald household at Armadale, he asked questions busily and settled himself to a general spirit of enquiry, the fruits of which he then presents in his *Journey*. He begins with a complimentary description of the walled orchard, which had survived the destruction of the castle in the years following the '45. A visiting fossilist from Aberdeenshire drew Johnson's attention to a species of ash tree, enabling the great man to support his recurring arboreal obsession: 'The present nakedness of the Hebrides is not wholly the fault of Nature.'

Johnson heard bagpipes at Armadale, and a story to accompany them – of a past Macdonald aggression against a family in Culloden, whom the Macdonalds locked in their church one Sunday morning and torched, this being the tune played while the flames danced. Johnson's commentary upon this tale airs his willingness to take in everything and give it back out again: 'Narrations like this, however uncertain, deserve the notice of the traveller, because they are the only records of a nation that has no historians, and afford the most genuine representation of the life and character of the ancient Highlanders.'

He next examines the Hebridean footwear – 'Brogues, a kind of artless shoes, stitched with thongs so loosely, that though they defend the foot from stones, they do not exclude water.' The wearing of Highland dress, the speaking of Erse, the weather – his observations begin with the commonplace and are taken by his mind up on to the plateau of thought.

In this, his value always exceeds Boswell's; Johnson the writer has no need to grind the axe of his ego, and thereby feels no qualms in conveying how confusing he finds the native Scots, who, decisive and firm in their answer to his first question, are likely to contradict it entirely in answering the second question. He observes, not unamusedly, 'such is the laxity of Highland conversation, that the inquirer is kept in continual suspense, and by a kind of intellectual retrogradation, knows less as he hears more.'

Boswell's reflections upon their first four days on Skye ring with a different clang, and behind his final edition of his *Journal of a Tour* lies a curly history. He disliked Sir Alexander Macdonald, a view shared by many: it originally stemmed from unfavourable comparison with Alexander's older brother, the late, much-loved, James. On his own account, though, Alexander possessed the opposite of generosity, had a pompous air, offensive self-importance and had embraced his Eton education and all things southern too warmly (not a word he otherwise inspired) for the liking of his fellow-Scots.

Boswell loathed him so much that his first edition of the *Tour to the Hebrides* had to be amended on acount of the unflattering position he took on Sir Alexander. Excisions, notes and actual published first edition refer to Sir Alexander's reputation for racking up his tenants' rents unfairly and harshly; and to noticeable meanness – 'he has disgusted all mankind by injudicious parsimony'; Boswell originally told of Sir Alexander asking a visitor whether the punch-bowl on the table in front of them were not indeed very handsome. The guest replied, 'It would be – if it were full.'

When he read the remarks in the first edition, the Lord of the Isles wrote angrily to Boswell; a duel might have been fought had Boswell not agreed to edit out offending passages next time around. At the Clan Donald centre in Skye, near whose grounds stood the house in which the pair stayed, some relevant legalistic correspondence between the two may be seen. Thomas Rowlandson capped the matter – which had become public knowledge – in his final Boswell cartoon, called 'Revising the Second Edition', which shows a terrified Boswell being grabbed by the throat; Lord Macdonald is pointing with his stick to the offending pages of the first edition and Boswell is complying in terror.

The edition of Boswell's *Tour* now generally available only refers obliquely to a lack of warmth, and to Boswell's own 'spleen' while staying there – all this notwithstanding that the beautiful (and pregnant) Lady Macdonald was a cousin of Boswell's. Although the clan is diffuse now, a cohesion lingers: Macdonalds all over the world contribute to the funding of the Clan Donald Centre, a well-run and surprisingly unembarrassing tourist, residential and archival institute for the celebration of the name.

* * *

On Monday, 6 September 1773, Boswell and Johnson left the home of Sir Alexander Macdonald and set off on horseback to a staging-post near their embarkation point for Raasay. Beyond Broadford (which Boswell calls 'Broadfoot'), past today's electricity installations, down a long roadway, lies the farm at which they stayed, and some remains of the original house still stand. The Mackinnons lived here, on land owned by the Macdonalds, 'of the first rank of tenants', Johnson wrote to Mrs Thrale, 'where we were entertained better than the landlords'. Shortened to 'Corry' nowadays, known locally as 'Old Corry', the pair's spelling again differed, with Johnson calling it 'Coriatachan' and Boswell 'Corrichatachin': the Ordnance Survey calls it 'Coire-chat-achan'. (The Mackinnons hosted them here twice, the second time being at the end of September after the pair had crossed the island to catch a boat for islands south of Skye.) 'From Armidel,' writes Johnson, 'we came at night to Coriatachan, a house very pleasantly situated between two brooks, with one of the highest hills of the island behind it.'

As if it had happened a few years ago, Mr Donal John Mac-Lennan, leaning on his metal gate as his sheep thronged the pens of today's farm at Corry, knew that Johnson and Boswell had been guests in this place, and that they had had good times here. On their first stay the Mackinnons gave them 'the comfort of a table fully furnished', and a party that night with songs in Gaelic, in whose choruses even Boswell joined. Other buildings have taken over at Corry, and at their rear the blond old wall of the original house stretches under the shade of a tree in this hollow full of little rivers. The travellers' response to this place was positive and warm, and this does not simply derive from the contrast with the pompous inhospitality they found at Armadale, where they were perhaps disgruntled at staying only in an estate official's house (the mansion had been burnt down), even if the laird and his lady stayed with them.

At the Mackinnons they entered the true spirit of the west of Scotland, the 'kindly and tooty' people of the song 'Westering Home'. Alexander Macdonald had clearly abandoned much of that hospitable tradition, perhaps owing to his embrace of southern education, or perhaps as a reaction to the affection in which his late brother had been held. The Mackinnons belonged closer to the ground of Skye, an open house where all strata mingled easily. Johnson wrote, 'We were treated with very liberal hospitality, among a more numerous and elegant company than it could have been supposed easy to collect.'

The Edinburgh effect had begun to work again, the great man come to visit, a fact which Johnson pleasedly concedes a couple of paragraphs earlier, when he observes, 'The arrival of strangers at a place so rarely visited, excites rumour, and quickens curiosity.'

In Skye, Johnson's text begins to grow denser, and he gives the appearance, almost, of wishing to record every moment. An impression also grows that when he reached Skye, having 'conceived', during his little mountain idyll, 'the thought of this narration', Johnson, emulating Boswell, has now begun to take notes. He made his eighteenth-century reader aware of the travel difficulties, and how they were surmounted – on steep hills by precipices the Highlander and his horse go carefully, the rider sometimes walking, always with a guide: 'The horseman has always at his side a native of the place, who, by pursuing game, or tending cattle, or often being employed in messages or conduct, has learned where the ridge of the hill has breadth sufficient to allow a horse and his rider a passage, and where the moss or bog is hard enough to bear them.' To Mrs Thrale he wrote, 'No part that I have seen is plain; you are always climbing or descending, and every step is upon rock or mire. A walk upon ploughed ground in England is a dance upon carpets, compared to the toilsome drudgery of wandering in Skye . . . The use of travelling is to regulate imagination by reality . . .'

He summarised continuously – the manners and *mores* of the people, the scale of hospitality, the diet, and the disposition of the household in which he stayed, the more 'ordinary' the folk the greater Johnson's detail. When all the consequences of his account are added up, it transpires that he created a permanent and invaluable record of an ancient way of life – not at first as antique as he had hoped, but he was not ungratified at the glimpses of the past that he caught.

Johnson's reflections under the heading of 'Coriatachan in Sky' amount to only eighteen hundred words or so, yet they constitute the clearest view of him I have had so far, the best opportunity to try and assess what made him. If great writing may principally be a matter of fine and large spirit expressed in outstanding technique, to my eye, as I still acquaint myself with him, Johnson triumphs by combining a welcoming mind with an economy of expression, so that he shares the maximum of observed experience in the minimum of words. In this, so difficult to achieve, he towers.

Never leaving us to feel that he has short-changed us, each observation complete in itself, as if it has been roundly considered before utterance, he manages to accommodate the following items of interest in that eighteen hundred words: a comparison between Hebridean manners of burial and Roman funeral rites; the weather (repeatedly); the literacy of the Hebrideans; how travellers are accommodated, there being no hotel system; diet – wild-fowl, fish, venison, beef, mutton, goat, poultry, bread; whisky for breakfast (the morning dram, known as a 'skalk'); the availability of tea, coffee, marmalade and other preserves, honey and cheese; trading practices – wine from the French in exchange for wool; culinary variety, short on vegetables other than potatoes, not good on custards; napery, crockery and cutlery; the abating fervour of the clans in the wake of Culloden; and he believed he saw the slow rise of prosperity under the 'unpleasing consequences of subjection'.

The 'Coriatachan in Sky' passage, the first of the great Hebridean discourses in Johnson's *Journey*, displays a writer confident that he is imparting information and reflection in sufficient quantities to excite both the reader's thought and imagination – and yet not so lengthy as to bore them, nor so brief as to frustrate them.

Boswell's counterpoint to this recitative divulges that among their books the Mackinnons had the shorter version of Johnson's own Dictionary, and that, notwithstanding the merry and warm respect they received from the household, the place began to feel like a prison on account of the adverse weather. By contrast, while Boswell fretted and twitched, Johnson wrote a brace of Odes, one to honour the Isle of Skye, the other for his friend Hester Thrale. Both in Latin, they received much admiration when they entered the wider world.

In conversation at Corry, Johnson heard the stories he longed for – of men seeing visions, of examples of 'second sight' on Skye; Mrs Mackinnon's father had once met some women who, while working in a field, heard ghostly voices, signifying imminent death; he later met two funerals at the predicted place.

Behind Boswell's published account of his fidgety stay at the Mackinnons' – he felt so lethargic that he did not encourage Johnson to talk so that he would not have to write it down – lies some oddity. Bearing in mind that after the stinginess of Armadale he had gone to the house of this 'hearty welcome', and had been pleased with 'a numerous and cheerful company' – why did Boswell prove less forthcoming than one might have expected about the Mackinnons? Snobbery may provide one answer: in his supposed solidarity with his own kind, he may not have wished to suggest that a tenant farmer could prove more generous of spirit than the laird. Fear may have contributed – fear of Sir Alexander's wrath. He could have been forgiven had he waxed much more lyrical. Indeed, he cut from his published version his original account of the hospitality they experienced – a pity because it constituted a valuable little sliver of social history, describing their arrival in 'a low parlour' of this two-storeyed house, to be greeted with tea from a silver service. Supper was as lavish as they had yet had in Scotland: 'A large dish of minced beef collops, a large dish of fricassee of fowl, I believe a dish called fried chicken or something like it, a dish of ham or tongue, some excellent haddocks, some herrings, a large bowl of rich milk, frothed, as good a bread-pudding as I ever tasted, full of raisin and lemon or orange peel, and sillabubs made with port wine and in sillabub glasses. There was a good table-cloth with napkins; china, silver spoons, porter if we chose it, and a large bowl of very good punch.'

When Boswell awoke on Wednesday, 8 September, the wind had died, but the rain persisted. It eventually cleared and after breakfast they prepared to go to Raasay; they would see the Mackinnons again in two weeks or so.

Boswell's account says they rode two miles to the shore to find a herring-boat which would take them out to Raasay. Today, a ferry crosses from the shore of Loch Sligachan, considerably more than two miles from Corry; waiting on the simple pier at Sconser, the vessel can be seen leaving Raasay, preceded by a small bow-wave.

The Raasay ferry takes only a handful of vehicles and rather more passengers, and travels frequently, and if the ferryman finds that he has no room for you on his last run of the day from Raasay back to Sconser he will return. On a fine mid-morning, the water at Sconser is glowingly clear, a kind of northern coral sea, and with boats bobbing on moorings near the back-gardens of their owners' cottages; a few lobster pots, a net drying in the light sunshine.

Boswell's and Johnson's footsteps can no longer be seen around Armadale and Sleat; so far, only Corry retains their memory, in that old stretch of white crumbling wall. Johnson found the whole island harsh and barren; to Mrs Thrale he wrote, 'though I have been twelve days upon it, I have little to say.' Yet his journey from the beautiful south to Corry took him through scenery which is today lovely. This part of Skye, wooded and lush, benefits from any warmth lingering in the North Atlantic Drift. Can it have changed much – or did it rain so pre-emptively that he cannot have noticed the lovely inlets at Isleornsay, their green banked lands sloping to soft-coloured waters? He ignites the imagination, nevertheless, with glancing observations of Skye '. . . so much indented by inlets of the Sea, that there is no part of it removed from the water by more than six miles'.

Before they left for Raasay, there arrived at the Mackinnons' a card and two visitors. The card was written by the Reverend Donald McQueen and told them that the Laird of Raasay had sent his own boat for them; the reverend gentleman himself arrived shortly afterwards; 'an elderly man,' says Boswell, 'with his own black hair, courteous and rather slow of speech, but candid, sensible and well-informed.' Mr McQueen, who would be with them for some weeks, was accompanied by one of the Macleods of Raasay to pilot them, Malcolm Macleod, aged sixty-two. To judge from Boswell's description, Macleod cut as representative a figure of Hebridean or Highland imagery as any folklore could have created, a hero straight out of Scott or Stevenson or Tranter: bearded, ruddy-cheeked, lively-eyed, wearing brogues, tartan stockings, 'a black waistcoat, a short green cloth coat bound with gold cord, a yellowish bushy wig, a large blue bonnet with gold thread button'. He also wore 'a purple camblet kilt': sartorial defiance: the kilt had been banned after the '45 in which the Macleods played a significant part, not least in assisting Bonnie Prince Charlie to escape. 'Camblet', a word as old as Marco Polo, or even springing from earlier Arabic associations, connects into 'Camelot', fine cloth, finer than camelhair with which it became commonly associated, finer than wool, as fine as silk itself and perhaps a combination of camel and wool and silk. To wear a kilt of camblet denoted a singular man – such as Malcolm Macleod of Raasay.

The boat had been made in Norway. 'The water was calm,' says Johnson, 'and the [four] rowers were vigorous.' Boswell, who says the high wind blew in their faces, described one of the oarsmen, 'a Macleod, a robust, black-haired fellow, half-naked, and bear-headed, something between a wild Indian and an English tar. Dr Johnson sat high on the stern, like a magnificent Triton.'

On Skye, Boswell's writing changed character, and became lyrical, more poised, vigorous and clear, as if the elements and the landscape lifted him. Perhaps his heart and mind leaped together at the daily realisation of his dream to take his beloved Johnson on this tour to these parts. The short journey to Raasay proved vivid. Malcolm Macleod sang a heroic song in Gaelic, with the boatmen and the Reverend Mr McQueen taking up the chorus. Passing Scalpay, Johnson suggested to Boswell that they buy the island, 'found a good school' on it, and an episcopal church, 'and have a printing-press where he would print all the Erse that could be found'. Rounding the corner of Scalpay, the weather of the open sea hit the boat and their faces, and Johnson, though uncomfortable, again reached for, and found, the humorous and positive: 'This is now the Atlantick. If I should tell at a tea table in London, that I have crossed the Atlantick in an open boat, how they'd shudder, and what a fool they'd think me to expose myself to such danger.'

Johnson increases in delight; how many edges he gives to an observation. A small boat journey becomes a crossing of the ocean; and continuing the mimicry of aggrandisement, he anticipates satirically the throwing-up of London's hands at his folly – and by implicit contrast, how much more adventurous and un-foppish he appears, while yet mocking himself.

In the open sea, Joseph Ritter – always there beneath the text or in the shadows of Boswell's narrative – mystifyingly lost Johnson's spurs overboard. How? Had he laid them in the bottom of the boat, or on the seat beside him – and a little wave swept them away? And why not have placed them for safe keeping in a pocket, satchel or valise? Johnson, after a moment of being stung at this carelessness, dismissed it as 'rather an inconvenience than a loss', and went on to use the incident to defend his views on the second sight. He had dreamt the night before of losing his walking-stick on the current of a stream. The Reverend McQueen countered, and spoke with the authority of one who, in order to rout the local belief in witchcraft, had had to preach aggressively from his own pulpit.

Near Raasay, a charming gleam comes from Boswell – 'the singing of our rowing was succeeded by that of reapers', the same song heard in a differently enchanting place by the Lady of Shalott. They must have had such a pleasing approach to Raasay House; the bay of their arrival seems unlikely to have changed, a wide and gentle place, now full of windsurfers – the mansion where they stayed now houses an Adventure School. The modern ferry comes in a good deal farther south, beneath slabs of World War Two concrete fortifications. A welcoming party of six walked down to the shore as the boating party disembarked not without difficulty; Johnson, after his six or seven hours on the Atlantic, found the rocks 'irregularly broken, and a false step would have been very mischievous'.

More intensely than Skye, the smaller canvas of Raasay plunged Johnson straight into the life of the islanders. The men greeting Johnson included the Laird, his doctor brother, and four other Macleod relatives, including one, known as Sandie, who had been exiled for his part with the Jacobites in 1745. It becomes clear from Boswell's descriptions that this family were considerably less Anglicised than the Macdonalds on Skye, and still remained on the side of the Gaels. In keeping with Sandie Macleod's fighting on behalf of the clans, the Laird himself, although straitened by low incomes from his estates, had never racked his rents and as a consequence, says Boswell, 'so far is he from distressing his people, that, in the present rage for emigration, not a man has left his estate.'

Up at the house waited Lady Raasay with her family – three sons and ten daughters. Brandy was poured immediately, and 'On a side-board was placed for us, who had come off the sea, a substantial dinner, and a variety of wines.' Boswell does not record whether Johnson accepted a drink; nor has he recorded Johnson taking alcohol on the journey so far. (Six years later, according to the *Life*, Johnson 'harangued' at Joshua Reynolds's house 'upon the qualities of different liquors', and coined the much-quoted 'Claret is the liquor for boys; port, for men; but he who aspires to be a hero must drink brandy.') Johnson told Mrs Thrale, 'We went up into a dining-room about as large as your blue room, where we had something given us to eat, and tea and coffee.'

Soon they rolled back the carpet and had a dance. A slight divergence appears here in the separate chronologies; Boswell gives the impression they danced *after* supper; Johnson says, 'When it was time to sup, the dance ceased, and thirty persons sat down to two tables in the same room. After supper the ladies sung Erse songs, to which I listened as an English audience to an Italian opera, delighted with the sound of words which I did not understand.' He had landed in the midst of the true hospitality and zest of the west of Scotland.

They came to Raasay House on the evening of Wednesday, 8 September, and stayed for four nights, a shorter stay than their first spell on Skye. Yet, as if some kind of mathematical progression took hold of him, Johnson's accounts of the several places in which he found himself, get longer, with Raasay the longest so far. He wrote a detailed set of observations – an entire territory, as it were, under his eye as a jewel to a watchmaker's glass. The society of Raasay was so self-contained that he could hold it in his palm and turn it this way and that. Thus, he acquainted himself with the meanings of the songs he heard them singing, songs of love and emigration; with inheritances and alliances between these western chieftains; with the size and topography of Raasay and its suitability for animal husbandry. He found trees on Raasay, and saw the trout from their streams but not the eels, which prompts him towards thoughts on national culinary abhorrences: 'The Neapolitans lately refused to eat potatoes in a famine. An Englishman is not easily persuaded to dine on snails with an Italian, on frogs with a Frenchman, or on horse-flesh with a Tartar,' and then leads into a discussion which philosophically connects the natural foods of nations with the natural development of man's society. Pondering the absence on Raasay of deer, hares and rabbits, and expanding to discuss beasts of prey, he begins to give a picture of a small island community in the eighteenth century as comprehensively and economically as any reader could desire.

The compactness of the place, as Johnson found it, may still be touched. He reckoned that the population of the day numbered somewhere between six and nine hundred people, but he based this on the fact that the laird pressed together an army of a hundred men for the '45, and according to Johnson 'the sixth part of a people is supposed capable of bearing arms'. Allowing for the fact that not every man would hear the call, and that the laird would wish to leave a number of men to guard the place, he then bumped up the arithmetic to suppose nine hundred inhabitants.

By the road from the ferry to Raasay House, small neat houses appear, bright colourful gardens, attentively tended, gleaming in the sunshine. Sports reporters are reputed to gauge crowds well; who measures populations at a glance? I cannot tell how many people live on Raasay today; nine hundred would seem a high estimate although in the interior of the island, houses appear unexpectedly like mushrooms in the grass. A quiet life, but an exquisite one visually, on this long narrow island, on whose southern forested hills the poet Sorley Maclean found that 'Time, the deer, is in the wood of Hallaig.'

Behind Raasay House there still stands 'a chapel unroofed and ruinous'. Is it the same as Johnson described? This small graveyard contains the 'repositories for the dead' of the Macleod generations. Once more appears the value of the difference between Johnson's discursiveness and Boswell's practical observations. Johnson used the little family cemetery to break into a contemplation of Martin Martin's journey and then lead to a consideration of roofless churches as an exemplar and a herald of the eventual decline of religion. Boswell brings us to the very bones – literally – of their excursion to the churchyard behind the stable-block. 'A little to the west of the house is an old, ruinous chapel, unroofed, which never has been very curious. We here saw some human bones of an uncommon size. There was a heel-bone, in particular, which Dr Macleod said was such, that if the foot was in proportion, it must have been twenty-seven inches long. Dr Johnson would not look at the bones. He started back from them with a striking appearance of horror . . .'

Excellent though Johnson has so far proven at the explorer's notes, Boswell threatens to outdo him regarding Raasay. It is from Boswell that we learn of the height of Dun Can, Raasay's peak on which he danced a Highland reel with old Malcolm Macleod who called him between five and six in the morning to go walking.

THE DANCE ON DUN-CAN.

Boswell is the one who tells us the legend of the seahorse from the lakes who devoured a man's daughter, and was eventually trapped by the lure of a sow on a spit; from Boswell we learn that of the hundred-strong little army the Laird of Raasay mustered, eighty-six came back from Culloden; Boswell chronicles the ash and plane trees, the limestone rocks, the caves and their stalactites, the black cattle, the plover, the pigeons and blackcock, the rainfall, nine months in a year, the juniper, the peat, the belief in the existence of a gold mine, and the women *wawking* or *waulking* the tweed, a tedious operation where the tweed is rubbed over and through water in order to shrink and thicken it (in the outer Hebrides they add their own urine to the vat, although Bozzie missed that one), and the women sang a worksong to accompany the rhythmic labour, and did not succeed in drowning out Johnson's deep voice as he asked them questions. From Boswell we learn that the Laird of Macleod was in debt to the tune of forty thousand pounds, and this Hebridean Micawber had an income of only thirteen hundred a year.

They danced every night. Boswell reported: 'The queen of our ball was the eldest Miss Macleod, of Rasay, an elegant, well-bred woman, and celebrated for her beauty all over these regions, by the name of Miss Flora Rasay. There seemed to be no jealousy, no discontent among them; and the gaiety of the scene was such that I for a moment doubted whether unhappiness had any place in Rasay.' Of the celebrated Miss Flora, Johnson wrote to Mrs Thrale that she 'dresses her head very high, and has manners so ladylike, I wish her headdress was lower'.

When Boswell had completed his own adventuring on Raasay, he turned his attention, as usual, to making Dr Johnson sparkle: 'Let me now gather some gold dust – some more fragments of Dr Johnson's conversation, without regard to order of time.' Raasay had a smaller familiarity with the topics on which Dr Johnson was likely to speak. Boswell tried all the same, but reported only one 'typical' conversation of any length. It took place on Friday, 10 September, and only between Johnson and Boswell; Johnson talked of four people, Richard Bentley, David Mallet, the Duchess of Marlborough and Joseph Hooke. It was an exchange of literary gossip, having to do with the finances of writing, and the 'ghosting' of the Marlborough memoirs, and would have meant nothing to the dancing, chattering folk in Raasay House.

Apart from that, and a brief exchange with Boswell on one of the Macleod family, it was now clear that Johnson found little stimulation on Raasay: 'There was not enough of intellectual entertainment for him, after he had satisfied his curiosity, which he did, by asking questions, till he had exhausted the island': does Boswell mean the topic of Raasay or its people? Johnson himself concluded that 'Raasay has little that can detain a traveller, except the laird and his family'; and in their 'feat of hospitality' he found a 'delightful contrariety of images. Without is the rough ocean and the rocky land, the beating billows and the howling storm; within is plenty and elegance, beauty and gaiety, the song and the dance.'

On a sunny Sunday morning they left Raasay. Despite their qualms of travelling on the Sabbath, they took the weather as it came to them and sailed back to Skye, landing in the harbour of Portree.

Beyond Raasay House today, the road winds inland, an excellent road for so small an island. Then, like hope, energy or money, the road runs out just when you need it. Small farms may be seen in the valleys, and, in patches at least, the crofters of Raasay would appear to have good, green land. From the first heights heading north, the sails of the Adventure School's windsurfers may be seen like pictures in a child's storybook on the glimmering water. This, rather than Inch Keith or Scalpay, would have been the island for Johnson. Raasay has an atmosphere of independence: had the Macleods ever declared a Republic of Raasay, the place feels as if the idea might have taken hold. Someone once felt it worth fortifying; beneath grey-white Dun Can, a castle stands at the roadside, formidable and hostile even in bright warm sunshine. Bees enquire within the heather overlooking the sea.

Boswell spent an energetic time on Raasay; he walked almost the entire island and had his dance on top of Dun Can. For once, if briefly, the biographical positions are reversed, when Johnson writes to Mrs Thrale describing Boswell's doings. 'On the third day Boswel [*sic*] went out with old Malcolm to see a ruined castle, which he found less entire than was promised, but he saw the country.'

The building they stayed in and entered from the (largely unchanged) foreshore may now be found behind a later front; the walls of the Raasay House Johnson slept in are held prisoner within the nineteenth-century accreted façade; one or two corridors may be seen and touched. After the Macleods' modest grandeur and great hospitality, Raasay House became a hotel, and now the bare boards of the Adventure School thud with young feet; they sleep in bunks and merry community where Johnson had a room to himself, which, as he told Mrs Thrale, 'in eleven rooms to forty people was more than my share'. He further speculated that with a room to Boswell, and one for the laird, 'there remained eight rooms only for at least seven and thirty lodgers. I suppose they put temporary beds in the diningroom . . . there was a room above stairs with six beds in which they put ten men.'

That night, I read again their separate accounts of Raasay, to see what I had missed: the streams of which Johnson wrote, 'One of the brooks turns a cornmill, and at least one produces trouts'; the garden, described by Boswell, 'plentifully stocked with vegetables, and strawberries, raspberries, currants, etc.'; and a swift passing observation in one of Johnson's letters to Hester Thrale, a reference he does not include in his official text. His politics, as exemplified by this omission, again prove intriguing and his almost furtive observation hands me on to my next destination. Johnson had told Mrs Thrale a little of the four-hundred-year history of Raasay (or 'Raarsa' as he calls it) – and then he divulged that Bonnie Prince Charlie 'was hidden in his distress two nights at Raarsa, and the king's troops burnt the whole country, and killed some of the Cattle'.

They made swift work of Portree where they landed on the Sunday afternoon. Boswell, but not, oddly, Johnson, looked over an emigrant ship in the harbour. After lunch they set off to Kingsburgh for one of their most memorable encounters. It merits the longest entry devoted to any one person in Boswell's account, and no more than two sentences in Johnson's: the person they met was Flora Macdonald, who had helped Bonnie Prince Charlie to escape after Culloden.

The harbour of Portree, the principal town on Skye, is, as Boswell observed, 'a large and good one', and from it the road climbs up into the town, now much built since 1773 – a square, several banks, a school, and many, many tourists. In the hotels at night they provide 'Highland Evenings' – kilts, pipers, stout balladeers, male and female, and little girls in tartan dresses and white socks dancing like precise, muscled wraiths between wooden swords to the music of accordion, fiddle and piano. One shy-faced fawn performed 'Flora Macdonald's Fancy'. The naming of tunes in Gaelic dancing has as much to do with the whim of the moment as with anything portentous: 'Upstairs in a Tent', or 'The Clock on the Dresser', or 'The Walls of Limerick' owe more to whimsy in the kitchen on the night than to any attempt by the musician to give his tune immortality. Likewise, perhaps, 'Flora Macdonald's Fancy' – 'A name,' wrote Johnson in his *Journey*, 'that will be mentioned in history, and if courage and fidelity be virtues mentioned with honour. She is a woman of middle stature, soft features, gentle manners and elegant presence.' She had borne seven children and was in her fifty-first year in 1773, when, on that September Sunday evening she entertained, and played hostess overnight, to her famous English visitor and his plump little annotator from Edinburgh, who wrote of Flora: 'She is a little woman, of a genteel appearance, and uncommonly mild and well-bred.'

The A850, having come north from Broadford, leaves Portree for the north-west of Skye and after a few miles, just beyond the standing stones by Borve, splits into the A856. After Kensaleyre, this beautiful road, a territory of hawks, runs by Loch Snizort Beag, and from the calm grassy uplands, well-to-do houses look down on the waters where the opportunities for boats seem infinite. The scenery up here has been arresting so far; now it takes on an unexpectedly serene beauty. Flora Macdonald lived in a small farm estate, off this road. Nothing remains of the house where the Pretender hid and where Johnson and Boswell stayed: a few stones peeping forth from grassy old mounds, within new unruly sycamores and sprouting ashes. Trees guard the house from the east winds; meadows slope down to the water. Nobody nearby knew the location of the well a little farther on, from which Bonnie Prince Charlie drank. The outlines of the old house can just about be traced: lumps in the ground, grass-covered old rubble. A reclusive woman lives on the site today, with a fierce and deterring desire to protect her privacy.

They stayed at Kingsburgh on Sunday night, having first been greeted by Flora's husband, another archetype of a fine Highland figure. Says Boswell, 'He had his Tartan plaid thrown about him, a large blue bonnet with a knot of black riband like a cockade, a brown short coat of a kind of duffil [thick-napped cloth], a Tartan waistcoat with gold buttons and gold button-holes, a bluish phili-beg, [or filibeg, or kilt] and Tartan hose. He had jet black hair tied behind, and was a large stately man, with a steady sensible countenance.' Flora Macdonald's fancy, Allan, had married her in 1750 when she was twenty-eight.

Born in South Uist, she became and remains a most famous woman in Scottish history, epitomising forever the more accept-able of the romances associated with the Stuart cause. On a June night in 1746, she disguised the haughty Prince as her Irish maid, 'Betty Bourke', and went with him/her in an open boat from Benbecula to the seat on Skye of Sir Alexander Macdonald. Flora's coolness carried her through a dinner attended by the head of a platoon of soldiers on Skye to apprehend the Prince, who was then conducted to Raasay. The Pretender nearly gave the game away by holding his skirts too high crossing a stream: 'some women whom they met reported that they had seen a very big woman, who looked like a man in woman's clothes.'

The Flora Macdonald section of Boswell's *Journal* lasts for over three thousand words, and in the detail of any one single meeting or encounter enjoyed throughout their whole journey, nothing else compares with it. It came about because, after an early night in the same bed as that slept in by the Prince, Dr Johnson, who had a cold and had been rendered a little deaf by it, 'spoke of Prince Charles being here, and asked Mrs Macdonald, "Who was with him? We were told, madam, in England, there was one Miss Flora Macdonald with him." She said, "They were very right."'

She then launched into an account so detailed that Johnson said to Boswell, 'All this should be written down,' and Boswell did, in a faithful rendition that traces every move made by the Prince and those who wished him to escape – every hardship, close call and incident, every hope, frustration and despair. Beneath the oral history lies a sad text of spies, betrayers, official reprisal and oppression, and heartrending devotion: 'Old Mrs Macdonald, after her guest had left the house, took the sheets in which he had lain, folded them carefully, and charged her daughter that they should be kept unwashed, and that, when she died, her body should be wrapped in them as a winding sheet. Her will was religiously observed.' Kingsburgh, Flora's father-in-law-to-be, gave the Prince a pair of new shoes and, when they were returned to him, kept them as treasured souvenirs. 'After his death, a zealous Jacobite gentleman gave twenty guineas for them.'

Bonnie Prince Charlie had a price of thirty thousand pounds on his head when he was being ferried hither and yon across many isles and sea-lochs of the Hebrides, and yet, and yet – the people of the west, such as Flora Macdonald and Malcolm Macleod of Raasay, risked their lives for a man they must have known in their hearts was a lost cause.

Where Johnson exercised great prudence in his remarks, both in his own text and in his letters to Mrs Thrale, Boswell took a different line; having concluded his great notation of Flora Macdonald's exciting tale, Boswell summarised that for all the Highlanders' dedication to the Stuart Cause, he 'found every where among them a high opinion of the virtues of the King now upon the throne, and an honest disposition to be faithful subjects to his majesty . . .'

Were he not so useful and entertaining on his main subject, Boswell might easily call all his facts into question by such a blatant lie, so blatantly told to curry Establishment favour in London. Did he sincerely hope to persuade his readers that the Gaels of the west of Scotland uncritically adored George III?

Moving down the open field at Kingsburgh, a view of the sea-loch comes into view, wide and bright, the view from her window every morning until Flora Macdonald and her husband left to try and increase their fortunes in America. They emigrated a year after they met Johnson. In this they had no luck; the War of Independence broke out while they were in the Carolinas, and they came home no richer, if wiser.

On the Monday afternoon, Flora Macdonald's husband conducted the travellers to his boat, and took them across Loch Snizort Beag, out a little into Loch Snizort, around what is now called Lyndale Point and into Loch Grishinish, or Greshornish. They might have fared more comfortably had they sailed a longer journey – from Kingsburgh up to Waternish Point, a journey which would then have taken them directly down into Loch Dunvegan – although local people told me the weather here can come up very quickly, and perhaps Allan Macdonald's boat was not adequately large. The Rev. Donald McQueen, 'the most intelligent man in Skye', was still with them, and while under sail he proceeded to give Johnson a pithy and useful outline of the landlord and tenant system as it operated, and as it proved unworkable. The tacksmen, he told Johnson, were emigrating, unable to comply with the exorbitant rents demanded by the lairds and deluded by the dreams of wealth they had promised their own tenants. (A tacksman, in Boswell's phrase, was 'a large taker or leaseholder of land, of which he keeps part as a domain in his own hand, and lets part to under-tenants': Flora Macdonald's father was a tacksman.) Their lands were now being occupied by poorer people, their former servants, who had not the means, nor, to judge from McQueen's words, the energies or capacities to work the land properly; by such measures were they witnessing the reduction of the great Scottish holdings. Boswell's observation that the King should intervene to stop people being forced from the land was augmented by Johnson's opinion that 'were an oppressive chieftain a subject of the French king, he would probably be admonished . . .'

On the boat, Johnson asked about 'the use of the dirk, with which he imagined the Highlanders cut their meat', and was told they also had knives and forks, that the men tended to hand the knives and forks to the women after they had cut their own meat which they then ate from their hands, and that one old Macdonald retainer always ate fish with his fingers, claiming that 'a knife and fork gave it a bad taste'.

At Greshornish, their horses, says Boswell, 'had been sent around by road to meet us. By this sail we saved eight miles of bad riding.' Johnson disliked the riding he had experienced on Skye, complaining of its 'unsocial' nature, owing to the usual narrowness of the way which never permitted two abreast; and, he said, 'you cannot indulge in meditation by yourself, because you must be always attending to the steps which your horse takes'. Greshornish lies at the end of a long narrow road connecting with the A850; a calm and green place with blue, long waters, and a profusion of rabbits on the lawns of the hotel. From there they rode to Dunvegan, either more or less as the crow flies by a drovers' trail, or coming down from Greshornish to join what is now the A850, at a point about half-way between Portree and their destination, Dunvegan Castle.

Johnson's cold, still in its first phase – three days coming, three days staying, three days going – was getting worse. He did not have a good journey from Greshornish; the ground proved so soft that he frequently had to dismount and walk. Nevertheless, his energy of observation remained constant and again inclined towards the economics of the area: he contemplated one piece of land, a 'watery flat', that seemed to have natural drainage possibilities – 'it had a visible declivity'; although he allowed that even if he felt it could be reclaimed without 'difficulty or expense', these were relative terms.

They made their way towards Dunvegan. Dismounting on a narrow pathway with a drop of ground on one side, Johnson had a fall, and although 'he got up immediately without having been hurt' the journey was wild, hard and fatiguing. Led the last stretches of the way by a guide using arcane local landmarks, they arrived at Dunvegan Castle in the later afternoon, and Johnson found himself much warmed by the reception.

He did not have to contend with hundreds of tourists. Today the sounds from the packed car park and souvenir shop must surely drown the water-music of Rorie More's Cascade, the waterfall which the thirteenth Macleod chieftain liked to hear roaring beneath his window before he slept. Dunvegan Castle stands on the edge of the sea, and looks up along the long narrow Loch Dunvegan to the north-west. They say that on a clear day you can see the Isle of Harris. Lady Macleod received the travellers in 'a stately dining-room', fed them and led them into the drawing-room for tea to meet the family. She made Johnson feel doubly at home, as she had 'lived many years in England', therefore he could expect English manners and sense of comfort. He stayed at Dunvegan for eight nights, from Monday, 13 September, to the morning of Tuesday the 21st, and may even have outstayed his welcome; Johnson more or less refused to leave the comfort of the castle and aplauded the weather's inclemency which kept him and his companions pinned down.

Dunvegan was the headquarters of the clan Macleod; the old castle, a ruin in Johnson's time, dated back to a time of Viking rule. A little earlier, the famous literary pair would have arrived by boat: the stairs of the land entrance only appeared during the reign of the previous chief. Pennant's *Voyage to the Hebrides* of 1772 carries an illustration by Moses Griffith which shows the castle almost separated from the land; since then, the approaches have been consolidated around to either side of the eastern, land-ward façade. Dunvegan impresses, despite both its grey colour and the obvious architectural tinkerings of the Victorians.

The feudal independence of the clans fascinated Johnson, even leading him into anecdote, deriving from the vendettas of Skye between the Macleods and Macdonalds. 'Before the reign of James the Fifth, a Highland Laird made a trial of his wife for a certain time, and if she did not please him, he was then at liberty to send her away' – which is exactly what took place when a Macdonald married a Macleod. The Macleods repaid the slight in vicious irony; the wedding, they said, 'had been solemnized without a bonfire, but that the separation should be better illuminated'. John-son reports this and other gory tales, tongue-in-cheek so firmly you can scarcely see his jaw bulge. He seems to have spent his time at Dunvegan listening to the winds and the women, and compares the waves off Dunvegan, even in a tempest, un-favourably with those on the coast of Sussex, and again finds no trees.

Dunvegan had a well; the water, Johnson found upon enquiry, was not brackish but hard; Rorie More's drinking-horn held two quarts of liquor, 'which the heir of Macleod was expected to swallow at a draught . . . before he was permitted to bear arms, or could claim a seat among the men'. When the laird returns after a long absence the shoals of herring fill the sea-loch outside the castle; if a woman departs for the islands opposite, the shoals will desert the Macleods. Guests came, one pair occasioning a hilarity reported soberly by Johnson. The laird and his wife from Muck, a small isle to the south, had a difficulty. He, family name of Maclean, should have been addressed in common with all lairds by his title – thus, Macleod, Laird of Raasay was known as 'Raasay', to distinguish him from all other Macleods. To come from an island called 'Muck' presented some problems, on account of the substance in which not to tread, and the animal with whose name in Gaelic it cross-fertilises – the pig. Therefore, poor Mr Maclean could hardly call himself 'Pig' or 'Ordure'; and he settled for 'Isle of Muck'. Johnson, in perhaps a fit of amending courtesy, reflects upon the excellence of 'Isle of Muck' as a landlord. To the people of his little island, two miles long and three-quarters of a mile wide, 'Isle of Muck' fetched a tailor from the mainland twice a year and a blacksmith from the Isle of Eigg (Johnson has not so far reflected upon the name of the laird of Eigg). And Isle of Muck had inoculated his tenants against the smallpox at a cost of two shillings and sixpence per head.

When their journey began, a crucial ingredient consisted in Boswell being able to show Johnson off to the people of Scotland who met him. And all along the route, beginning at James's Court in Edinburgh, they gathered at Mr James Boswell's invitation to watch the pearls fall from the Great Bear's jaws. Dunvegan became for Johnson his most successful visit of the Tour so far. They gave him a good room, and 'here therefore we settled,' he said, 'and did not spoil the present hour with thoughts of departure.' In his last note on the place he says, 'At Dunvegan I had tasted lotus and was in danger of forgetting that I was ever to depart.'

Boswell at Dunvegan vacillates between huge enjoyment of his friend's celebrity and performance, and acute discomfort at some of the conversational and social occurrences. His rendition of the approach journey from Kingsburgh fills in more detail than

Johnson's, with the revealing observation – still visibly under-standable – that their guide navigated across the moors 'much in the same manner as, I suppose, is pursued in the wilds of America, by observing certain marks known only to the inhabitants'.

Boswell should have written fiction. Where Johnson utters statesmanly reflections, Boswell lets us see the small events – 'we dismounted' – and then captures the detail of their arrival, their welcome by Lady Macleod (the laird's mother, not his wife). Her son had been detained on his way to Dunvegan, so they lunched in a stately dining-room, and then went to the drawing-room to meet the family. He shows us Johnson in a delighted state, thrilled because the 'entertainment here was in so elegant a style, and reminded my fellow-traveller so much of England'.

On the dining-room walls today hang generations of Macleods; Boswell and Johnson were entertained by the 23rd chief, Norman, who did not marry for a decade after the travellers stayed here. He was nineteen in 1773, and had been tutored at Oxford by George Strahan, a friend of Johnson. His father, also Norman, who died a year earlier, in 1772, is portrayed in Allan Ramsay's portrait as if he might have been Bonnie Prince Charlie – in wrap-around plaid, curly white wig, a gold-hilted claymore at his left hip, right hand outflung, and he stands in a landscape of rock, sky and water. His wife, Ann, a Martin from Ross, was the Lady Dunvegan who hosted Dr Johnson.

Next morning, Tuesday, they slept late, and after breakfast they walked in the garden. The local clergyman called, and two further Macleods, Claggan and Bay, 'two substantial gentlemen of the clan', stayed to lunch of venison and wine. Boswell's father had rendered Lady Macleod of Dunvegan some legal service in a dispute with the laird of Brodie and James basked in the repayment of the compliment. The host raised an interesting topic – 'the subject of making women do penance in the church for fornication': Johnson, who does not mention this conversation, uses the word 'infamy' and relates sexual morality to laws of property. 'Consider what importance to society the chastity of women is. Upon that all the property in the world depends. We hang a thief for stealing a sheep; but the unchastity of a woman transfers sheep,

and farm and all, from the right owner. I have much more rever-
ence for a common prostitute than a woman who conceals
her guilt.'

Neither man reveals whether Lady Macleod took part in this
somewhat lubricious conversation. When Boswell sought to
establish a distinction between 'the licentiousness of a single
woman, and that of a married woman', Johnson intensified his
analogy, comparing the loose single woman to a thief, and the
randy married woman to a thief who first murders the victim,
and says that among women the infection of licentiousness spreads
from the single to the married. Boswell tried to rally by saying
that in India there is a distinction, and Johnson put him down hard.
'Nay, don't give us India. That puts me in mind of Montesquieu' –
the French philosopher and belle-lettrist whose *Persian Letters* may
have formed the inspiration for Goldsmith's *Citizen of the World*:
both employed the satirical device of having their society scruti-
nised by visitors from a far-off land. Johnson claimed that whenever Montesquieu 'wants to support a strange opinion, he quotes
you the practice of Japan or of some other distant country, of
which he knows nothing'.

Dinner conversation that evening took in gout, on which a
distinctive book had been published some years earlier. Both Johnson and Lady Macleod found the book wanting, her objection
being that the author did not practise what he preached. This drew
from Johnson the observation that what a man does has nothing
to do with how he instructs. 'No man practises so well as he
writes. I have, all my life long, been lying till noon; yet I tell all
young men, and tell them with great sincerity, that nobody who
does not rise early will ever do any good.' He reinforces the point
by asking Lady MacLeod to consider whether she needed to know
the author of every book she read in order to agree with herself
its value. Typically, he summarises aphoristically the question of
whether writers lose authority if they are found not to practise
what they preach. 'There is something noble in publishing truth
though it condemns one's self.'

Boswell entered the argument. The gout writer had recommended addressing the ailment with good humour, 'as if,' says
Boswell, 'it were quite in our power to attain it.' Johnson believed

good humour an acquired quality, one which came with the ageing process, and came of learning to please others rather than the
child's instant gratification of pleasing itself.

> Lady MacLeod asked, if no man was naturally good.
>
> JOHNSON: No madam, no more than a wolf.
> BOSWELL: Nor no woman, sir?
> JOHNSON: No, sir.
>
> Lady Macleod started at this, saying, in a low voice, 'This is worse
> than Swift.'

As the evening progressed the clan gathered, and 'listened with
wonder and pleasure while Dr Johnson harangued'. Boswell
reveals another sliver of his biographical method by complaining
of frustration that he cannot take it all down.

Next morning, through the sheets of rain, another glimpse of
Scottish eighteenth-century life: the men of the Macleods left the
castle early bound for the next large sea-loch south of Dunvegan,
Loch Bracadale, to say goodbye to emigrants bound for America.
Johnson and Boswell sauntered through the castle, as they could
today, where many of the artefacts are preserved in a museum;
they looked at Rorie More's drinking-horn – Boswell's description
is clearer than Johnson's – 'a rather large cow's horn, with the
mouth of it ornamented with silver curiously carved'. They saw
his bow, and his claymore – which they both spell with a 'g', a
mispronunciation if the word derives from *cliamh mor*, the 'big
sword'. Boswell observes that when the clans were disarmed after
Culloden, they used the old broadsword as covers for their butter-
milk barrels: 'a kind of change,' he says, 'like beating spears into
pruning-hooks'; swords turned sadly into ploughshares.

The pair discussed a book found lying in the dining-room, the
works of Sir George Mackenzie, a predecessor of Boswell both
at the Scottish Bar and in literature. Boswell, as he did frequently,
used the works of one writer to provoke Johnson into an opinion
of another, in this case Edmund Burke.

Burke, a Dublinman, was twenty years younger than Johnson and politically opposite to him, a member of the party
Johnson called 'vile Whigs'. Yet, as Boswell records in the *Life*,

'As Johnson always allowed the extraordinary talents of Mr Burke, so Mr Burke was fully sensible of the wonderful powers of Johnson.' Repeatedly, their mutual admiration surfaces, and Johnson always found Burke a challenge, always felt it necessary to raise his game in Burke's presence. Of Burke's politics Johnson believed, as he did of any political opponent, that honesty deserted him when embroiled politically, only to return when engaged conversationally or intellectually. On this occasion in Dunvegan he repeated his earlier assertion that Burke never made a good joke. The laird, Macleod, asked Johnson therefore to define 'the particular excellence of Burke's eloquence', and Johnson's reply summarises not only Burke, but all men of such gifts, and it hymns education and the acquisition of learning: 'Copiousness, and fertility of allusion; a power of diversifying his matter, by placing it in various relations. Burke has great information, and great command of language; though, in my opinion, it has not in every respect the highest elegance.' On another occasion he described Burke as 'an extraordinary man. His stream of mind is perpetual.'

That evening, Johnson's cold was worse, and the Macleods of Dunvegan cosseted him. He both wore and drank night-caps: the one made of flannel by one of the Macleod ladies, the other a little unaccustomed brandy, which occasioned him to reveal to his hostess why he never drank. He said he had been unable to take it in moderation, and then, in a long illness, he was forbidden liquor, so when the habit had been broken he never returned to it.

Next morning, Johnson gave a fine performance of talking. He held the company spellbound (or so Boswell says) with detailed accounts of how to mint coins and how to brew beer. The impressed Reverend McQueen thought Johnson had somehow done both. Since patronising behaviour always contains a curious element of innocence, Boswell was inflated with pride, 'elated by the thought of having been able to entice such a man to this remote part of the world', and his tongue, thus loosened, flicked out a memorable simile of himself. 'A ludicrous, yet just image presented itself to my mind, which I expressed to the company. I compared myself to a dog who has got hold of a large piece of meat, and runs away with it to a corner, where he may devour it in peace, without any fear of others taking it from him.' Before the day was over, Boswell would pay for his flush of righteous enthusiasm.

At table that evening, the current Macleod seemed depressed; he was having difficulty with relatives. Boswell rattled on about the prospect of other travels with Johnson, perhaps to Sweden, where, hoped Boswell, they would see the King. Johnson said he doubted if the King would speak to them and Colonel Macleod had a go at Jamie: 'I am sure Mr Boswell would speak to *him*' – Boswell underlines the pronoun. 'But seeing me a little disconcerted by his remark, he politely added, "and with great propriety".' Realising that Macleod had perceived him clearly, Boswell introduces a short *apologia pro vita sua*, 'a short defence of that propensity in my disposition', in which he justifies his pursuit of the great and famous as 'nothing more than an eagerness to share the society of men distinguished either by their rank or talents', and calls it a search for knowledge. Whether Boswell means this sincerely, or as sleight-of-hand to deflect people from calling him a mere snob, must be measured against the remarkable and immortal results of his association with the one man who allowed him to share his company relentlessly.

Boswell walked into another wall that evening. When the ladies had withdrawn from the dinner-table, a conversation began about the Highlanders and their linen. Johnson, outlining a preference for vegetable derivatives rather than animal, said, 'I have often thought, that, if I kept a seraglio, the ladies should all wear linen gowns, or cotton – I mean stuffs made of vegetable substances,' and declared a hatred for silk: 'you cannot tell when it is clean.' Boswell burst out laughing and could not stop – the very idea: that Johnson, 'that majestic teacher of moral and religious wisdom', should keep a harem, and had *often* thought of it.

Johnson tore him apart. Boswell does not tell us what he said, other than that it included 'a variety of degrading images'. It must have been a savage attack; Boswell had offended Johnson's pride and held him up to ridicule; now Johnson retaliated with such force that Boswell says, 'though I can bear such attacks as well as most men, I yet found myself so much the sport of all the company, that I would gladly expunge from my mind every trace of this severe retort.' Outside, the rain of Skye beat on.

Boswell's portrait of Johnson at Dunvegan shows an elderly man with the snuffles, easily tired, and happy to savour some of the comforts of home. In the security of the castle, run under the English training of Lady Macleod, and as long as he could potter from room to room, with the occasional short foray out beneath the weather, Johnson relaxed, and flexed his muscles for his hosts and the other guests who called to see him. At its best the structure of one of his perorations follows this pattern: he begins with a general statement and summarises it with an accessible example; then he moves to a narrower statement and concludes with a final example taken from everyday life. On Friday, 17 September, he performed in a series of conversations in which the style of his thought clearly appears, the manner of his arguments, his journey from proposition to summary, thesis, antithesis and synthesis.

They began at lunch with a conversation on cunning. Johnson related its effectiveness not to the trickery of the practitioner but to the credulity of the recipient: 'It requires no extraordinary talents to lie and deceive.' Developing the thought into consideration of wickedness, Johnson's one-two punch summarised the presence and shape of evil within the human spirit, and he returns, if obliquely, to his recurring theme of the difficulty in being good, rather than succumbing to the natural *animus* all humans share. Once again he is worth quoting in full; the italics are Boswell's:

> It requires great abilities to have the *power* of being very wicked; but not to *be* very wicked. A man who has the power, which great abilities procure him, may use it well or ill; and it requires more abilities to use it well, than to use it ill. Wickedness is always easier than virtue; for it takes the short cut to every thing. It is much easier to steal a hundred pounds, than to get it by labour, or any other way. Consider only what act of wickedness requires great abilities to commit it, when once the person who is to do it has the power; for *there* is the distinction. It requires great abilities to conquer an army, but none to massacre it after it is conquered.

Johnson's next disquisition arose from a subject brought back by Boswell after a short excursion. He and the Reverend McQueen set out after breakfast to find the ruins of what McQueen believed had been an ancient pagan temple to the goddess Anaitis. Boswell's description of the location corresponds with today's scenery: wild heathland has altered little on Skye: 'The country around is a black dreary moor on all sides, except to the sea-coast, towards which there is a view through a valley . . . the place itself is green ground, being well drained, by means of a deep glen on each side, in both of which there runs a rivulet with a good quantity of water, forming several cascades which make a considerable appearance and sound.'

Forestry has now been applied to the upper slopes (Johnson would have been pleased), and in sunshine the views of the distant coast sparkle to the north-west. The waters described by Boswell flow powerfully beneath deep banks reached after a walk of some hundreds of yards from the B886 north of Fairy Bridge. From a height to the east the land's patterns show more clearly, and the remains of some ancient structure may be discerned in the heather. When Boswell and McQueen walked out – the site is north-north-east from Dunvegan Castle over very rough, near-impassable ground – they were accompanied by McQueen's servant. He must have been with them all the time from Corry, to Raasay, to Kingsburgh, to Dunvegan: 'a fellow quite like a savage' – and they were followed, 'as colts follow passengers upon a road', by local lads, barefoot, ragged, lazy and not wholly unmenacing.

McQueen found the ruins, and then claimed to trace the road along which the goddess's statue would have been borne in procession from the temple to the river for the ceremonial washing attributed to worship of Anaitis. Boswell puts into perspective the size of ancient sites of worship, by assessing the entire site at two acres and the 'whole extent of the building' as no larger than 'an ordinary Highland house'.

After lunch, Boswell, knowing McQueen's passion for the place, introduced the subject of Anaitis. Johnson questioned the clergyman closely – then, first disagreed with him and finally trumped him. McQueen relied on the name of the locality, Ainnit, or Annait, to prove, using the traditional antiquarian reliance upon linguistics, that it had truly been a temple of the goddess. Johnson extracted from him the English meaning of the Gaelic place-name; it signified a place of, or near, water, conforming, claimed McQueen, to 'all the descriptions of the temples of that goddess, which were situated near rivers that there might be water to wash the statue'. Johnson, contradicting him, took him from the particular belief to the general likelihood: from the possibility of a singular holy place to the generic derivation from water: 'Had it been an accidental name, the similarity between it and Anaitis might have had something in it; but it turns out to be a mere physiological name.' It could have been, he argued onwards, a fort, or even an early Christian site, or even a pagan place of votive offering, 'for there is such a multititude of divinities, to whom it may have been dedicated, that the chance of its being a temple of Anaitis is hardly any thing. It is like throwing a grain of sand upon the sea-shore to-day, and thinking you may find it to-morrow.'

Did Johnson know Anaitis, sometimes called Anahita, to be the name of a Persian and pan-European goddess associated with water, in the way that Sequanna gave her name to the river Seine? His dismissal of McQueen's argument contrasts the man of the world with the islander, the widely-read man of learning and classical scholarship with the local pastor who had an amateur interest in the etymology of his own language.

Even when Mr McQueen said that since Asia Minor had been populated by Celts, could not the same religion have come with the Celts to Skye, Johnson defied him, and the point he made remains valid to this day. He dismissed any such link for lack of proof; for him there was 'no tracing the connection of ancient nations, but by language; and therefore I am always sorry when any language is lost, because languages are the pedigree of nations. If you find the same language in distant countries, you may be sure that the inhabitants have been the same people, that is to say, if you find the languages a good deal the same; for a word here and there being the same will not do.'

Before that, Boswell reports two other Johnsonian performances, on portrait painting and the techniques of historians. On the former Johnson wished for accuracy of representation, by which means the portrait painter also creates a piece of history; on the latter he applauded developments in which historians had begun to consult and interpret factual record instead of merely culling from other histories.

In the evening Johnson, as he did when in defence of a figure he admired, delivered one of his acutest perceptions. One of the dinner guests found Pennant, the travel writer, superficial. Johnson counter-punched, landing three telling blows. One – that 'Pennant has told us more than perhaps one in ten thousand could have done in the time that he took.' Two – when the laird complained that Pennant described how rents drained the Highland economies without saying how they should be refurbished, Johnson said, in effect, that Pennant was obliged to report, not to cure; 'If I tell that many of the Highlanders go bare-footed, I am not obliged to tell how they may get shoes.' Three, and Johnson's knock-out punch – Pennant's descriptions went as far into detail as Pennant wanted them to, and therefore they should be seen for what they are, not what they might have been: 'Here is a man six feet high and you are angry because he is not seven.'

Next morning, Saturday, Johnson walked early into Boswell's bedroom 'to forbid me to mention that this was his birthday'. He was 64 – and too late: Boswell had already told Lady Macleod, therefore Johnson could not avoid the embarrassment he obviously felt at the prospect of congratulations. Boswell assumed that Johnson's displeasure at Lady Macleod knowing came 'from wishing to have nothing particular done on his account'. We do not know what, if anything, took place celebratorily: neither man mentions gifts, birthday toasts, felicitations, not even from the Macleod children.

As Saturday passed Boswell talked of leaving Dunvegan on the Monday; Johnson said he would not budge until the Wednesday. Mr McQueen left, heading south in time to preach next morning at Bracadale, and saying he would wait for them at Ullinish. He and Johnson parted with warm expressions of mutual regard. In passing, Boswell asked McQueen whether he felt content as a clergyman on Skye, and the reverend man answered – or so Boswell interprets – that much of his satisfaction with his lot derived from his Skye ancestry. In a rare occurrence, the accounts of Boswell and Johnson overlap on this Saturday, on the matter of 'Muck', the laird thereof. They share the information about the isle's dimensions, population, inoculation (against smallpox) and services.

Sunday morning at Dunvegan brought the worst weather so far – and the most valuable insight yet into Johnson's influence on Boswell's writing. Before breakfast he went to Boswell's room 'to read my *Journal*, which he has done all along. He often before said, "I take great delight in reading it." Today he said, "You improve: it grows better and better."' Johnson dismissed a compliment-hunt by Boswell, who worried whether he had acquired slovenly habits. To apply the principles of this meeting, and the crucial facts that its seemingly casual remarks convey – 'which he has done all along' and 'it grows better and better' – is to unveil a picture of Johnson, on the road, casting his eye repeatedly over Boswell's entries. From the knowledge I have acquired so far of Johnson, I cannot imagine him forbearing to make comment, nor can I imagine Boswell not seeking advice and guidance. Does not this short exchange at Dunvegan account fully for Boswell's never-ending flattery of Johnson? He *knew* the Great Bear would see every word. Yet, credit to Boswell, for all his lapses into near-hagiography, we get a sufficiently rounded picture of Johnson to survey him and to judge.

Sunday's conversation involved the manner in which men choose wives; strange associations with the island of St Kilda; the further travels of Johnson; and a dissertation upon prize-fighting, leading into observations upon combat and duelling. Memorable among these exchanges: Johnson believed that men choose weak and ignorant women as their wives because they 'know that women are an over-match for them'; he thought little of poetry he had heard from St Kilda: 'it must be poor, because they have very few images.' Boswell countered this critique, suggesting that genius may also reside in the inventive distribution of sparse material. Johnson: 'Sir, a man cannot make fire but in proportion as he has fuel. He cannot coin guineas but in proportion as he has gold.' On travel, Johnson hoped to go to Italy in 1775. When the Laird said he preferred Paris, Johnson said there was 'not a Frenchman of letters now alive he would cross a sea to visit'.

Johnson also read a little – in his room he had works by his erstwhile host Lord Monboddo, and Laurence Sterne's *Sermons of Mr Yorick* (interestingly, Boswell does not give the full title, merely calling it *Sermons*, a deference perhaps to the scandal the book had caused when it appeared in 1760). Johnson even complained a little – or so Boswell suggests – that he was not seeing enough of Boswell: 'He asked me today, how it happened we were so little together.' Bozzie blamed the time-consuming *Journal*.

As happens many times throughout, and frequently in footnotes, one sentence of Boswell's from the after-dinner conversation contains the seeds of a novel – even, potentially, a saga: 'We talked of the extraordinary fact of Lady Grange's being sent to St Kilda, and confined there for several years, without any means of relief.' Maddening, such a tantaliser. Boswell's footnote, even if extensive by his standards, frustrates further.

Lady Grange was unharmoniously married to a Law Lord. 'For some mysterious reasons, which have never been discovered, she was seized and carried off in the dark, she knew not by whom.' She did, but Boswell for all the legal and social reasons in the world, could not say, nor could he expand beyond a sketchy account of her long, forlorn imprisonment. Sir Walter Scott, however, had no such constraints upon him fifty years later, and he had the added advantage of seeing Lady Grange's journal. Lady Grange's husband had been a Jacobite and during one of their marital battles she hinted that she would expose his seditious leanings – for which he could be hanged. He, knowing of vindictive blood in her family, got her kidnapped and dumped on St Kilda, where she spent several years, with a waiting-maid for company. Eventually she escaped, by means of a message for help hidden in a twist of tweed yarn, but she and the Catholic priest who agreed to assist her were both intercepted and imprisoned on another remote island where Lady Grange died. It is part of the enjoyment of Boswell that again and again he sends his reader's imagination flying, like God, in all directions at once.

Monday, their last day in the Macleod castle, dawned with higher winds. These abated a little around nine o'clock, and the sun came out; then it rained again. At breakfast Johnson reminisced about early days in London, and suddenly, with a surprising ungallantry, disparaged a previous hostess, Lady Macdonald, wife of Sir Alexander from Armadale. Boswell is careful not to identify her; she is 'a lady, whose name was mentioned'. Johnson said she should be sent to St Kilda, that she 'stood in the way of what was good'; he called her beauty 'insipid', and said that a skilful craftsman could cut a better face out of a cabbage.

When the young laird of Dunvegan, Norman Macleod, came down late for breakfast, Johnson ticked him off, saying laziness was worse than toothache: 'I have been trying to cure my laziness all my life, and could not do it.' Breakfast over, Johnson returned to one of his favourite themes on the trip – Scotland's economy. Now that feudalism had collapsed, taking with it the traditional form of power, the great lairds had better make themselves rich, he believed, and land and its development offered the only way forward. He dismissed commerce: 'Depend upon it, this rage of trade will destroy itself. You and I shall not see it; but the time will come when there will be an end of it. Trade is like gaming. If a whole company are gamesters, play must cease; for there is nothing to be won.' If it feels like an extreme observation – and, in parts, not unprescient for the great financial débâcles of the nineteenth and late twentieth centuries – Johnson was also voicing an intellectual's fashionable enquiry into the lastingness of common interest. He had chosen to see trade as linear rather than circular, upward rather than lateral, egotistical rather than mutual: 'When all nations are traders, there is nothing to be gained by trade, and it will stop first where it is brought to the greatest perfection.'

Today, Dunvegan means to attract tourists, and the castle museum panders energetically with memorabilia of Bonnie Prince Charlie, including a blond, round lock of his hair, or possibly his wig. The drinking-horn of Rorie More; his Cascade in the gardens; the means by which attention is drawn to cannon and architecture; the tight directions which the visitor must follow – this is no casual throwing-open for the curious and homageous, this is big business, as at Cawdor, although less kempt. The literature of the castle, published by the 29th Laird of Dunvegan, John Macleod of Macleod, makes the business plain: 'Since the castle was first opened to the public more than forty years ago, the number of visitors has risen from a few hundred to tens of thousands' – many of them Macleod descendants from the New World.

Such developments keep Johnson and Boswell at a further remove, although on the wall of the castle hangs a framed letter in which Johnson, with his attractive spidery writing, gives thanks to his host: 'The kind treatment which I have found wherever I go makes me leave with some heaviness of heart an island I am not likely to see again . . . I hope you will believe me thankful and willing, at which ever distance we may be placed, to show my sense of your kindness by any offices of friendship that may fall within my power. Lady Macleod and the young ladies have by their hospitality and politeness made an impression on my mind which will not easily be effaced. Be pleased to tell them that I remember them with great kindness and great respect. I am, Sir, your most obliged and humble servant.'

Lady Macleod (whose title was a courtesy one) kept serving Johnson tea. She was wrong about Dunvegan being unsuitable for gardening – she wanted to move to a less rocky place: today it blooms and blows. The rocks beneath the castle, on account of the form they seem to have in high seas and foam, are called Macleod's Maidens. Johnson slept in the fairy tower where hangs the Zoffany copy of the Joshua Reynolds portrait in which poor Johnson looks so grumpy. From his bedroom he could see Macleod's Tables, two flat-topped hills, Healaval Mhor and Healaval Bheag to the south-west.

One last memorable portrait to carry away from Dunvegan: Johnson wore his wig turned inside out as a night-cap, and Lady Macleod said, 'I have often seen very plain people, but anything as ugly as Dr Johnson with his wig thus stuck on, I never have seen.'

CHAPTER VII

'On grave subjects not formal, on light occasions not grovelling'

THEY LEFT DUNVEGAN CASTLE on Tuesday morning, 21 September. Boswell complained of being uneasy at having received no letters from home. On the way south, roughly along the line of the modern A863, they passed the church and graveyard of Durinish, in which they inspected the Lord Lovat memorial pyramid with what Boswell called a 'pompous' inscription, in Latin that Johnson called 'poor stuff, such as Lord Lovat's butler might have written'.

They were now heading down along an isthmus, towards the inner western flank of Skye, through the most beautiful scenery. Islands lie out to the west, the outer Hebrides, and nearby, the shores have façades of low cliffs; on a sunny afternoon, the rocks and grasses of the headlands sparkle, with tremors of snow-white foam at their feet. The Reverend McQueen appointed himself their guide to the area's antiquities and took them to see a broch.

These notable and architecturally intriguing prehistoric fortifications look like ancient Martello towers, or the bases of truncated Irish round towers: squat, wide, powerful buildings, of two layers, an inner and an outer skin built in the traditional un-mortared drystone technique, each layer clipped to the other with rays of horizontal slabs. They may have been Pictish, Orcadian or Celtic. Some had galleries, some one floor only. Almost five hundred have been counted, with a similarity of design: they taper like power station cooling towers. Unique to Scotland, all seem to have been built within a span of a couple of hundred years, by and large from about 100 B.C. They might have been created by a small dynasty, or family of itinerant construction contractors commissioned by wealthy families who wanted fortifications against the Roman legions. Usually they occupy situations of powerful visual advantage, and thus they maximised defence possibilities. On hillsides, or ocean promontories, or clifftops, the broch's occupants could see approaching invaders in time to batten the hatches.

Johnson was not uniquely impressed, although in his description of its physical composition and possible history, he again displays his gift for deriving an idea from a newly-discovered fact. He considers how the primitive builders might have raised the heavy stones with wooden lifters. Then comes the philosophy: 'Savages, in all countries, have patience proportionate to their unskilfulness, and are content to attain their end by very tedious methods.' He then contemplates what the broch might have been and, having dismissed its uses as a fort because it had no water supply nearby, concluded that it was a fortified animal pen, with the inner rooms 'the shelters of the keepers'.

Nearby, McQueen showed them an artificial cave, whose entrance seems nowadays permanently closed. Johnson dismissed the notion that such burrowings may have been early Skye-man's habitation – too low, too narrow, too damp – and believed them bunkers, 'places only of occasional use, in which the Islander, upon a sudden alarm, hid his utensils, or his clothes, and perhaps sometimes his wife and children'. He apologises to his readers for not investigating this 'bunker' to its fullest extent, and then rewards them with a Gothic legend – the story of a Highland intrigue by heir against laird.

A ruined castle prompted McQueen to tell it: a young Macdonald, growing impatient, initiated a conspiracy to kill the incumbent. His cohorts wanted something for themselves, therefore a contract was drawn up and signed by all. It was given for safe keeping to a Macleod man who could not read. He held a bond from a cattle drover who owed him money; the drover produced the cash and demanded his bond back – Macleod gave him the contract, and the drover, when he read it, took it to the target of the conspiracy, the laird Macdonald, 'who, being thus informed of his danger, called his friends together, and provided for his safety'. He then gave a banquet, invited the conspirators, seated each one between two of his friends, revealed that he knew of their compact, but forgave them, provided that the heir, Hugh, swore undying fealty – which he did.

But later he reneged, was pursued and imprisoned in Macdonald's dungeon. They lowered him a meal of salt meat; 'and when, after his repast, he called for drink, conveyed to him a covered cup, which, when he lifted the lid, he found empty. From that time they visited him no more, but left him to perish in solitude and darkness.'

One of the pleasures in reading Johnson lies in the fact that he includes the reader in his thought processes. Such a tale, which he takes some trouble to tell, generates the word 'Gothic' – and then a few pages later in his narrative, Johnson describes how the landscape of Skye inspires Gothic imaginings.

Ullinish had a cave with a famous echo and they took Johnson to see it. The boatmen had some fun at his expense, and he none at theirs. When they learned their cargo's nationality, they asked 'if the Englishman could recount a long genealogy'. They took a further rise out of him. Having undermined his pedigree, they now played games among themselves: one of them claimed he heard 'the cry of an English ghost. This omen,' says Johnson, 'I was not told till after our return, and therefore cannot claim the dignity of despising it.' The cave disappointed him, too: no echo, although he did see limpets and mussels in their natural habitat, as distinct from on a London stall, and Boswell, borrowing a rod from a little boy fishing, caught a pollock or 'cuddy'. Johnson turns the catch into an economic matter, pointing out how the locals used it for food and lamp-oil, and that if the islanders could only fish all the year round they need never fear famine.

They got to Ullinish about six o'clock, the guests of a local magistrate, another Macleod (Louis MacNeice's poem 'The Hebrides' applies: 'where a few surnames cover a host of people'). The house at Ullinish still stands, now The Ullinish Lodge Hotel at Struan, with wide and pleasing views over the land and the sea, and a large saloon bar, and the brochure tells of the famous two who stayed upstairs in 1773; and of the oystercatchers, sandpipers, redshanks, whales and golden eagles, with alpine rock cress on the Cuillins.

Mr Macleod of Ullinish comes across as silent but dry-witted; Mr McQueen met them here. Next morning, Boswell hands us an invaluable historical snapshot; when out walking, he saw an emigrant ship, 'the Margaret of Clyde . . . a melancholy sight'; *en route* to North America, it surely contained folk forced out of their homes by landlordism; as with the Irish emigrants, many may have taken the roof-trees of their cottages in the hope of establishing foundations in a New World. Next Boswell records the visit to the *souterrain* and agreed with Johnson that those who constructed it intended a bunker, not a dwelling-place – it being more difficult to build than a house – and in any case Mr McQueen was 'always for making every thing as ancient as possible'.

Boswell does essay a description of the landscape here, but in a short factual paragraph, and even if lyricism in writing touched neither him nor Johnson, he might have done better than this prosaic offering, given the materials he had to hand: 'From an old tower, near this place, is an extensive view of Loch-Braccadil [*sic*], and, at a distance, of the isles of Barra and South Uist; and, on the landside, the Cuillin, a prodigious shape of mountains, capped with rocky pinnacles in a strange variety of shapes. They resemble the mountains near Corté in Corsica, of which there is a very good print. They make part of a great range for deer, which, though entirely devoid of trees, is in these countries called a forest.'

He made no mention of the wonderful light; or the sparkle of the sea as if it belonged in a story book; or the way the green of these fields, more than any other on this journey, seems to take on a golden glow under the sun; or the inviting undulations of the headlands; or how the islands seem to beckon like a mariner's fate. The name 'Hebrides' comes from a scribe's misreading of Pliny's *Hebudae* (a similar mis-reading turned *Boudicca*, Queen of the *Iceni* in east Anglia, into *Boadicea*), and at the sight of the islands out in the sea off Ullinish, I wish they could have been 'Hesperides' instead, because if ever distant isles seemed to have golden apples on offer, these did on a sunny morning. Even their location seems to suggest that they were, as with those Fortunate

Isles guarded by the daughters of Hesperus, as far to the west as the earth could reach.

Boswell also describes the afternoon's cave exploration, adding that the loss of echo was temporary owing to the heavy rain dampening the walls: 'Such are the excuses,' he remarks tartly, 'by which the exaggeration of Highland narratives is palliated.' By now, Johnson's preoccupation with trees seems to have abated a little; Boswell reports many, plus a garden, as well as something Johnson must have appreciated but did not report – a hill on which 'justice was of old administered', as in the presence in place-names of the suffix '-law', still widespread in Scotland. And Boswell makes a good remark: 'It is singular that the spot should happen now to be the sheriff's residence.'

The evening took on its familiar shape – conversation designed to display Johnson. One remark adds further to the evidence of his role in Boswell's *Life*. 'Talking of Biography, he said, he did not think that the life of any literary man in England had been well written. Beside the common incidents of life, it should tell us his studies, his mode of living, the means by which he attained to excellence, and his opinion of his own works.' In other words, he was urging method upon Boswell, as he would himself observe when a group of booksellers banded together to produce collectively an anthology of the poets they all published individually, and asked Johnson to write the headnotes to each. He organised his material according to the theories he propounded to Boswell, causing the work, originally entitled *Prefaces, Biographical and Critical, to the Works of the English Poets* to become known as *Lives of the Poets*; the prefaces largely take the form of a short factual biography, an assessment of the poet's moral and creative approach, and a view of the actual work. As they make their way down the shank of Skye, it becomes ever clearer that Johnson, as a teacher showing a child how to write, had long clamped his own fingers over Boswell's biographical pen-hand.

Inevitably, given where they had been travelling since mid-August, James Macpherson's name came up again. When the *Fingal* controversy first broke, Johnson had been among the most scathing of the denouncers, saying the works did not possess genuine antiquity. Believers who challenged his dismissals asked, according to Boswell's *Life*, 'whether he thought any man of a modern age could have written such poems?' Johnson replied, "Yes, Sir, many men, many women, and many children."' Here at Ullinish a decade later, Macpherson's name would continue to irritate Johnson; he simply believed that Macpherson had invented the ancient poet, Ossian, whose works he claimed to have discovered and translated. 'I look upon Macpherson's *Fingal* to be as gross an imposition as ever the world was troubled with. Had it been really an ancient work, a true specimen [of] how men thought at that time, it would have been a curiosity of the first rate. As a modern production, it is nothing.' Thus he challenged the Reverend McQueen, who, according to Boswell, 'always evaded the point of authenticity'.

Next morning, before Johnson rose, Boswell set in motion a trial of Macpherson suggested by his son's host. They asked Mr McQueen, who had said he knew some ancient verses, to find a passage in *Fingal* that he recalled from work known before Macpherson had 'discovered' Ossian. McQueen obliged: Boswell and young Macleod compared and found similarities. When Johnson showed his face for breakfast, Boswell told him that Macpherson's translation was not dissimilar from the original verse in Gaelic McQueen had been reciting. Johnson still repelled all boarders: 'Well, sir, this is just what I always maintained. He [Macpherson] has found names, and stories, and phrases, nay passages in old songs, and with them has blended his own compositions, and so made what he gives to the world as the translation of an ancient poem.' Johnson was proven right. When challenged to produce the original scraps of manuscript from which he quarried his 'discoveries' and then translated, Macpherson could not.

Macpherson was six feet three inches tall, florid, voluptuous and hedonistic. He provoked name-calling: sullen, lecherous, bullying, coarse; a man, said one contemporary, who 'kept only tavern company, the prey of toad-eaters and designing housekeepers'. In 1759, then in his early twenties, Macpherson told a playwright, John Home, that he had been out in the west, talking to old Highlanders who rendered for him in Gaelic the poetry of the Celtic Ancient, Ossian. Home, who spoke no Gaelic, asked Macpherson for translations, and excitably showed them to a publisher. When the verses appeared, critics waxed until they fell over: 'The two great characteristics of Ossian's poetry are tenderness and sublimity. It breathes nothing of the gay and cheerful kind; an air of solemnity and seriousness is diffused over the whole. Ossian is perhaps the only poet who never relaxes, or lets himself down into the light and amusing strain . . . The extended heath by the seashore; the mountain shaded with mist; the torrents rushing through a solitary valley; the scattered oaks; and the tombs of the warriors overgrown with moss; all produce a solemn attention in the mind, and prepare it for extraordinary events.'

Except in Dr Johnson. Unlike David Hume and Thomas Gray (men whom Johnson disliked anyway), he reached for the opposite of admiration, and repeatedly denounced Macpherson as a publicity-seeker and a liar; 'Sir, when he leaves our houses, let us count our spoons.'

They stayed at Ullinish two nights, during the course of which they baited poor Mr McQueen for his support of Macpherson; they also debated Garrick's contribution to Shakespearean revival – Johnson minimalised it, saying Garrick was a performer of the plays, not a Shakespearean scholar; and Boswell, seeing how the others in the house glowed in the light of Johnson's eloquence, squeezed an extra dance out of his bear. Johnson had been giving them 'an account of the whole process of tanning, and of the nature of milk, and the various operations upon it, as making whey, &c.' when Boswell began to wonder whether Johnson knew anything of another business, 'an art, or whatever it should be called, which is no doubt very useful in life, but which lies far out of the way of a philosopher and poet; I mean the trade of a butcher.'

Would a duck swim? Johnson duly danced, telling them the different ways animals are slaughtered. And he then proceeded to instruct Boswell how a man in London must behave if he has a public image: 'A man who is not publicly known may live in London as he pleases, without any notice being taken of him; but it is wonderful how a person of any consequence is watched', citing two instances where he himself, supposedly clandestinely, advised a Member of Parliament and visited the Prime Minister – yet within days of each event could hear back from third parties about both encounters.

They toasted Johnson at Ullinish, and Macleod told Johnson that if he would agree to come for three months of every year, or even one month, he would give him the pretty island of Isa in Loch Dunvegan. They raised a glass and hailed him as laird: 'Island Isa, your health!' they cried. Johnson bowed, and said he would sally out and take the Isle of Muck, at which he fell about, and continued laughing long after the others had stopped smiling. Boswell reports that when Johnson did something similarly disproportionate one night in London, Garrick said acidly, '*Very* jocose, to be sure!'

'Sept. 23. We removed to Talisker,' wrote Johnson to Mrs Thrale, having told her a paragraph earlier that at Ullinish 'we were well entertained, and wandered a little after curiosities'. On the sharp bend of the road outside the hotel that was once the house of Mr Macleod the magistrate, MacNeice is back in my mind: 'The houses straggle on the umber moors'; had he written 'struggle' it would have cost him nothing in accuracy, and even though the landscape comes from the floor of Paradise, this is not easy living. A mile farther on, I digress – to a man sorting sheep in a series of small stone pens, and the timbre of his voice is softer than any other speech I have ever heard. But neither he nor I could find a boatman who would take me out to the little isle of Wiay where they saw the cave with the English ghost.

They now took another of their little sea-voyages, which, curiously, Johnson does not mention. From Ullinish they sailed to Fernilea (they call it 'Ferneley') on Loch Harport, bound for Talisker as guests of Colonel Macleod whom they had met in Dunvegan. One of his kinsmen, the farmer of Fernilea, met them at the shore with a horse for Johnson; Boswell, the Rev. McQueen and their two servants walked. Farmer Macleod gave them lunch, and they then travelled the three miles to Talisker for a stay of two nights. To Johnson's pleasure, Colonel Macleod and his wife were cultivated people; he, scholarly, 'having been bred in physick'; she spoke several languages, having lived with her husband on his military postings abroad. Just as well; Johnson found Talisker the most remote and joyless place of all, ideal for hermits. 'It is situated very near the sea, but upon a coast where no vessel lands but when it is driven by a tempest on the rocks. Towards the land are lofty hills streaming with water-falls.'

At Talisker Johnson met and liked a young man who, Boswell excepted, becomes perhaps the most significant figure during Johnson's Scottish tour – Donald Maclean, heir to the island of Coll; Johnson approves of him in every sentence. To begin with, Coll had studied farming in Hertfordshire and Hampshire, thereby conforming with several of Johnson's tenets – that the Scots could and should learn from the English; that Scots noblemen should Anglicise, meaning 'civilise' themselves more; that, as he said at Dunvegan, the chieftains now had to generate their wealth from their land, exactly what Coll sought to do by improving his knowledge of agriculture.

Trees, shrubs and crags protect Talisker's corner of Skye. Across a long moor, the house, private and wishing to remain so, still has, as Johnson described to Mrs Thrale, 'a garden well cultivated, and what is here very rare, is shaded by trees'. One feature described by Boswell also remains unchanged: 'The court before the house is most injudiciously paved with the round bluish-grey pebbles which are found upon the sea-shore; so that you walk as if upon cannon-balls driven into the ground.' Strong and white-painted and known in the language of local architecture as a 'polite' house, meaning gentrified, the building has many accretions which encase the original structure that Johnson and Boswell visited. Two nights before their arrival, drama knocked upon the door. In a storm, two boats foundered just along the shore, and, as Johnson told Mrs Thrale directly and his readers only obliquely, 'the crews crept to Talisker almost lifeless with wet, cold, fatigue and Terror, but the Lady took care of them.'

Boswell, Johnson and McQueen had sailed from Ullinish, by the lee of Wiay, round the point to a landing just short of Talisker bay. Aboard, Johnson delivered himself of a typically infuriating opinion: as Boswell calls it, 'one of his fits of railing at the Scots'. He maintained that Scotland had once been a learned and cultured country, but had never developed concomitantly until the Union with England: 'the arts of civil life did not advance in proportion with learning . . . they had hardly any trade, any money, or any elegance . . . "We have taught you," said he, "and we'll do the same in time to all barbarous nations, to the Cherokees and at last to the Ouran-Outangs"' – their running Monboddo joke. Johnson's insensitivity often amazes: did his idea of teaching 'barbarous nations' embrace the near-genocide that followed Culloden? Boswell tried to fight back, but obeisance to Johnson had long made him feeble, and McQueen obviously said nothing.

The couple of days at Talisker yield further revelations of Johnson's character and life – that he had a physical bravery; that he did not always fight fair and was perfectly capable of trying to shift the argument to another ground where he felt he had a better chance of winning; we see further evidence of his talent for avuncularity; and an inconsistency in his concerns which may have stemmed from his political opinions.

This last could account for his lack of interest in the lunchtime conversation when they disembarked from their Ullinish boat. The Macleod who met them spoke to Boswell in a way that suggested he, Macleod, would manage all estates in an egalitarian, even a socialist, way: he could not see why he should raise his rents just for his own comfort, better by far that the profits of the estate be shared. Bizarre that Johnson did not contribute to this conversation, given his proven interest in the subject, given that the economics of lairdship and Scottish estate management formed such a concern in his own *Journey*.

His unfairness in argument materialised after dinner that evening at Talisker House. Boswell and Macleod of Talisker had begun to praise the Scottish clergy for their excellence as pastors. Johnson took exception and complained, not quite in so many words, that the Scottish clergy were an unlettered and ill-read lot, that the English clergy possessed superior learning and therefore could not be compared. Boswell said they had been discussing the clergy from a pastoral, not an intellectual, point of view; 'But, sir, we are not contending for the superior learning of our clergy, but for their superior assiduity.'

Johnson said, 'I see you have not been well taught; for you have not charity.' As Boswell put it, 'he conquered by deserting his ground and not meeting the argument as I had put it' – but Sam had been sailing, and he was sixty-four and still recovering from his cold, and he was shaky on his feet, and anxious to get back to the comforts of London, and troubled by the incessant inclemency of the weather; it rained and it blew and it bothered him. By now he had had enough.

'Friday, 24th September. This was a good day. Dr Johnson told us, at breakfast, that he rode harder at a fox chase than any body.' Talisker House belongs in children's adventure stories, a wide and friendly building. High rocks guard it, Boswell climbed them and had views out to Barra due west, Dunvegan north and Raasay behind them due east. It rained on me, and the streams intensified, silver ribbons growing broader and thicker, tumbling down from the heights. Boswell, lucky enough not to be impeded by rain, found Cuchulainn's well; the old Ulster god-hero must have been around these parts, and Boswell drank from its 'admirable' waters. 'On the shore,' he said, 'are many stones full of crystallizations in the heart.' They still lie there.

At Talisker he answers a question that has been across my mind more than once. 'Our money being nearly exhausted, we sent a bill [cheque] for thirty pounds, drawn on Sir William Forbes & Co. to Lochbraccadale, but our messenger found it very difficult to procure cash for it.' How did they manage? Johnson obviously brought a large float with him from London, otherwise they would not have been able to pay the board, lodging, transport, guides, tips and *largesse* demanded of them since Edinburgh. The island, according to Boswell, had no cash: 'There is a great scarcity of *specie* in Skye,' and the Reverend McQueen told them how difficult he found it getting enough coin to pay wages.

In this Pepysian insight from Boswell, we learn that the economy of Skye swung between the animal drovers paying by cheque, and the people needing cash to pay the pedlars who, there being no shops on Skye, supplied all the snuff, tobacco and other personal luxuries.

'Saturday, 25 September. It was resolved we should set out, in order to return to Slate [or Sleat], to be in readiness to take boat whenever there should be a fair wind.' I can now trace quite clearly their footsteps since Dunvegan, and if Dr Johnson rode at all here, then salute him for heroism – such tough countryside, such hard terrain. No wonder Johnson delayed as much as possible at Talisker House; by the time I turned the high-angled cross roads near Talisker Distillery, a building as neat and sturdy as a thatched whitewashed cottage, though a deal more salubrious, the rain alone would have sapped a regiment's strength. 'Dr Johnson remained in his chamber writing a letter, and it was long before we could get him in motion.'

This must be the letter he wrote to Mrs Thrale, dated the previous day, because when Boswell went up to fetch him Johnson quoted the song, 'Every island is a prison' and to Mrs Thrale he began likewise, the letter which gave her all the details of Raasay. When, six days later, he wrote his long, long letter to her, he gave details of Talisker, and of it said, 'A place where the imagination is more amused cannot easily be found' – the waterfalls, the mountains and the beating of the waves upon the shore.

In Ullinish and Talisker, western Skye, therefore, holds two consecutive places where little change has taken place since Johnson came by. The rooms at Talisker House have been altered in reconstructions, but the building still sits in its sheltered nook, with trees planted against the west wind, and the gardens angled to take full advantage of whatever warmth comes in from the south-west on the North Atlantic Drift. Of the places Johnson and Boswell visited, this house, and the landscape north of here, that is the road down from Dunvegan through Ullinish, will remain in my mind as the most enticing and memorable. Talisker House fires the imagination, not explosively or pyrotechnically, but with the good power of reflective imagination.

They again had dreadful weather, and they left their departure until so late on the Saturday that they had to travel through darkness much of the way, and here comes Johnson's Gothick reflections: such a journey, through wild and craggy solitude is fine, he argued, if you are cheerful and have a good guide; woe betide you if you wander 'benighted, ignorant and alone. The fictions of the Gothick romances were not so remote from credibility as they are now thought' – meaning, he explains, that in olden feudal days, nobles lived in fortified castles dotted at intervals throughout the savage country, so that it became perfectly feasible to pass from the desolation of rocky, windswept moorland to the table-groaning firelit elegance of a castle such as Dunvegan.

With this thought, and no further details, he arrives at Ostig (Ostaig) and the longest, most absorbed reflection of Highland life he was to write in any one place. Weatherbound waiting for a boat to islands farther south, he spent only three days at Ostaig, and although he wrote the final version of *A Journey to the Western Islands* when he returned to London, the forced inactivity of a rather dull house in Skye seems to have prompted him to use the occasion for extensive reflection. With leisure, *in situ*, Johnson drafted his chapters.

Boswell's accounts of the four days immediately after they left Dunvegan, from Tuesday the 21st until they left Talisker on Saturday the 25th, further unveil Johnson's character and his contribution to the way in which Boswell wrote about him. Again, Boswell's amplifying function succeeds. Sometimes he and Johnson overlap, and in doing so disagree; more than once Boswell includes a fact or detail which Johnson, surprisingly, neglects. For example, in that churchyard of the Lovat memorial, they saw a funeral, and watched the mourners dig the grave using an implement which sounds, from Boswell's description, very like an Irish *slane* or *slean* (pron. 'shlaan'), used for cutting turf; fashioned like a spade it has an extra, right-angled blade. Boswell also observes that on Skye they carry home the harvest either on horseback or on a kind of sled.

Now their journey presents some practical difficulty to a follower in their footsteps, as Johnson's mind expanded in contrary proportion to the activities in which he was involved – that is to say, he wrote most about the places where he did least. The peak of his Scottish literary achievement takes place chronologically between Sunday, 26 September and Wednesday, 13 October. yet he never did so little in the whole journey. First he spent three nights at Corry, in the farmhouse they had visited on the way into Skye; then he spent three nights at Ostaig; then two nights at Armadale, 1 and 2 October. On Sunday the 3rd, they set sail for the isle of Coll, spent that night weather-bound at sea, landed on the island on Monday morning, and spent ten nights there, unable to travel on account of storms. Conversely, Johnson's greatest and longest accounts of Scotland relate to that period of his journey. At first glance, this is misleading; the lengthiness of his account gives the impression that he found Skye and the western isles at their most absorbing in undramatic places such as Ostaig. In effect, Johnson employed the technique of recollection in tranquillity: writing his *Journey to the Western Islands* in his London rooms, but having almost certainly drafted some of it during his enforced longueurs *en route*, he cast his mind back to where it was least occupied, and used the comparative inactivity of, in particular, Ostaig, to give his readers his fullest account of Scotland, economically, socially, philosophically.

The passage, 'Ostig in Sky [*sic*]', runs to more than seventeen thousand words, his major essay on the state of Scotland and its people as he found them, and felt he must report. 'Ostig in Sky' comprises all the qualities of a great essay: authority, clarity, individuality, arresting charm, purity and the essential paradoxical combination of immutability and flexibility; that is, it may be read with the reader's own imagination dancing to its tune and making up his own steps as he goes along, but the tune remains the same. To find Johnson ever again – this, the object of my journey – I need look no further, because, as Montaigne did when he made those *Essais* to divine what he believed, Johnson measures his own judgments against the power and content of the great, wide and often untamed territory he had been visiting. In this, another great property of the essay materialises: he is writing not about Scotland or the Isle of Skye, but about the world and his own view of it. Above all, he wrote it to be read, and his style shows it; the writer draws his reader forward as if entrancing him with the plot of a novel; the essay is a model in how to make mundane matter enjoyable with the application of imagination, learning, perception and excellent prose.

To summarise 'Ostig in Sky' would be impertinent, and rob my own readers of the joy of its anticipation should they go on to read the original book I have been tracing. It would also give offence to those already familiar with the piece. To those who have not yet found it, be prepared for an essay in which Dr Johnson seems to leave not a corner of human existence ignored, and does so in a style which contains a worthwhile aphorism every two lines or so; several permanent wisdoms; a model of how to inject the personal pronoun 'I' without egotism or intrusiveness; a willingness to move with ease from the moral to the frivolous: when Johnson once described Addison's prose as 'the model of the middle style; on grave subjects not formal, on light occasions not grovelling', he might have been defining this essay.

Which component of the piece most appeals? Is it the structure? From geography, climate, weather and geology, he moves through fertility, agriculture and lost mineral and industrial potential, on through the history, the social module, the economics, the folklore, the food, the general conversation – a linear tracking across the west of Scotland and its way of life as he saw and understood it. Is it the power of the content? Once read, it is difficult to imagine a clearer picture of this edge of Britain in the eighteenth century. Is it the style, his enviable art concealing his art? 'As the mind must govern the hands, so in every society, the man of intelligence must direct the man of labour.' Few words: large thought.

One short paragraph, on the curse of those parts, emigration, bears quoting in full for its beauty and pithiness and political compassion. 'Let it be inquired, whether the first intention of those who are fluttering on the wing, and collecting a flock that they may take their flight, be to attain good, or to avoid evil. If they are dissatisfied with that part of the globe, which their birth has allotted them, and resolve not to live without the pleasure of happier climates; if they long for bright suns, and calm skies and flowery fields, and fragrant gardens, I know not by what eloquence they can be persuaded, or by what offers they can be hired to stay.'

This is the Johnson I am discovering, this overlord of language, who draws thought and feeling together in a prose whose principal technical characteristic is clarity, and whose principal emotional characteristic is consideration for his reader, whether discussing peat, water-mills, bagpipes, superstition or barley broth.

While Johnson was composing his great thoughts for 'Ostig in Sky', Boswell pressed on, recording the autumn days and their

little events. He prised Johnson out of Talisker House, and at
Saturday mid-day they set off to ride to Sleat. By leaving late
they added to the roughness of the journey, which took them
across country east to Sconser where they ate, then took a boat on
Loch Sligachan and sailed round the coast to Strolimus. Boswell is
not clear on the timescale here, but it is possible to work out that
they may have got to Sconser about half-past five or six, because
he says they climbed into the boat at seven. In which case they
made good ground from Talisker; that first leg of the journey
from Talisker House – I am assuming they headed due east to
Loch Harport and met some kind of better road – is tough going
even today, much more so if you are creaky and unaccustomed
to riding. On the way they stopped at a hut and watched an old
woman grinding corn on a quern.

Boswell takes over the Johnsonian mantle here briefly; he
describes the construction of Skye cottages – a double stone wall
with earth in the sandwich, thatched rooves secured by ropes from
which stones have been suspended, and he reaches for a simile
from, no doubt, his own life: 'These stones hang round the bottom
of the roof, and make it look like a lady's hair in papers.'

At Sconser Boswell had a letter from his wife: did she tell him
of her pregnancy? He does not say. The Reverend McQueen, that
local pastor often buffeted by Johnson, said goodbye to them and
Johnson took him by the hand, said 'Dear Sir, do not forget me!'
(a redundant plea) and they said they would help Mr McQueen
with 'an account of the Isle of Sky, which Dr Johnson promised
to revise'. Then, in the showery dusk, they sailed inside Scalpay
to Strolimus, whence they headed for the Mackinnons' at Corry,
that house of great previous hospitality to them, and arrived at
eleven. The Mackinnons had prepared for bed, but they rekindled
the fire and put a midnight supper on the table for Johnson,
Boswell, the young Maclean of Coll, and the servants whom
Boswell only occasionally mentions.

Johnson went to bed after this late supper, but Boswell, Mackinnon and Coll stayed up drinking punch and Boswell did not get
to bed until five in the morning. Mr Donal J. MacLennan from
Harris, whom I met at Old Corry as he corralled his sheep with
the sun shining on the fair-skinned ruins of the walls within which

THE RECOVERY.

Johnson had slept, told me that they 'had a good time that night in the old house', and that Boswell had a hangover in the morning.

'Sunday, September 26: I awaked at noon, with a severe headach. I was much vexed that I should have been guilty of such a riot, and afraid of a reproof from Dr Johnson.' Instead, Johnson amusedly called him 'a drunken dog', and as the others gathered in Boswell's room, his host carrying the cure of a brandy dram, Johnson told them to make Boswell drunk again. Bozzie eventually struggled to his feet, quarried for a little worshipful feeling inside him to honour the Sabbath and in Johnson's room found his hostess's prayer-book and opened it at the epistle which read, 'And be not drunk with wine, wherein there is excess.' Boswell remarks in a dry tone, 'Some would have taken this as a divine interposition.'

At this point, there is a footnote of great value in later editions of Boswell's account. When his *Journal of a Tour* first appeared, his intemperance at Corry seems to have occasioned comment both jocose and serious. The 'banterers' he dismissed, but he took on the serious critics, and to some effect. They seem to have complained that he included the description of Johnson's indulgence towards his drinking. Boswell shows his biographer's stuff by saying he was prepared to show all sides of Johnson, regardless of how he appeared: 'In justice to him I would not omit an anecdote, which, though in some degree to my own disadvantage, exhibits in so strong a light the indulgence and good humour with which he could treat those excesses in his friends, of which he highly disapproved.'

Not much to see of their footsteps at Old Corry, or Ostaig, so again I content myself with imaginings of the way they spent their days, fuelled by Boswell's details. His *Journal* is as useful as a screenplay: he moves his characters in and out of the action, we see them in close-up or in long shot. At dinner Mrs Mackinnon reminisced about Flora Macdonald, and gave Boswell the words of a song her father sang in his cups. Outside, it blew and rained.

Monday dawned still unsuitable for travelling, and they read. It had become one of Johnson's more agreeable discoveries that Skye had so many books; at Corry he renewed acquaintance with the books he had found here three weeks ago, just before they crossed to Raasay.

Boswell makes a further four useful records of the day: the wealth of provisions in the house at Corry, even though the Mackinnons had no garden, 'not even a turnip, a carrot or a cabbage'; Johnson holding forth on the uselessness of their garden spade, too heavy for good land; his ease with the ladies who danced and drank his health: one of them sat on his knee and kissed him and he said to her, 'Do it again and let us see who will tire first.' Finally, he comes to Boswell's room, reads his *Journal* and compliments him upon it: 'The more I read of this, the more highly I think of you.' The evidence – that Johnson oversaw Boswell's biographing – is becoming irresistible. And so to bed, while below the house roistered on punch so loudly Boswell regretted not joining them.

Next day, Tuesday, rained again – but we can see vividly from Boswell how they had to conduct their lives at the Mackinnons'.

'On grave subjects not formal, on light occasions not grovelling'

A Skye farmhouse had few pretensions to the accommodation of great guests; in the busy hospitality, as people came and went, as servants and family milled easily about, few had ever imagined the need for moments of solitude, and all rooms came into use. By day, the ladies sat, and servants ate, in the room in which Johnson slept, and Boswell's bedroom was 'a kind of general rendezvous of all under the roof, children and dogs not excepted'. Boswell went to Johnson's room for quiet, and, before Johnson rose, sat there writing his Journal, and even when the ladies took it over after breakfast they chattered away without minding him. It is a clear picture – Boswell in a corner of a farmhouse bedroom, the ladies talking to each other, probably in Gaelic, Johnson's strong voice booming from another room as he talked to young Coll, or to his host and hostess, while Boswell recorded the talk of the previous night.

This was their last day at Corry; I try to count the people in the house: Mr and Mrs Mackinnon, young Coll, Boswell and Johnson, Boswell's servant, Joseph Ritter, Donald Macleod whom they had last seen at Dunvegan, others of the Mackinnon family, and assorted servants. At any one time there must have been up to twenty people under that roof. It rained all morning.

Boswell's desire to show all sides of his great companion comes through rewardingly once more, and shows us – obliquely, therefore with brilliant clarity – Johnson's political philosophy, and one of its contradictions. Johnson talked (obviously, to judge from the topic, within the general company although Boswell does not say so), of threshing and thatching, an economic matter on Skye and in the Highlands. He moved from the particular matter of how best to hire a thresher, by the day rather than by the grain he produces – 'I would rather trust his idleness than his fraud' – to the ever-vexed business of wage control, and Johnson the Tory said, 'It would be of very bad consequence to raise the wages of those who procure the immediate necessaries of life, for that would raise the price of provisions,' and went on to conclude that 'if wages are once raised, they will never get down again.'

Then came the contradiction in terms if not in words. After midday the weather cleared, suggesting departure; the Mackinnons insisted upon lunch, at which Johnson engaged Mrs Mackinnon in a whispered conversation. The topic – and he had dwelt upon it before on his journey – did not accord with Johnson's politics: further details of Bonnie Prince Charlie's escape. Mrs Mackinnon, being the daughter of the old Laird Macdonald of Kingsburgh, and thus Flora Macdonald's kinswoman by marriage, had much to tell: she was actually at her father's house when the Prince stayed there.

All at table could hear, and they began to tease Mr Mackinnon about Johnson and his wife colloguing. 'She, perceiving this, humorously cried, "I am in love with him. What is it to live and not to love?" Upon her saying something, which I did not hear, or cannot recollect, he [Johnson] seized her hand eagerly and kissed it.'

They left Corry at four, with young Mackinnon to keep them company, bound for Ostaig again where they were to stay in the minister's house until Friday night. Another *ceilidh* greeted them, with the minister's sister, a Miss Macpherson, accompanying her own Gaelic songs on the guitar. Both Boswell and Johnson praised their host. Johnson said, 'He has a great deal of Latin, and good Latin,' and Boswell pays him the ultimate compliment: 'He appeared to be a man of such intelligence and taste as to be sensible of the extraordinary powers of his illustrious guest.'

On Wednesday and Thursday at Ostaig, the weather again confined them to the house, where they had better accommodation than at Corry, with space to be alone. Visitors called to see Johnson, whose mood swung a little, between the enjoyment of performing his opinions and the confinement which delayed his return to the mainland and then home.

They say on this island that the traveller will always return to Skye. We know that Dr Johnson would not, did not. His age and the exceptional travel rigours dictated a flouting of the old saying. I shall have no such difficulty, and already have fulfilled the return, and will do so again and again. For what reason I cannot say; therefore any intention to return rises from the emotions and the imagination. Recalling the place now, every rough texture and salt-and-pepper heather colour comes back, and every landscape, those wide sloping lands to the sea in the north-west, the honey shore near Ullinish, the violet-blue of the waters and skies near Dunvegan, and the softness of the accents of the crofters that I met.

It had already cornered my imagination. The bonny boat had been speeding over the sea to Skye since childhood, when the stories of Bonnie Prince Charlie hiding out in a cave and in all his awkward aristocratic tallness, disguised as an Irish maid, had a place alongside Jim Hawkins, Dr Livesey and Long John Silver. Adventure aside, Skye obliges the traveller to absorb it. The Cuillins personalise the island, with all points referring and deferring to them, and if not the Cuillins, other mountains. For instance, at the end of the long lane leading down to Old Corry rises two and half thousand feet of a hard and immediate cone called Beinn na Caillich: that name could be translated in a number of ways – the mountain of the old woman, or old head of the witch, or even, with a poetic stretch, the widow's peak. From the moment you find the electricity sub-station near Broadford and move down to Corry it takes command, and like all the other peaks on Skye, it holds you subject. In cities we lose touch with the usefulness of mountains: they tell you when the rain is due, they film the clouds as they pass over, and with a little help they chart the watcher's mood. Huge, rigid wizards, they cast spells, and in the mornings they invite adventure – a walk, a hunt, a fossil search – and in the evening they invite reflection, as they hide the sun and call the shadows forward. And the waters of Skye, the omnipresent waters. Apart from those small, woody lanes at the end of which might have been the ruin of the house at Ostaig – apart from those little verdant excursions, the water never leaves the field of vision. Wherever you go, look ahead or turn back, and there seems to be a sea-loch, or an interloping curled digit of silver, or a brackish stream, or a wide sound, or a distant stretch that might reach to Stavanger or Manhattan for all you know, and whatever state the light is in at that moment, the water is giving it back to you, telling you. That is the imagination's photograph that will take me back to Skye, a dancer of an island if ever there were one.

*　　　　*　　　　*

From Corry, to dull Ostaig, to Armadale for twenty-four hours. Dancing to bagpipes; eager listening by the hosts and their friends to Johnson's wit and wisdom; compliments to Boswell, from himself and from Johnson: 'He said today, while reading my *Journal*, "This will be a great treasure to us some years hence."' Sniping at Goldsmith: for his talking too much on all occasions whether or not he understood the subject in hand. One fascinating and tragic glimpse from Boswell, carried over from Corry: Mrs Mackinnon told him that the previous year in Portree, people seeing off their emigrating relatives, rolled on the ground with grief 'and tore the grass with their teeth' – but this year, 1773, nobody did that, giving the impression that perhaps they soon meant to follow suit. They danced a dance called 'America', a whirling dance involving all, and Boswell interpreted its circular absorbing motion as being intended to show how all the people get caught up in emigration. And how they gathered round to sip from every sentence Johnson uttered, even delaying topics of interest until Johnson came to hand and uttered.

This is the last I shall see of Johnson among the ordinary folk of Scotland, at home among the circumstances of people not unfamiliar to him, as being of the same class, or somewhat better off, than his own origins in Lichfield. He had obviously given much thought throughout his life as to how he should conduct himself in the homes of the great; in the farmers', clergymen's and factors' houses of Skye, we see a more modest Johnson, performing more naturally, under less pressure to impress. He entered different debates among them, took different soundings, struck different notes, less the statesman, more the student of humanity. He puzzled, for instance, as to the truth of the rumour that the islanders of St Kilda caught a cold every time a stranger came among them, and he teased the Skye folk that perhaps they felt the same when Sir Alexander Macdonald came to stay. His knowledge was doled out in friendly and amused ways; he even contemplated his own position, laughing to think of himself wandering around the islands at sixty, and wondering where he would be roving to at eighty. At Armadale on the morning of Sunday, 3 October, they were alerted suddenly to the possibility of a favourable wind, and Dr Johnson, with many thanks to all within reach, took his leave of memorable Skye as a potentate concludes a state visit.

The next leg of the journey contained significant failure for me, and for reasons not dissimilar to those which caused Johnson and Boswell such difficulty. Their schedule, however loose, had been thrown aback by the weather on Skye, and they set off for Mull. Intending to visit only two other islands – the holy isle of Iona, and Inchkenneth, the home of Coll's father – they ran into further bad weather, and suffered a severe setback to their travels, if not their writings. I failed to follow their footsteps, because the weather also prevented me from taking the course onto which they had been blown: a storm, often dangerous, forced them off the coast of Mull, and they had no option but to land on Coll. They effected that landing in darkness and swiping rain; Johnson had been seasick, and Boswell terrified: 'I now saw what I never saw before, a prodigious sea with immense billows coming upon a vessel, so as that it seemed hardly possible to escape.'

Boswell's account of their dangerous little voyage has genuine dramatic force, and excellent comedy. Out on seas notorious to mariners, and near midnight, they were certainly in grave danger; their sails grew ragged, the boat heeled to within an inch of the waterline off the low rocky shore of Coll. Comically, the steering was done by a man with one eye; Coll had five dogs aboard, one of whom lay at Johnson's back, 'keeping him warm'. They waved burning peat as a signal and Boswell, also seasick, feared that Coll's sporting munitions might ignite from a flying spark. In the wind and beating rain, Boswell asked Coll for something to do and Coll put into his hands 'a rope which was fixed to the top of one of the masts, and told me to hold it till he bade me pull'. Upon reflection, Boswell realised that Coll had handed him a meaningless task, as if keeping a child busy.

Safe at last, Johnson slept aboard, and Boswell and Coll were accommodated by the captain of a larger vessel moored in the same harbour. Assessing their journey now, they had given them-selves a problematic task: today's Skye ferries from Armadale go south-south-east to Mallaig: they essayed a journey eleven times longer, aiming to land at Iona that night, a distance of, according

SAILING AMONG THE HEBRIDES.

to the modern map, about fifty-five miles. When the wind failed them, they then thought to round the point at Ardnamurchan, slip into the Sound of Mull, and anchor at Tobermory. All of this they tried to do at a time still within the period of equinoctial gales: a crazy ambition, and we nearly lost Boswell, Johnson and all the literature that issued from their relationship.

Their time on Coll has the value of microcosm, and I am told that the house in which they mainly stayed still stands. Notwithstanding the friendliness of young Coll, a man whom Johnson so loved that all of London would, on his behalf, mourn the young man's death by drowning a year later, the island proved a greater inconvenience than they could ever have expected. They were bound to it from Monday, 4 October, until Thursday the 14th. Johnson's pliability suffered, and he chafed terribly: 'This is a waste of life.'

My own journey took me straight to Mull, but on mainland

roads from Mallaig, roads where the white tips of waves may sometimes be seen through the woods, by Loch Ailort, Loch Moidart, and Loch Sunart, and then an inland climb to Lochaline where a ferry crosses to Fishnish on Mull, a long way from Coll. I can only read about it now, their scraggy, uneven time on Coll, where even the well-meaningness of those who gave them hospitality seems thin against poor Johnson's frustration. Coming up from the boat on the morning after the night before, they got soaked to the skin; they had several false starts before they got away again – and yet they both exploited the inconvenience professionally to give their readers memorable images.

Both Johnson and Boswell observe that they could have sailed from Coll next morning, but they chose to chance fortune with the winds, and since they had come to explore islands, they would investigate Coll (both write 'Col'). Curiously, my failure to land on Coll brought me closer to them than I had so far come, as if the geography, economy and society they recounted became the colour and brush-strokes by which we see the artist through the painting. In a way, Coll fulfilled my journey's intention. By the time I got to the shores of Mull I had become habituated to reading what they wrote and then locating what they observed. By not seeing Coll, but with the habit of standing in their footsteps now formed, added to the way they stimulate the imagination, I got a clearer view of the island than I might have done, and the clearest view of all of their individual methods, and of each man's nature. Taken together, their renditions of Coll coalesce elegantly into a study of the pair and their individual arts.

Each man's account of Coll brings the reader in touch with the feel of the island – sandy, rocky and wet with pools, low, with a shortage of hills and thus open to the winds of the Atlantic. The islanders seemed caught in a life without reason or intent, they drifted in and out of argument, with not even sufficient facilities for prayer to sustain them in some sort of purpose-giving belief: their minister, Hector Maclean, deaf, ageing and dogmatic, had only the front room of his ramshackle house in which to hold services. 'He was about seventy-seven years of age,' writes Boswell, 'a decent eclesiastick, dressed in a full suit of black clothes, and a black wig. He appeared like a Dutch pastor, or one of the assembly of divines at Westminster.' He and Johnson argued about the philosopher-theologians Samuel Clarke and Gottfried Wilhelm Leibnitz. The minister supported the latter and Johnson defended Clarke, but since each man was somewhat deaf and did not fully apprehend the other's argument, no dangerous collision occurred. Johnson, in one of his perfectly-phrased observations, records the minister with due acknowledgment: 'I honoured his orthodoxy, and did not much censure his asperity. A man who has settled his opinions, does not love to have the tranquillity of his conviction disturbed; and at seventy-seven it is time to be in earnest.'

Claustrophobic experience when travelling brings forth unforgettable character studies. Coll is only a dozen miles long by four and a quarter miles wide – Johnson says thirteen by three, but by what measure I cannot fully say; the isle confined them so long that they could not avoid close observation of the few people they met. After the minister, their next greatest treasure, observed by both, is Mrs Macsweyn, the wife of the farmer at Grishipoll, in whose household Johnson says he 'saw more of the ancient life of a Highlander than I had yet found'. Mrs Macsweyn spoke no English 'and had never seen any other places than the islands of Sky, Mull and Col'. She gave Johnson a spoon made of horn to stir his tea, and Boswell says she wore tartan and taught him songs in Gaelic. Just before they left Coll, Johnson was told, in her presence, that Mrs Macsweyn had never been on mainland Scotland:

JOHNSON: That is rather being behind-hand with life. I would at least go and see Glenelg.
BOSWELL: You yourself, sir, have never seen, till now, any thing but your native island.
JOHNSON: But, sir, by seeing London, I have seen as much of life as the world can show.
BOSWELL: You have not seen Pekin.
JOHNSON: What is Pekin? Ten thousand Londoners would *drive* all the people of Pekin: they would drive them like deer.

Johnson met one other man on Coll whom he found memorable, another Mr Maclean, of Corneck, whose brother was the much-renamed laird of the Isle of Muck. Boswell reports a Johnsonian discourse occasioned, evidently, by Corneck, again a classical exercise in the relationship between thought, commonsense, idea and conciseness, some of the more prominent medals worn by Johnson: 'The rent must be in a proportionate ratio of what the land may yield, and the power of the tenant to make it yield.' Boswell then reports Johnson as considering Corneck 'the most distinct man he had met in these isles', on account of the fact that Corneck, he said, 'did not shut his eyes, or put his fingers in his ears', unlike 'most of the people whom we have seen of late'.

Coll, son of the laird, governed the island in his father's absence at Aberdeen. The young man strides in and out of their narratives. Johnson notes his kindness and effective conduct as a host, and his venturesome building of a carriage-road. He observed closely and with approval Coll's conduct among his people – nothing showy or domineering: 'his only distinction was a feather in his bonnet'; and an ease of greeting that drew people to him. Coll maintained the customs of a Scottish chieftain's household, including a piper at dinner.

Boswell went galloping with Coll, and climbed one of the isle's three hills, out of which adventure there comes from Boswell a picture that fixes Johnson, big, lumbering, talking-to-himself, curt and courteous Johnson, as effectively as any description so far.

On Saturday, 9 October, after a week of talk and small, weather-permitted excursions, Boswell asked Coll to show him a local curiosity, a huge boulder said to have been hurled by a giant up a mountain at his mistress. Johnson, 'who did not like to be left alone', went with them, even though he remarked of the legend, 'There are so many more important things, of which human knowledge can give no account, that it may be forgiven us, if we speculate no longer on two stones in Coll.' When all dismounted to continue on foot, Johnson stood himself 'against a large fragment of rock. The wind being high, he let down the cocks of his hat, and tied it with his handkerchief under his chin.' Thus disported, he took a book out of his pocket and began to read, while Boswell and Coll climbed up to inspect the giant's rock. Presumably Johnson wore his brown coat, and what a daft and endearing sight he must have looked, a large, and probably not very clean, handkerchief passing around the top of his head-gear and tied beneath his chin – like one of those old comic strips of a man with a gumboil wearing a hat.

Boswell says the population of Coll had increased much in the previous thirty years: Johnson assesses the numbers as somewhere between eight hundred and a thousand – close: an official count in 1771 said twelve hundred. The typical socio-economic structure prevailed – laird, some farmers (Boswell reports no more than three tacksmen of significance) and many smaller tenants. To which must be added some extras, by way of a floating population, and once more there enters the narrative one of those fleeting, sidelong details from which a novel could uncoil. Johnson mentions that the farmers pay for their labour drawn from the lower orders by way of food – money not being a commonplace on Coll – and yet, he says, the island had beggars, something of a plague. And even more so in the neighbouring island of Tiree, so tormented by beggars that the islanders drew up an agreement to give no more alms. Here comes the fascinating snippet: they did not make their compact simply because they had grown sick of giving alms, or because these islands in general saw beggars as sinister, but because on Tiree 'they had among them an indigent woman of high birth, whom they considered as entitled to all that they could spare'.

Who was she? Johnson does not say. Where did she originate, and how did she fall upon her hard circumstances? I have so far found no mention of her in Boswell's *Journal*.

We can count the number of people they met on Coll, and with the exception of aristocracy they typify the social range of people encountered by the pair throughout their jaunt. There was the young acting laird, Coll himself; then, their first host, a retired colonial, Captain Lauchlan Maclean, and his wife; her father, the aged Reverend Hector Maclean who stood with his back to the fire and tugged the peak of his wig as he talked; the heavily-built octogenarian Mr Macsweyn, and his untravelled wife, and their fifty-year-old son, Hugh; an unnamed man, wife and their children living in a hut alongside the old castle of Coll – 'Dr Johnson gave them some charity'; and the realistic Mr Maclean of Corneck.

The island of Coll gave them the accumulated specimen of the life they had hoped to see in the west of Scotland.

Their joint picture of Coll is completed by their references to the island's texture and geographical composition: in this low, wet, gritty and rocky place, agriculture seemed an adventure rather than a commonplace. One significant feature interfered, brought about by the confluence of weather and terrain – high wind blew sand great distances, and it piled up, according to Boswell, on meadowland. Johnson disagrees with the extent of the sandblown damage: he claims that the islanders exaggerated, that because rain usually accompanied wind, the sand grew too heavy to blow.

Again I wish that, inside the simple mechanisms of a time machine, he had met David Thomson at Nairn. Thomson would have challenged Johnson's scepticism as to the damage sand can do. Along the Moray Firth, it attacked like a foe, especially on an October day in 1694 where fifteen out of sixteen farms on one hillside alone were wiped out. People rose in the mornings to find their windows and doorways darkened: sand lapped the eaves. The storm went away, and, no pasture left, they drove their animals inland, then returned to try and salvage their homes. This time they believed the end of the world had come, because the storm returned and, records Thomson, 'the huge sandhills it had created during the previous day and night were now shifting; the westerly gale lifted them and blew them along in massive blinding clouds . . . Next morning there was nothing to be seen but sand, not even the tops of trees, nor even the chimneys of the laird's big house. The church had been deeply buried . . .'

On Coll, Boswell, perhaps owing to time on his hands, offers the reader an account of the island's physical and animate life, something he has rarely essayed in his *Journal*, most notably so far only on Raasay. He seems not to have feared overlapping Johnson, and if he gives no impression of having chosen to supply what Johnson did not, it yet transpires that their accounts, though with similarities, may be read each as an amplification of the other. Boswell records 'forty-eight lochs of fresh water'; Johnson says 'many lochs'. Johnson says 'they have neither deer, hares nor rabbits'; Boswell notes 'a rabbit-warren on the north-east of the island'; he gives details of the horses – small and so numerous that some are exported; the cattle – black and rough-haired; the sheep, some for the table, and 'goats in several places'; Johnson merely observes, 'Their quadrupeds are horses, sheep, cows and goats.' Johnson ignores the bird-life; Boswell shot starlings and knew of snipe, wild-duck, wild geese, swans, wild pigeon and plover.

They overlap when discussing the islanders' domestic occupations, giving their readers an ideal moment to compare their styles and minds. Johnson, habitually concise, says, 'Several arts which make trades, and demand apprenticeships in great cities, are here the practices of daily economy. In every house candles are made, both moulded and dipped. Their wicks are small shreds of linen cloth. They all know how to extract from the Cuddy, oil for their lamps. They all tan skins, and make brogues.' Boswell uses almost exactly twice as many words. 'Every man can tan. They get oak, and birch-bark, and lime, from the main land. Some have pits; but they commonly use tubs. I saw brogues very well tanned; and every man can make them. They all make candles of the tallow of their beasts, both moulded and dipped; and they all make oil of the livers of fish. The little fish called Cuddies produce a great deal. They sell some oil out of the island, and they use it much for light in their houses, in little iron lamps, most of which they have from England; but of late their own blacksmith makes them.'

Not for the first time, I wonder whether Johnson did not need Boswell more than Boswell needed Johnson; the biographer not only told us about his subject, he amplified the life they both saw, and gives us the man in his times, whereas had we only Johnson's writings, and those of standard biographies, we should have been deprived of many of our powers to measure him.

Nevertheless, the chief tool – and virtue – in Boswell's biographical kit has always been his reporting of Johnson's conversations. On Coll they seem to have been fewer than one might have expected: Johnson certainly never hit his Dunvegan form: perhaps the company did not adequately stimulate him. Therefore, confined by the weather, Boswell, as well as reporting the Coll conversations such as they were, used his journal-writing time to recall other aspects of the man. One detail had hilarious possibilities. Johnson told him of a man in Northamptonshire who had gained a considerable influence in life by calling himself Johnson's brother. Only when the impostor grew too brash did anyone think to ask Johnson, and the man was routed.

In the ten days they spent on Coll, Boswell only reports fourteen occasions of conversation, none of great moment. If most consist of brief exchanges, they still add the touches that help the general picture: how Johnson as a young man in London often went without food for two days, subsisting on tea; Johnson's refusal to visit Blenheim because he would not give the Duke of Marlborough the satisfaction of saying 'Johnson was here; I knew him, but I took no notice of him'; Johnson's view on the relationship between landlord and tenant – 'the poor man is always much at the mercy of the rich'; Johnson's intolerance of low life and coarseness, which, given how much he had knocked around, he found a little inexplicable in himself; and Johnson's praise again for Boswell's *Journal* – 'I wish thy books were twice as big.'

Best of all, and in some ways almost the most illuminating so far, is one short paragraph in which Boswell sets forth a little anthology of Johnson's peculiarities. No night-cap – he commonly wore a handkerchief in bed; on horseback leaving Talisker he stopped, turned the horse's head back towards the house, stayed for a moment or two then caught up with the others. Even in freezing weather Johnson opened windows and stood at them. And how he talked to himself, all the time: muttering and mouthing and murmuring, sometimes bursting with laughter at some recollection, or gesturing to accompany fragments of prayer, at which moments his *voce* was anything but *sotto*.

There stands the isle of Coll, across from the lushness of Mull, a sable-coloured island the day I first saw it, and wished I could get on it. I could see buildings at Arinagour, ('the pasture of the goats', I presume) but it was a frightful day of high wind and driving rain and, unlike the man in the song I could not 'find me a handsome boatman to ferry me over my love and I', and have had to be content with that gap in my itinerary, although the three forces – of their two accounts and my own imagination – have more than amply given me a picture of this island where there was hardly any window-tax because there were hardly any windows, where there was a profligacy of whisky stills, where the young laird grew turnips to the scorn of the lady who had never seen even Glenelg, where Boswell without further comment from himself or Johnson shot starlings – was this with one of Coll's fowling-pieces, and were the birds picked up by one of Coll's five dogs? – where Boswell reported 'no serpents, toads, frogs or any other venomous creature', where Johnson's imagination was fired with the stories of old family feuds and attacks, where the wind roared and blew not sand but rain in my eyes, and I could just make out that there were other houses on Coll, and they may even have been the very ones in which Johnson met that old minister who looked like something out of a Dutch painting. Coll became, if not the full stop, the last semi-colon on my journey, and I had now, by not visiting it, gleaned so much of these two wonderful characters that I could go home and spend the rest of my life including them in my pleasures – and that, after all, was why I came.

Johnson wrote to Mrs Thrale, 'There is literally no tree upon the Island. Part of it is a sandy waste, over which it would be really dangerous to travel in dry weather and a high wind' – so he did believe the stories about the blowing sand? Every village, he said, had 'a small garden of roots and cabbages'. He ends on a touching note: 'I have not good health, I do not find that travelling much helps me. My nights are flatulent, though not in the utmost degree, and I have a weakness in my knees, which makes me very unable to walk.'

On Wednesday, 13 October, young Coll called Boswell early: they could probably make Mull. They did not: the wind forced them to wait for the morning tide, and they slept on board the boat upon which they had bought their passages, a sloop with a cargo of kelp, anchored a little offshore. Boswell records the night as an enjoyable, almost boyishly adventurous experience; Johnson says they spent the hours 'not very elegantly or pleasantly'. On the Thursday, they sailed before seven and got into Tobermory – Johnson calls it 'Tobor Morar' – just as the wind was rising again at mid-day. Not a lot of footsteps left now: mainly some trekking across Mull. There is a feeling in both of their reports that the thrust has gone from the journey, as if their appetites had been satisfied by the meal they had come to eat – but I may be projecting my own feelings upon them.

They lunched in Tobermory, by a harbour full of ships. Even if he has by now written for his readers the greater and more crucial parts of his travel experiences, Johnson remains true to his own powers of enquiry and observation. He summarises the virtues and faults of Tobermory from a shipping point of view – a safe, natural harbour, but a compression of mountains brings fast winds from the landward side. Johnson's spirits had been foul on the little voyage from Coll. Tea with bread and butter revived him and Boswell humoured him, teased him, fearing the black mood might deflect Johnson from visiting Iona. In fairness to Boswell, like some intellectual *impresario*, he does also seem to have wanted posterity to get the benefit of Johnson's observations in such places. Next day they were due to visit Coll's uncle, Sir Allan Maclean, on the little isle of Inchkenneth, a sizeable distance south-west of Tobermory, and in line with the direction of Iona. Horses had been hired.

CHAPTER VIII

'After death the art of making friends'

A WHOLLY ACCURATE, STEP-BY-STEP, hour-by-hour replication of their journey is probably impossible today. Not all the roads they travelled have remained the same. In any case, time has altered knowledge, and in the strictest terms of Johnson's wish for discovery, we cannot be expected to feel the same wonder at the Highlands and islands as he did; the tone and scale of revelation he brought to his readers began to grow redundant from the moment he published his *Journey to the Western Islands*, and even then others, his favourites such as Martin Martin Gent. and Thomas Pennant, had gone before. Once swift transport became commonplace, the words he wrote to Mrs Thrale – 'The use of travelling is to regulate imagination by reality, and instead of thinking how things may be, to see them as they are' – began to lose their particular application to the Scotland he saw: it is now possible to 'regulate imagination by reality' at a remove not even Johnson's great mind could have envisaged.

Following in their footsteps was for me, in any case, always more a matter of imagining them 'on location', rather than gaping in wonder at any of their places still intact. Envisaging Johnson physically in Scotland was ultimately made possible by Boswell, who described the figure in the landscape; 'a large bushy greyish wig, a plain shirt, black worsted stockings, and silver buckles. Upon this tour, when journeying, he wore boots, and a very wide brown cloth great coat, with pockets which might have almost held the two volumes of his folio dictionary, and he carried in his hand a large English stick.' Glosses may be found in the *Life*, appealing glimpses. With such descriptions in mind, Johnson becomes easy to spy on, in inns, farmhouses, great houses and castles, or clumping along roads and tracks: his 'countenance was the cast of an ancient statue', says the concluding passage of the *Life*.

More importantly, Johnson's own words, in his text, conversation and letters, fix the emotional and intellectual man. We may all choose the parts of people we wish to like and dislike: Johnson has both, and before long on the journey, I chose. Now, the very thought of Johnson is like warmth and intelligence, not only for his learning, and the size of his mind, and the intense curiosity – the eternal teacher also being the eternal student – but for his view of himself. Who can dislike, for all his shambles, Goldsmith blessed with 'a knack at hoping'? Similarly endearingly, Johnson wrote to Hester Thrale, 'You remember the Doge of Genoa [he may have meant Venice] who being asked what struck him most at the French Court, answered, "Myself." I cannot think many things here more likely to affect the fancy, than to see Johnson ending his sixty-fourth year in the wilderness of the Hebrides.' He ended the letter on a plaintive note; 'My eye is, I am afraid, not fully recovered, my ears are not mended, my nerves seem to grow weaker, and I have been otherwise not as well as I sometimes am, but think myself better lately.'

Samuel Johnson was a loving man, and he bent his great intellect to pluck from his observations facts which would interest a woman of whom he was especially fond, and in writing to Mrs Thrale thus, he also gave her the opportunity, when reading his letter, to feel a little love for him.

His own affections took many forms. That morning at Slains castle, at breakfast before they presseed on to Aberdeen, Johnson pulled one of his little stunts of courtesy. To avoid praising an ode he did not like, written for Lady Errol on the birth of her son, he read the piece aloud with bravura. His late wife, the bibulous and unevenly loved Tetty (having married a widow, Johnson spent long periods away from her), had a daughter, Lucy Porter, with whom Johnson stayed in lifelong touch. Lucy, Sam's stepdaughter – Tetty and Sam had no children – told Boswell that when Johnson was first introduced to the widowed Elizabeth Porter, he was wigless, with stiff straight hair, 'separated behind', he was 'lean and lank, so that his immense structure of bones was hideously striking to the eye', and he often had 'seemingly, convulsive starts and odd gesticulations, which tended to excite at once surprize and ridicule'.

Mrs Porter was so much engaged by his conversation that she overlooked all these external disadvantages, and said to her daughter, 'This is the most sensible man that I ever saw in my life' – this rawboned awkward man who proposed marriage at twenty-six, to a woman twenty years older than him, against fierce opposition from her kin. (One wonders how sheltered a life she had led with the late Mr Porter.) Boswell's *Life* relates Tetty's belief in Sam, evidenced by her reaction to Johnson's great solo periodical, *The Rambler*.

'Johnson told me, with an amiable fondness, a little pleasing circumstance relative to this work. Mrs Johnson, in whose judgment and taste he had great confidence, said to him, after a few numbers of *The Rambler* had come out, "I thought very well of you before; but I did not imagine you could have written any thing equal to this." Distant praise, from whatever quarter,' concluded Boswell, 'is not so delightful as that of a wife whom a man loves and esteems.' Tetty's praise was uttered three days before her death in 1752; Sam was over twenty years a widower when he reached Scotland.

Boswell, like all Johnson's friends, knew the receiving end of his affections. When he wrote to Boswell to congratulate him on passing his Bar examinations – 'You have done exactly what I always wished when I wished you well' – he went on to bestow a piece of memorably kind and shrewd advice, displaying not just the size of his own heart, but his perception of Boswell's psychological mechanisms. Understanding that Boswell hoped that at last he had pleased his lawyer father (who destroyed most of James's necessary childhood feelings of self-importance), Johnson urged him on, observing, 'We all live upon the hope of pleasing somebody; and the pleasure of pleasing ought to be greatest, and at last always will be greatest, when our endeavours are exerted in consequence of duty.'

When in funds, Johnson bailed out impecunious friends like his beloved Goldsmith, of whom he clucked, 'No man was more

Raasay House. The laird, his wife and their three sons and ten daughters hosted the travellers. Johnson wrote to Mrs Thrale: 'We went up into a dining-room about as large as your blue room, where we had something given us to eat, and tea and coffee.'

A small carved stone on Raasay. Boswell wrote of Johnson on Raasay, 'There was not enough of intellectual entertainment for him, after he had satisfied his curiosity, which he did, by asking questions, till he had exhausted the island.'

Raasay. 'A little to the west of the house is an old, ruinous chapel, unroofed, which never has been very curious. We here saw some human bones of an uncommon size. Dr Johnson would not look at the bones. He started back from them with a striking appearance of horror . . .'

Portree harbour on Skye, described by Boswell as 'a large and good one'.

Suisnish on Skye. The scenery did not enchant Johnson, who wrote,
'Though I have been twelve days upon it, I have little to say.'

Isle Oronsay on Skye, an island,
Johnson found, 'so much indented
by inlets of the Sea, that there is no
part of it removed from the water
by more than six miles'.

Dunvegan Castle today. 'At Dunvegan,' said Johnson,
'I had tasted lotus and was in danger of forgetting that
I was ever to depart.'

Rorie O'More's cascade. Boswell observed
Johnson delighted with Dunvegan, because the
'entertainment here was in so elegant a style,
and reminded my fellow-traveller so much of
England'.

The Hebrides. Boswell at Ulinish wrote, 'From an old tower, near this place, is an extensive view of Loch Bracadil [sic], and, at a distance, of the isles of Barra and South Uist.'

The island of Coll, to which they had a terrifying journey. BOSWELL: 'I now saw what I never saw before, a prodigious sea, with immense billows coming upon a vessel, so as that it seemed hardly possible to escape.'

The bay on Iona where Columba landed. Boswell, on this holy island, 'hoped, that, ever after having been in this holy place, I should maintain an exemplary conduct'. He failed.

The post office at Lochbuie: on a wall nearby a plaque reads, 'After leaving Moie Castle the Lochbuie family resided in this house from 1752 to 1790 and it was in this house that Dr Johnson and Mr Boswell were entertained in 1773 by John Mclaine XVII Laird of Lochbuie.'

Lochbuie. Boswell described the journey across Mull to Lochbuie as 'a very tedious ride, through what appeared to me the most gloomy and desolate country I had ever beheld'.

Inveraray Castle, Argyll, where Boswell solicited an invitation to lunch for himself and his great friend: 'I was most politely received, and gave his grace some particulars of the curious journey which I had been making with Dr Johnson.'

Rest-and-be-Thankful. Johnson wrote a thank-you letter to the Duke of Argyll for his help in this leg of the journey: 'That kindness which disposed your grace to supply me with the horse, which I have now returned, will make you pleased to hear that he has carried me well.'

Eglinton Castle, Ayrshire, where the travellers met the 85-year-old, six-feet-tall Countess of Eglintoune, who washed her face every day in sow's milk and trained rats as a hobby. 'Her figure', says Boswell, 'was majestic, her manners high-bred, her reading extensive, and her conversation elegant.'

Auchinleck House, Ayrshire, scene of the great altercation between Johnson and Boswell's father, notwithstanding Johnson's promise, 'I shall certainly not talk on subjects which I am told are disagreeable to a gentleman under whose roof I am.'

foolish when he had not a pen in his hand, or more wise when he had.' Johnson also had gifts of domestic attentiveness, and even in old age, as we know, could prove incongruously entertaining with the children of his companions, being whatever animal – elephant or kangaroo – they wished.

After an early life filled with difficulty on all the usual fronts of love, money and understanding, he learned how to measure and control his expressions of affection over a long period, and he seems to have found and managed the degrees of intimacy he needed – so that those in his regard knew they were loved. Equally, those whom he excoriated felt the lash unmistakably: he was a full man, as thoughtful as he was pompous, and often massively both, turn and turn about. He had wisdom in abundance but was not above forcing it upon people. His capacity for forcefulness in argument was wryly summed up by Goldsmith, adapting a quotation from a contemporary play: 'There is no arguing with Johnson; for, if his pistol misses fire, he knocks you down with the butt-end of it.' This ungainly man was warm and dismissive and advisory and depressed and patronising and intelligent and not infrequently philistine: he once urged that a carving of the Venus de Milo be thrown into a pond 'to hide her nakedness and cool her lasciviousness'. Boswell said, when seeking reminiscences of Johnson from Fanny Burney, 'We have seen him long enough on stilts; I want to show him in a new light. Grave Sam, and great Sam, and solemn Sam, and learned Sam . . . gassy Sam, agreeable Sam, pleasant Sam . . .' A newcomer to Johnson finds all these men in Scotland.

Johnson and Boswell sat in their 'tolerable inn' (which can still be traced behind main street buildings in Tobermory) and talked of European literature and its practitioners, with Johnson showing the breadth of his reading; they discussed Racine, Molière and Voltaire, whom Johnson felt yet unproven. At this juncture Boswell adds to the evidence of Johnson choosing his own biographer. Boswell recollects that 'the Sunday evening that we sat by ourselves at Aberdeen, I asked him several particulars of his early years, which he readily told me; and I wrote them down before him.' (This took place at that introspective moment when, finding the conversation of Aberdeen less than gripping, the two with-drew by themselves to the New Inn.) Now, in Tobermory, Boswell made some more enquiries and made his notes while Johnson looked on. In a footnote, Boswell then remarks, 'It is no small satisfaction to me to reflect, that Dr Johnson read this, and, after being apprized of my intention, communicated to me at subsequent periods, many particulars of his life, which probably could not otherwise have been preserved.' But – in the main text of the *Journal* comes Boswell's great statement, the one which advertises what was to become Literature's most famous biography: 'I shall collect authentic materials for the *The Life of Samuel Johnson LL.D*; and if I survive him, I shall be one who will most faithfully do honour to his memory. I have now a vast treasure of his conversation at different times, since the year 1762, when I first obtained his acquaintance [Boswell got the year wrong: it was 1763]; and by assiduous inquiry, I can make up for not know-ing him sooner.' With these sentences, it finally seems incontro-vertibly true that Boswell had Johnson's co-operation and approval, and even if Johnson has never been portrayed in this Scottish journey as censoring Boswell's text, or in any way caus-ing it to be adjusted, his very reading of it will have been enough to control, dictate, and guarantee the tone in which he desired his life to be portrayed.

As they sat over their dishes of tea, 'the young Laird of Col', as Johnson calls him, had gone about a mile out of Tobermory to visit his aunt, the wife of a doctor. He came back with an invitation that Johnson and Boswell spend the night there. A pass-ing stranger, known to Coll, took their letters to the mail at Inveraray. When they got to Dr Maclean's house, where, says Johnson, they found 'very kind entertainment, and very pleasing conversation', Johnson asked Boswell for some paper to write more letters, and got irritable when Boswell told him to write short letters, as they had to leave early next morning. Johnson reflected that they had not seen as many islands as they had hoped.

The weather next day imprisoned them again; rain, they were informed, had made the rivers impassable. Johnson expressed little concern, content, he told Boswell, now that he had a means of posting letters to his friends at home. He read for part of the day and in the evening Dr Maclean's daughter read him some poems in Gaelic and translated them; Johnson calls her 'the only interpreter of Earse [*sic*] poetry that I could ever find'. Then she sang for him, accompanying herself on the spinet and Johnson reflected enjoyment. The music over, Johnson, Boswell and Coll enjoyed a bitchy conversation about a 'penurious gentleman of our acquaintance', presumably Sir Alexander Macdonald. Then Boswell, as he has begun to do at times of quiet and inaction, catches up on moments of recent conversation with Johnson, understanding that biographical chronology does not need to be rigid: memoir stalks, rather than snatches, its subjects. Johnson on preparing for death: 'If one was to think constantly of death, the business of life would stand still'; Johnson asked Boswell if the Scottish 'jaunt had answered expectation'. Boswell told him it had exceeded it: 'I expected much difficulty with him, and had not found it', and Johnson observed that they had been treated like 'princes in their progress'.

On Saturday, 16 October, the weather lifted and they set out to cross the northern crest of Mull. Johnson called Miss Maclean 'the most accomplished lady that I have found in the Highlands. She knows French, music, and drawing, sews neatly, makes shell-work and can milk cows.' A black mood returned as, astride his little horse, he found the country drearier than Skye. Boswell had no bridle, his servant Joseph Ritter no saddle, as they crossed waterlogged land and flooded roads.

Today, it seems impossible that they even considered the journey; Mull, though beautiful, has much rough territory and is subject to water and rock. I still do not know how they did it but I am assuming, in the absence of accurate directions from either man, that they took what is now the B8073 from Tobermory as far as Dervaig, and then up by Ardow, down to Achleck, and afterwards along the coast by Loch Tuath.

Since that road today hardly counts as a wonder of the western world, what can it have been like when they travelled? The journey took them eight hours, and, if the mileage they were given to expect is accurate, they progressed at only a mile an hour. Johnson, whose spurs went overboard on the boat to Raasay, now lost his walking stick. He had given it to 'a fellow' who was to hand it over to the baggage-man following on behind; but they never saw it again. Against all Boswell's persuasions, Johnson insisted that it had been stolen, that such a piece of timber was worth a lot – trees, again – on account of Mull's barrenness. The loss hurt; Johnson needed the stick as a crutch for his weak legs – and, with its foot and yard measurements, as a tool for his enquiring mind. As he would observe later, 'no man should travel unprovided with instruments for taking heights and distances.'

On this leg of the journey, Johnson exercises for the last time his writerly tactic of drawing general economic conclusions from particular experience of landscape or terrain. Some years before, Mull had known famine in a winter when, unprecedentedly, frost had kept snow on the ground for eight weeks; it was a late reverberation of a freak climate lasting a century and a half, when the general temperature dropped several degrees winter and summer during a period which became known as 'the little Ice Age'. Johnson had not heard of this, and, taking the intense wintriness to be a recent and isolated phenomenon, he summarises the island's economy by pointing out that such an unusual spell of hard weather would cause no more than small difficulty in a fertile land. 'But where the climate is unkind, and the ground penurious, so that the most fruitful years will produce only enough to maintain themselves', such freak conditions would produce catastrophe, avoidable if such communities developed alternative economic means, such as manufacturing industry.

The creaky old bear found the journey hard going; 'This was a day of inconvenience, for the country is very rough, and my horse was but little.' He says they had no road to follow, but if their journey took them even loosely in the general track of today's un-numbered route from Dervaig down to Fanmore, no wonder he found it tough. And no wonder they did not make Inchkenneth, which they had expected to reach easily that night. None of the land they had hitherto traversed since Johnson entered Scotland two months earlier could have been as inhospitable as this rocky, wild, undulating, bleak route. Back in the warmth of his rooms in London, when recalling this piece of travel, Johnson wrote his lengthiest peroration on the virtues of forestry.

He begins with a rhetorical question: 'It is natural, in traversing this gloom of desolation, to inquire, whether something may not be done to give nature a more cheerful face, and whether those hills and moors that afford heath cannot with a little care and labour bear something better?' He proceeds to his next sentence offering no surprise whatever: 'The first thought that occurs is to cover them with trees,' and there is no stopping him for the next page, as he considers trees from all sides: the lack of satisfaction occasioned by the length of time between seeding and abundant tall growth; it merely serves to remind the forester of the shortness of human life. The expense bears thinking about, the length of time to which that acreage must lie committed to its seedlings before a return on investment may be expected. He takes into account the vigilance required to defy the teeth of the deer, the goat, the hare, the rabbit. Trees were one of Johnson's solutions to Scotland's economic problems, although he entered a sad note of caution: Sir James Macdonald, apparently, had planted 'several millions, expecting, doubtless, that they would grow up into future navies and cities': lack of care, including less than adequate fencing, were about to cost Sir James his investment.

Johnson acknowledges that these were not the thoughts coursing through his head across Mull; nor did he appreciate the scenery: that novelty had long worn off, and he said he had now a 'mind employed only on our own fatigue'. When they got to the shore of Loch Tuath, a strong wind blew in their faces, and as they would not risk crossing the mouth of Loch na Keal to Inchkenneth, their difficulty intensified. A house in which Coll knew they could spend the night became inappropriate out of respect and courtesy – they had heard *en route* that the owner lay, as Johnson put it, 'in bed without hope of life'. Not wishing to embarrass the family of a dying man, they finally decided to put up at the house of a Mr McQuarrie on the island of Ulva. This also presented a difficulty: the ferry had gone, and their shouts could not be heard against the wind, nor their signals seen in the darkness. Fortunately, sailors off an Irish boat from Derry, moored in the sound of Ulva, rowed them over, and they spent Saturday night hearing mariner's tales from the Irish sea-captain, and stories of second sight from their host. McQuarrie came from a family of Gaelic warriors; one man from Ulva, who had fought with the McQuarries at Culloden, brought his clan banner back and swam across the sound with the flag wrapped around him. Boswell and Johnson shared a bedroom with good beds but an earthen floor which, wet from recent rain pouring through a broken window, made Johnson's bare feet a match for his habitually coal-coloured hands. If he listened carefully, and provided some of the second-sight stories had convinced him, he might have heard a faint cry across the sound; Ulva is the island of 'Lord Ullin's Daughter', the tragic heroine of Thomas Campbell:

> Come back, come back, he cried in grief
> Across the raging water
> And I'll forgive your Highland chief
> My daughter, O, my daughter!

But she did not come back in this island melodrama, she drowned, and Johnson would have needed not second, but third, sight, to have heard the windswept cries, because Campbell was not even born in 1773. (He might have approved, though, of Campbell's most famous remark, 'Now Barabbas was a publisher.') Incidentally, many, if not most, novelists use snatches of song in their works; 'Lord Ullin's Daughter' is almost the only song or ballad Graham Greene ever includes in his work, and he does so twice. Perhaps he fastened on these parts because his ancestor, Robert Louis Stevenson, shipwrecked David Balfour in *Kidnapped* on the island of Erraid not far from Ulva and made him trudge across the Ross of Mull.

Even an island as tiny as Ulva could provoke Johnson to make comments valuable and interesting to his readers. Staffa stands nearby, a romantic, geological curio; Johnson comments that because they did not daily reflect on the wonders of Staffa, the islanders of Ulva had been 'reproached [by visitors] with their ignorance, or insensibility', a matter he felt unfair as the Ulva folk saw Staffa in their eyes every day. 'How it would surprise an unenlightened ploughman, to hear a company of sober men, inquiring by what power the hand tosses a stone; or why the stone, when it is tossed, falls to the ground!' He allows another observation to fall tantalisingly short, when he reports that Ulva still retained the old practice of *mercheta mulierum*, 'a fine in old times due to the laird at the marriage of a virgin'. On Ulva, the laird had the right to every bride on her wedding night. This had been replaced, as in parts of England, with a tax – and, cash being scarce, Ulva paid in kind: it was known as 'The Wedding Sheep'. (I found no trace or mention of such a practice today along Mull's occasionally lush shore.)

Next morning, Sunday, they crossed the loch to Inchkenneth, and were greeted by Sir Allan Maclean and his two daughters. In his house they found recent newspapers, books and comfort. Boswell, in full confidence now that he had begun his great life's work of recording Johnson, continues to give us glimpses of Sam from earlier stages on their travels, snatches of conversation and insight which he had either neglected or feared to include. One shows how Johnson behaved when he felt he had met some kind of a match. A Dr John Campbell came into the conversation on Inchkenneth: he had done some research on that notorious head-cold the people on St Kilda were supposed to contract when a stranger landed among them. On Raasay, Boswell now reveals, Dr Johnson told them that he and Dr Campbell were about to have an argument stimulated by mention of Jethro Tull's book on farm husbandry. As Johnson began to argue, Campbell cut in and said, 'Come, we do not want to get the better of one another; we want to increase each other's ideas,' and Boswell summarises Johnson's telling of the anecdote as a proof that Johnson 'could be persuaded to talk from a better motive than for victory'.

Boswell then gives us one of the many unforgettable physical portraits of Johnson, akin to the kangaroo imitation in Inverness. On one night in Coll, Johnson strutted about the room, making passes with a broadsword; on another evening, Boswell planked a large Scottish bonnet on Johnson's head and his general appearance under this, with his wig sticking out all round beneath it, made him look, according to Boswell, like one of the old storytellers who used to belong in a Highland chief's household. That Sunday on Inchkenneth, they had prayers; Johnson had earlier told Boswell that on the Sabbath he could never read anything that was not theological. These prayers – Boswell reading from his ubiquitous Ogden – would later move Johnson to Latin verse commemorating the evening.

They stayed on Inchkenneth all day Monday. Boswell found some human bones in a ruined chapel, and gave them a new burial. They talked of commerce. Johnson disliked a man growing rich by sitting at a desk. 'If a man returns from a battle, having lost one hand, and with the other full of gold, we feel that he deserves the gold; but I cannot think that a fellow, by sitting all day at a desk, is entitled to get above us.' Once more, Johnson fantasised aloud about owning an island such as Inchkenneth – he would need it fortified, he said, against ruffians who might raid, steal or even cut his throat. Boswell told him to get a dog; Johnson thought not; he had little respect for dogs, and Boswell quotes a story of Johnson forcibly separating two savage dogs fighting. The Monday passed thus in unimportant conversation, as if Johnson were running out of steam, or Boswell now lacked intellectual energy. None of the conversations had anything of the consequence earlier recorded.

Yet Johnson observed Inchkenneth with vigour: a short first paragraph giving the geography, topography and population – Sir Allan, his daughters and their servants in a little *Arcadia*; then a comment upon the romantic fact that this remote spot contained a gentleman rather than a shepherd; expansion into Sir Allan's place in his clan, the life he led on Inchkenneth; a smidgen of history, some ruins, a little boating to the oyster-beds – Johnson gathered some shells 'for their glossy beauty'. On the Monday evening, Sir Allan told them tales of 'the American campaign' (presumably that of 1756—63), for which he had mustered a hundred men; the young ladies played tunes on their harpsichord, inspiring a twist of a jig from Coll and Boswell, and in general an impression materialises of the genial mood of Sir Allan and his entourage on this little island on an autumn Sunday and Monday in the inner Hebrides.

The piece, though short, is complete. It also possesses a courtliness. Although Johnson's compliments may have derived from his good humours as his insults derived from his ill ones, when he wrote about leaving Inchkenneth he did so in a form of manners perfectly suited to a departing guest: 'We could have been easily persuaded to a longer stay upon Inch Kenneth [*sic*], but life will not be all passed in delight. The session at Edinburgh was approaching from which Mr Boswell could not be absent.' How well rough Sam from Lichfield had trained himself – to incline to his hosts that he would willingly have stayed longer, had not a more pressing duty than pleasure, namely Boswell's practice at law, supervened.

They said goodbye next morning to the two young daughters of the island, and to Coll, for whom Johnson had developed great affection. Just under a year later Coll drowned in these very waters, 'perished', says Johnson, 'in the passage between Ulva and Inch Kenneth'. Boswell's footnote indicates that too many sailors, drunk from McQuarrie's house, climbed into the boat with Coll, and sank it.

With four oarsmen Sir Allan Maclean took them along the coast of Mull. Here, Johnson uses the type of brief phrase that characterises him: 'This part of our curiosity was nearly frustrated; for though we went to see a cave, and knew that caves are dark, we forgot to carry tapers, and did not discover our omission till we were wakened by our wants.'

A man was sent for candles, and they braved this cave, so deep, Mull legend said, that twelve men and a piper once entered it and never returned. Inside, in a second cave, Johnson, without comment, observed that there was 'a square stone, called, as we are told, Fingal's Table'; he did not amplify, perhaps not wishing to raise the name of James Macpherson again. High waves rendered nearby Staffa inaccessible, although it was populated at the time; the name 'Staffa' derives from the Norse word for the staves of basalt rock that form Staffa's most unique sight. They picnicked on the shore of Mull and spent the rest of the afternoon twibbling along the coast, or, as Johnson put it, 'roving among the Hebrides'. When the moon rose – Boswell reckons they must have sailed forty miles – they were still on the sea, and soon, to their relief, saw the lights of the tiny village on Iona, or, as they both call it, Icolmkill. As they approached, the tower of the old monastery loomed placidly out of the night. Their landing on the island moved both men to embrace each other. Iona's hallowed name had played a substantial part in their earliest considerations of a trip to Scotland.

The little island's inhabitants, for all their warm welcome, had no domestic accommodation to offer them. Johnson called them 'remarkably gross and remarkably neglected' and he, Boswell and Sir Allan, presumably attended by their servants and oarsmen, slept in a barn on hay, with some blankets provided by the villagers, and each man used a piece of their luggage for a pillow. Boswell recalls: 'When I awaked in the morning, and looked round me, I could not help smiling at the idea of the chief of the McLeans, the great English Moralist, and myself, lying thus extended in such a situation.'

They spent Wednesday morning examining Iona's ruins, Boswell superficially, Johnson minutely. He had prepared his readers for the eventuality that he might find Iona a place where the traveller would be – and should be – moved: 'Far from me and from my friends, be such frigid philosophy as may conduct us indifferent and unmoved over any ground which has been dignified by wisdom, bravery or virtue.' Boswell at one point tiptoed away from the breakfast Sir Allan and Johnson were having in the barn, and returned to the ruined church 'to indulge in solitude and devout meditation . . . I hoped, that, ever after having been in this holy place, I should maintain an exemplary conduct.' Impossible to dislike by now, Boswell becomes more touching as the journey draws to an end. In a kind of Augustinian prayer for God to send chastity – but not just yet, he mused that he would fix a moment some short time thence at which 'a better course' of his life might begin: needless to remark, he rarely achieved it, and once Johnson and his own constant Peggie were dead, Boswell drank more and more.

Yet, they both found much to criticise on Iona, and Boswell, in his disappointment – much of the advance information they had been given proved untrue – compared the headstones and their inscriptions unfavourably and therefore unjustly with those at Westminster Abbey. Johnson's account of Iona is so detailed that he must have taken notes, even though some paragraphs earlier he says he wished he had had the convenience of writing to make greater observations upon their sailing to Iona. He does hint that when they rose to survey the ruins after their night in the haybarn, he 'brought away rude measures of the buildings'; and how he must have missed his lost walking-stick, because, he laments, the measurements were 'inaccurately taken, and obscurely noted'.

The main impression Boswell and Johnson give cumulatively of Iona does not now apply. They complain of grievous dilapidation; some of the old buildings served as cowsheds; accumulations of mud and rubbish had replaced the odour of sanctity with something more pungent. Johnson observed that some edifices could easily have been repaired, which suggests that long before the care of heritage became official policy, Johnson understood all its implications. He would be happier to visit the island now, where the flagstones and the buildings have been so nurtured as to give a more powerful impression of Iona's former eccelesiastical greatness.

Had Iona come earlier in his tour, Johnson must surely have dwelt upon it at greater length. Not that he treats it lightly – but the island contained much, had he interrogated, that suited his mind. It had a great ecclesisatical history, concomitant with his interest in formal religion. Iona also had significant political relevance in the formation of early Britain, and even though the various conversations Boswell recorded on the journey show Johnson's intellectual and educational orientation to have been Mediterranean, he could have quarried riches from enquiry into Iona and its place in the Celtic Church.

Columba would have caught his imagination, a monkish wheeler-dealer of true power. He had to leave Ireland because one of his political intrigues turned out bloodily, but then from Iona, he and his monks – they began to write the history of the islands – infiltrated the politics of Scotland comprehensively, and to such a degree that their power carried south of the border. Within the grey walls Columba slept on a stone slab, a stone his pillow, on ground raised a little above his monks. He was born on the feast of Pentecost; he came to Iona on the feast of Pentecost; and he died on the feast of Pentecost 597 – he was exactly, magic number, seventy-seven years of age. Would Johnson not have been fascinated by the way Columba ruled his monastery, in a hierarchy of elders, worker novices and juniors, with, among them, scribes and political advisers? Would Johnson not have had much to say about Columba's deliberate interfacing of church with temporal power? How he used his reputation for sanctity to gain influence with kings? More surprisingly, given Johnson's interest in Shakespeare, he was content to observe that 'Iona has long enjoyed, without any very credible attestation, the honour of being reputed the cemetery of the Scottish kings' – but he never remarked, or perhaps had not been told, or perhaps it is a later story, that Macbeth is supposed to lie here. To play Johnson at his own game, there are times when reliance upon 'credible attestation' robs the imagination of enjoyable speculation and adventure.

Johnson conceded some force in Iona: 'That man is little to be envied . . . whose piety would not grow warmer among the ruins of Iona' – but that is not the whole story. History and legend meet here: the secular and the holy join forces, and the fabric and geography conspire. While remarking upon the poverty of the three hundred and fifty or so inhabitants, and their exports of corn and cattle, he missed the beauty of the sea, whose light gives Iona another kind of brightness and somehow reinforces the whiteness of sanctity. Boswell did make an excursion; he wanted to see the little bay at the southern end of the island where Columba (or Colmcille or Colmkille) had landed, so he got a horse and a guide and set out, a journey he says of two miles, accurate enough by today's measurements. He anglicises the name of the little bay, Portawherry; more likely the islanders called it Port a'Churaich, the Bay of the Currach, the large hide-covered willow coracle which bore Columba here from the Irish diocese where he had been causing trouble, for which he was exiled. If Johnson had only accompanied Boswell and stood on a high hill looking out to sea, Iona's tranquillity would have impressed itself upon him more than the poverty and dilapidation he recorded; he would have seen the uncommon whiteness of the sands, rendered brilliant by deposits of calcium carbonate, stretching peacefully along the lip of Iona's green turf.

At noon they departed; an ebb tide had grounded their boat 'at a great distance from the water', but Johnson was gratified to note how eagerly the islanders helped to push it down the beach. The night would be spent on Mull, in the house of a Minister, the Reverend Neil Macleod who, familiar with Johnson's writings, said, to the Great Bear's pleasure, 'I have been often obliged to you, though I never had the pleasure of seeing you before' – meaning, as Boswell suggests, that he admired Johnson's work and knew it thoroughly. Johnson says the man's 'elegance of conversation, and strength of judgment would make him conspicuous in places of greater celebrity'. Mr Macleod had been a minister on St Kilda, but regrettably they seem not to have thought of asking him about the mysterious head-cold, or the woman banished there so that she could not betray her highly-placed husband's Jacobite sympathies.

On Thursday morning, 21 October, in Mr Macleod's house, 'the subject of politics,' says Boswell, 'was introduced,' and thus we have the record of the Hebrides' last experience of Johnsonian discourse. Given the subject matter, the Great Bear produced his biggest paw-swipes. One politician was 'as paltry a fellow as could be. He was a Whig who pretended to be honest; and you know it is ridiculous for a Whig to pretend to be honest.' He called Pitt a 'meteor', Walpole 'a fixed star'; of another, he said the liverymen of London 'knew he would rob their shops, knew he would debauch their daughters'. Sir Allan Maclean made the error of suggesting one matter in which Scotland excelled England – the possession of more water. Johnson routed him with one of his trumpeting ridicules: 'You have too much! A man who is drowned has more water than either of us,' and thus hammered poor Sir Allan into subjection.

They left the house of the minister, bound for the Macleans of Lochbuie (whom both Johnson and Boswell call Lochbuy), Lady Maclean being an older sister of Sir Allan. Lunch was taken at the home of a Dr Maclean – 'in this country,' says Johnson, 'every man's name is Maclean' – and after what Boswell called 'a very tedious ride, through what appeared to me the most gloomy and desolate country I had ever beheld', they reached Lochbuie (Johnson says 'without any difficulty') between seven and eight in the evening. The laird's fame had preceded him, and though hearty and garrulous, he proved not the Falstaffian figure they had been led to expect; 'rough and haughty', Johnson calls him, 'and tenacious of his dignity.' Warned to attend Johnson's deafness, but getting his man utterly wrong, the laird yelled, 'Are you of the Johnstons of Glencro, or of Ardnamurchan?' Boswell says that Johnson gave Lochbuie 'a significant look'.

Were the Macleans of Lochbuie initially disappointed in the famous Dr Johnson? Exhausted after the day's hard travel, and possibly with the accumulation of hardships, Johnson went to bed early, leaving Boswell to hold the conversational fort. None the less, Johnson had said enough already to impress Lady Lochbuie, who told Boswell next morning before breakfast that she thought Johnson 'a dungeon of wit'. (When Boswell reported the conversation to Johnson later, he had to take some pains to assure Sam that this was a well-known form of compliment.) To Sir Allan's intense irritation, the hostess also suggested that they have cold sheep's-head for breakfast. Boswell joined forces with her 'from a mischievous love of sport', and she desisted only when Johnson, who came in later, 'confirmed his refusal in a manner not to be misunderstood'.

After breakfast, they looked at Moy, the castle of Lochbuie, and at the dungeon where, taking the law into his own hands, the laird had imprisoned people some years before. The legal authorities in Scotland, Boswell's father among them, had fined him and made him release them; smilingly, he now acknowledged to Boswell Lord Auchinleck's say in the matter.

Johnson uses Moy castle at Lochbuie as a point of departure for a discussion of castles in Scotland. As if describing Austria or Transylvania, he tells his readers the height, composition and defensive facilities. He discusses the social history of the castle, the behaviour of the chieftains who commissioned and occupied them, and he drew conclusions to paint a lawless age, 'fierce with habitual hostility, and vigilant with ignorant suspicion'. By the time Johnson got to Mull, the castle at Lochbuie had been uninhabited for a generation, and the Macleans lived in stone buildings nearby, over one door of which (it is no longer a residence) a stone plaque is still discernible: 'After leaving Moie Castle the Lochbuie family resided in this house from 1752 to 1790 and it was in this house that Dr Johnson and Mr Boswell were entertained in 1773 by John Mclaine XVII Laird of Lochbuie.'

So came their last moments among the western isles. They rode away from Lochbuie, and at last, on Friday, 22 October, went from Mull to Oban by boat, 'the bottom of which,' observed Boswell, 'was strewed with branches of trees or bushes, on which we sat,' or, in Johnson's words, 'the seat provided for our accommodation was a heap of rough brushwood.'

The crossing from Mull to Oban has more of Sir Walter Scott than Boswell or Johnson in it – glimpses of old castles on rocky necks of the sea, a large bird wheeling, the sea not as jade in colour as the bright flashing waters off Iona, but iridescent and magical. Mull, with some of the oldest rock in the world, so old it has few fossils, having been there before God created the fish of the sea and the fowl of the air, has grown richer and more planted than the desolate heathland Johnson and Boswell largely report; but it still has rain unprecedented in its inhibiting force. From the Fishnish ferry point, a long road takes the pilgrim past the Oban ferry port of Craignure and on to Iona across the Ross of Mull. Down against the sides of the high bare slopes the rain came in sheets, slanting, white-and-silver flanges, borne in great Mexican waves on the wind. For several hours, it came relentlessly by, sideways, and soon the streams of the roadside became little Niagaras of cold, brilliant-white spume.

Iona takes its prisoners by using atmosphere. I have been here before for another writing journey. A short distance from Mull by the ferry at Fionnphort, it might be a thousand miles off in the Atlantic, like a mirage. The square tower of the abbey, now a cosseted building filled with hymns, dominates the island, and there are crosses, ruins, headstones and holiness in this place of unusual confluence between the forces of legend and the history of antique religion. If Columba impressed all who saw him with the power of his prayer and self-denial, all of which contributed to his political reputation, yet this is the island where a young man, in common with many a young man in Scotland and Ireland and Wales and Cornwall, had a fairy sweetheart; and on Iona, too, in Wagnerian style, lived a smith who made for the young man a steel arrow. As long as he concealed that arrow in his garments, no foe could damage him. But one day, the hero of this little opera of oral history changed his clothes to go to a wedding. Along the way he began, as young men will, to hunt rabbits. His fairy sweetheart, jealous of the bride with whom he would dance as wedding guests do, jealous of the fact that she could not persuade her swain to join her in the faery world, killed him. Neighbours returning home next evening found his body in a grassy hollow by the shore, the face strewn with petals, the torso covered with little bright seashells.

Moy castle still stands a sulky hulk by the water; the hill yonder may turn yellow with vegetation from time to time, but not under this grey light. But the place is enchanted, with deep woods of dripping trees, and long overhung avenues leading to unseen houses amid the trees, and the quaintest post office in the realm, a shanty, almost hidden by foliage, and stone walls that suddenly forget what they are, and peter out, or collapse. Behind rises a hill where surely eagles must have flown, *Creag na h-Iolaire*, the rock or height of the eagles. To find Lochbuie you must mean to get there; it discourages unfocused travellers – and then rewards them with its long winding road, trees trailing leaves into the water. Mull has three thousand people, three and half thousand deer – sometimes to be seen swimming across one sound or another – and five thousand sheep.

I got to Oban about three weeks earlier in the autumn than they did, and on a much more luxurious boat. The water outside Oban harbour was so still, of grey satin, that each ripple from the ferry reached a destination on the shore. Iona's pull has brought commercial blood to Oban's cheeks; Christians pour through here, singing and praying their way to the holy island; odd mixture of European echoes in Oban, Norse boatnames, and a Roman Colosseum-type folly overlooking the town. The A85 faces north, then east through Connel, and at Taynuilt a small road, the B845, picks up their south-easterly spoor. Crossing the slopes by Loch Nant, the moorland was turned to gold by sunlight pouring down the hills like an elixir. The small road winds down to Kilchrenan and, near Annat (the Reverend McQueen's goddess again?), on to the shores of Loch Awe at the Taychreggan Hotel where, with suitably proportionate respect, there is a Dr Johnson *suite* – but a Boswell *room*.

They made good time from Oban, and got soaked. At the Taychreggan site, they boated across dark Loch Awe. In a hut at Portsonachan on the other side, Boswell changed some of his wet clothes, but Johnson did not, 'letting them steam before the smoky turf fire'. They then took the most direct available route, possibly a drovers' trail, to Inveraray, where their 'excellent inn' still stands, even if altered by fire since they stayed there: Johnson still did not change out of his wet clothes. Cheerful, though, at being back in good and impersonal accommodation, Johnson, whom Boswell 'had not seen taste any fermented liquor during all our travels' (wrong, Boswell: he had brandy at Dunvegan), called for a Scotch, to see 'what makes a Scotchman happy!'

Boswell got a letter from home, and one from David Garrick in London – in reply to the one he had written Garrick from Inverness, which Boswell quotes in full, and which begins, 'Here I am, and Mr [*sic*] Samuel Johnson actually with me.' The letter plays to Garrick's Shakespearean interests, with references to *Macbeth*, but Boswell also slips in the shaft of glee about his exclusivity with Johnson, who was 'in excellent spirits, and I have a rich journal of his conversation'.

Boswell wrote that letter on Sunday, 29 August and Garrick's reply, which he also quotes in full, was written on 14 September. Garrick began, 'You stole away from London, and left us all in the lurch; for we expected you at one night at the club, and knew nothing of your departure.' Does this suggest that Boswell told nobody of his tour with Johnson lest someone try to dissuade the Great Bear? What a shame Garrick wrote such a short letter: he had 'gout in the hand'.

Next morning being Sunday, they prayed – Ogden's *Sermons* again – and Johnson asked a waiter to bring him some books. He then argued with Boswell on the merits of one of the authors, James Hervey, a clergyman and Methodist activist, who had written a work called *Meditations among the Tombs*, something of a vogue a generation earlier. Hervey's style and approach call to mind those wreaths encased in glass one sees placed upon graves, and Johnson ridiculed him. Boswell claimed to have been a devotee of Hervey when young; now he conceded Johnson's skill at parody, when, dismantling Hervey's contemplation of the moon, Johnson voiced a 'Meditation on a Pudding'.

The scene may be imagined with facility in the main rooms of the Great Inn at Inveraray today. Change the furniture, remove the man in the green jumper and red face who whistled 'Rhapsody in Blue' spasmodically all through the smoked trout, and hit 'Begin the Beguine' as they brought him coffee. Accept the regimental drums above the bar; get a period costume for the lady whose spectacular conical bosom caught most of the fallout from the salad she was eating. The green walls and white cornices, the tartan coverings and the deer's head, might get by; remove the piano, and the lighting, bring in candles; take the framed sheet music of *La Bohème* and Franz Lehar off the walls and sit back within the sonorous earshot of Johnson, as he says, 'Let us seriously reflect of what a pudding is composed. It is composed of flour that once waved in the golden grain, and drank the dews of the morning; of milk pressed from the swelling udder by the gentle hand of the beauteous milk-maid, whose beauty and innocence might have commended a worse draught; who, while she stroked the udder, indulged no ambitious thought of wandering in palaces, formed no plans for the destruction of her fellow-creatures.'

On my right, a man tells his wife, 'They say there are whirlpools out near Jura,' and through the window the afternoon sunlight falls on a pretty, arched bridge.

Before lunch, Boswell raised a sticky matter: should he call and pay his respects to the Duke of Argyll in the castle a hundred yards away? He feared the Duchess might receive him coolly: Boswell had been involved in a disputed will on the opposite side to the Duchess's family. Boswell says that Johnson always behaved perfectly well when he met the aristocracy, but never courted them. Now, willing to come forward while hanging back, Johnson told Boswell, By all means go to the castle, but not before lunch, as that would look as if he were angling for an invitation to eat.

Directly after he and Johnson had lunched in the Great Inn,

Boswell walked to the castle and found the Duke at his table among gentlemen; the ladies had just withdrawn. 'I was most politely received, and gave his grace some particulars of the curious journey which I had been making with Dr Johnson. When we rose from table, the duke said to me, "I hope you and Dr Johnson will dine with us to-morrow." I thanked his grace; but told him my friend was in a great hurry to get back to London.' Boswell then had tea and was indeed frozen by the Duchess, who, 'sitting with her daughter, Lady Betty Hamilton and some other ladies, took not the least notice of me', but Boswell was 'consoled by the obliging attention of the duke'. Another stroke pulled, he went back to the Great Inn, and the pair of them spent the rest of that evening, Sunday, 24 October, in political gossip.

Next morning, one of the Inveraray clergy collected them, a brother to the Rev MacAulay they met at Cawdor manse. As Johnson meets the Duke of Argyll, Boswell says, 'I shall never forget the impression made upon my fancy by some of the ladies' maids tripping about in neat morning dresses.' The Duke arranged for them to be driven through the grounds of this, one of the most significant seats in Britain, where Johnson said, 'What I admire here, is the total defiance of expense.'

Halberds with red plumes flank the doorway; the suit of armour would fit a man five feet five inches tall. In the hallway hangs a portrait of the Duke of Cumberland, red-coated, black-cockaded, and fat-faced with protruding eyes, as ugly as I hoped the Butcher of Culloden might have looked. 'Dr Johnson took much notice of the large collection of arms, which are excellently disposed'; a lavish armaments display, the Armoury Hall, still dominates the castle, a copious arrangement of equipment for killing people. Wheels and fans of guns and halberds are fastened to the walls, the bayonets forming the hub, the muskets, fifty at a time, the spokes. Crossed claymores sit lower down; sabres occupy statue niches. On the long dining-room table sail four gold galleons and a huge silver rose bowl, watched over lifelessly by Tussaud-esque footmen in coats of cloth-of-gold brocade. Gentle baroque medallions on the walls embody such vivid representation that the stuccodores might have been the eighteenth century's photographers; Johnson did not see these embellishments: they came later. The creamy rooms provide a silken oasis in a castle whose principal historical atmosphere is arrogantly punitive.

The Duke sat beside Johnson, and Boswell first passed the dishes to the cold Duchess, then pushed his luck by raising his glass to her and, against the fashion of the day, toasting her. He says it was 'perhaps, rather too much; but some allowance must be made for human feelings'. She made no such concessions. When Johnson answered her query as to the lateness of their trip – 'You know Mr Boswell must attend the Court of session and it does not rise till the twelfth of August' – the Duchess replied, 'I know nothing of Mr Boswell' (and someone else muttered, 'She knew too much of Mr Boswell'). Boswell says that to be thus punished by such a beautiful and dignified woman was like being strangled by a silken cord.

He cannot have reported the conversation at Inveraray fully; the few uncompelling exchanges conflict with his remark that 'Dr Johnson talked a great deal and was so entertaining that Lady Betty Hamilton, after dinner, went and placed her chair close to his, leaned upon the back of it and listened eagerly. It would have made a fine picture to have drawn the Sage and her at this time in their several attitudes.'

Johnson says even less. 'At last we came to Inverary, where we found an inn not only commodious but magnificent. The difficulties of peregrination were now at an end. Mr Boswell has the honour of being known to the Duke of Argyle, by whom we were very kindly entertained at his splendid seat, and supplied with conveniences for surveying his spacious parks and rising forests.' Gainsborough painted the fifth duke, who according to his dates must have been Johnson's host: a handsome man, long-nosed and not unkindly. Neither Boswell nor Johnson discusses the Duke's politics, nor the Argyll political history, with its many twists and turns. Their host's father fought with Cumberland at Culloden; the Argyll soldiers, Royal and loyal Scots Campbells, stood in the front line; to add insult to injury, they wore clan clothing of plaid, kilt, and bonnet.

When he lunched with the Duke of Argyll, Johnson had therefore encountered both sides of the Stuart cause. At Kingsburgh, when he arose the morning after his night in the tartan-curtained

bed in which Bonnie Prince Charlie had slept, Johnson told
Boswell that he would have given 'a good deal rather than not
have lain in that bed'. Boswell also found in the room 'a slip of
paper, on which Dr Johnson had written with his pencil these
words: *Quantùm cedat virtutibus aurum'*. Boswell translates, 'With
virtue weighed, what worthless trash is gold.' (Ben Jonson had
written, 'Whilst that for which all virtue now is sold,/And almost
every vice – almighty gold.') Boswell adds a footnote to the effect
that when his *Journal* was published 'an ingenious friend' suggested
that Johnson's pencilled Latin tag referred to the £30,000 reward
on the Pretender's head during the Jacobite rebellion. This suggests a greater warmth on Johnson's part to the Jacobites than
Boswell explicates, or perhaps than Johnson would have wished
people to know. Boswell had already established the contrast: 'To
see Dr Samuel Johnson, the great champion of the English Tories,
salute Miss Flora Macdonald in the Isle of Skye, was a striking
sight' – and then he slips in the thought of both being 'somewhat
congenial in their notions.'

As to his own sympathies, even if he ran with the hare and
hunted with the hounds, what Boswell does not say has as much
value as his actual words. He evidently feared being labelled a
Stuart sympathiser, even though by now such affections had
become relatively safe, and already almost romantic. Yet he could
not wholly disguise his feelings on the matter, hence the long
account of Flora Macdonald's adventures. Nor did he fully conceal, notwithstanding that he only gave fleeting glimpses, his travelling companion's responses, nor did Johnson – evidently – ask
him to cut them from his *Journal*. Now, after lunch with the
Campbells – who from Inveraray Castle ran Highland spies against
the Jacobites – Boswell and Johnson said nothing political. The
family motto at Inveraray is 'Do Not Forget.'

Johnson went on to Edinburgh with Boswell, and stayed several
days there, being more dined against than dining. He had fretted
much, chafed, talked of by-passing Edinburgh in favour of taking
the mail-coach to London directly, alarming Boswell, who had
lined up yet more luminaries. From Inveraray, Johnson felt safer,
knew he was going home. On the Monday evening after that lunch,

he quarrelled with Mr MacAulay who kept interrupting him, and who, for his naive views on the difference between what people say (and may even believe) and what they do, Johnson called 'grossly ignorant of human nature, as not to know that a man may be very sincere in good principles, without having good practice'. Next morning the Duke of Argyll sent round one of his good horses to replace the little pony on which Johnson felt uncomfortable and ridiculous; Joseph Ritter said Johnson now looked 'like a bishop', and leaving Inveraray they headed north-east along the shore of Loch Fyne, then south-west over the Rest and Be Thankful where Stevenson had Alan Breck hold out his left hand to take his awkward manly leave of David Balfour.

The riding party, Johnson's spirits rising all the time, lunched at Tarbat or Tarbet at the junction of the A82 and A83, where Words-worth and Coleridge also stayed, and on to Rossdhu (Boswell calls it 'Rosedow'), now under transformation to the Loch Lomond Golf Club, then the home of Sir James Colquhoun, an industrialist who gave them a boat to explore the islands on Loch Lomond. Again they got drenched, and again Johnson enjoyed his little recurring fantasy of owning an isle: 'Had Loch Lomond been in a happier climate, it would have been the boast of wealth and vanity to own one of the little spots which it incloses, and to have employed upon it all the arts of embellishment.'

In the Colquhoun household, Johnson wrote a letter of thanks to be taken back to the Duke of Argyll; it is a model of its kind. He had undertaken to acquire for the duchess a copy of a religious book of which she had spoken.

My lord

That kindness which disposed your grace to supply me with the horse, which I have now returned, will make you pleased to hear that he has carried me well. By my diligence in the little com-mission with which I am honoured by the duchess, I will endeavour to show how highly I value the favours which I have received, and how much I desire to be thought –

My lord, Your grace's most obedient,

and most humble servant.

Saml. Johnson.

Earlier on the tour, Johnson spoke on the education of a chieftain's family, said it should be conducted as if at a court, with the girls learning 'pastry and such things from the housekeeper, and manners from my lady'. He recommended that Boswell read 'the best book that was ever written upon good breeding', Castiglione's *The Courtier*. Given his own 'ordinary' upbringing in Lichfield, it may be that Johnson learned manners from this sixteenth-century text. Baldassare Castiglione had a very Johnsonian ring to him, and it would not prove surprising had Johnson memorised Castiglione. (This is not to say that even if Johnson chewed and digested Castiglione, he could necessarily have swallowed him whole: 'It is better to be on the small side than unduly large; for men who are so huge are often found to be rather thick-headed.')

Johnson never again rode a horse in Scotland. From Rossdhu they went in the Colquhoun coach down Lomondside to Cameron, the house of the Smollett family, now a luxury hotel and country club. Johnson told Boswell that with Mr Smollett, a cousin of the more famous Tobias, he had 'more solid talk here than at any place we have been'. Boswell says that Johnson gave 'an able and eloquent discourse on the origin of evil, and on the consistency of moral evil with the power and goodness of God'. He was obviously in a religious frame of mind; his last two significant conversations, with the Duchess of Argyll and with the pious Lady Helen Colquhoun, had been of a theological nature.

At Cameron, Johnson was told that the family contemplated a monument to Tobias Smollett and that a Latin inscription had been prepared and would he cast an eye over it? According to Boswell, 'Dr Johnson sat down with an ardent and liberal earnestness to revise it, and greatly improved it by several additions and variations.' The obelisk stands in a nearby village, behind a grubby wire fence in the grounds of a school; presumably these had once been green fields in the vale of the river Leven which connects with Loch Lomond. The inscription, as amended by Johnson and with amendments to Johnson's amendments, can still be read. If Boswell has rendered Johnson's contribution accurately – his account of the inscription is uncharacteristically confusing – then the Smollett family did not accept all of Johnson's adjustments.

But it is impossible to tell; for instance, Boswell reports that he has 'happily preserved every fragment of what Dr Johnson wrote', and immediately quotes several lines as if they were the very beginning of the inscription as written by Johnson: *Quisquis ades, viator, vel mente felix, vel studiis cultus, immorare paululum memoriae Tobiae Smollett, M.D.* ('Traveller – as you draw near, whether you possess richness of intellect or whether you strive for refinement, dwell a little on the memory of Tobias Smollett, M.D.') However, the actual inscription on the obelisk begins: *Siste viator si leporis* (or *lepores*: the stone is smudged, but Boswell says *lepores*) *ingeniique venam benignam, si morum callidissimum pictorem, Unquam es miratus, immorare paululum memoriae, Tobiae Smollett, M.D.* ('Stand, traveller, if ever you be astonished at charm, genius, and abundant talent, at a painter of warmest character, dwell a little on Tobias Smollett, M.D.') Thereafter – the inscription is a long one – only a few flashes of Johnson's old Latin appear, and the whole feels not as influenced by him as Boswell would have us believe.

Nevertheless, when Johnson sat down so ardently, he exhibited a scholastic acumen not consistent with the man who told Lady Dunvegan, 'I inherited a vile melancholy from my father, which has made me mad all my life, at least not sober.' The scholarship in Johnson was extraordinary, an amazing and elastic intellect, which he directed frequently towards moral concerns. Did he flex his brain by working so much, every day some kind of moral cryptic crossword, some theological conundrum, puzzling, and figuring out, and thereby so occupying himself that he kept his famous temptations at bay, conserving his strength for his work? Perhaps – as he monkishly forsook all emotional involvement, lest he be swayed towards voluptuals, preferring to adhere to the rigour of education. Boswell's *Life* reports that Johnson himself, as a young teacher – with his wife's money he founded a school in Lichfield: it failed – had drawn up a list of ideal reading matter, with remarks such as 'Ovid's *Metamorphoses* in the morning and Caesar's *Commentaries* in the afternoon'; and, 'The Greek authors I think it best for you to read are these: Cebes, Aelian, Lucian, Xenophon (Attick), Homer (Ionic), Theocritus (Dorick), Euripides (Attick and Dorick) . . . in the study of Latin . . .

Terence, Tully, Caesar, Sallust, Nepos, Velleius Paterculus, Virgil, Horace, Phaedrus.'

Now that the notion of such education as 'general' has been lost to Western man forever, and with it a wide and bright pool of refinement has been choked with weeds, will we ever again encounter a mind so furnished in a spirit so bountiful, and a personality so lively and interested? With what late twentieth-century traveller could one range, in three months, over such a brilliantly wide ambit as Johnson's in Scotland? Witchcraft, reason, emigration, oratory, debt, responsibility, flattery, contentment, trees, trees and more trees, faith, lemons, Shakespeare, poems, cider, stockings, Jesus Christ, forgery, the disciplining of children, money, evil, gunpowder, Arabs, theatre, excise duty, feudalism, vermin (all kinds), mountains, insularity, sensation, spurs, miracles, death, Bonnie Prince Charlie, knives and forks, women who fornicate, gout, good humour, translation, Edmund Burke, the wearing of linen, cunning, etymology, duelling, literary etiquette, the humane slaughter of domestic animals, clean hair, hunting, Whigs, digging with a spade, kissing, drunkenness, threshing, thatching, night-caps (liquid and sartorial), government and the monarchy, attacks from critics, catching cold, libel, joking, Art, the landlord-tenant relationship, trade, Laplanders, dogs, sermons, luxury, good principles *vis-à-vis* faulty practice, Cromwell, Presbyterian theology, literary and antiquarian forgery, the taking of oaths, generosity and literary fame – of which Johnson said, 'It is advantageous to an author that his book should be attacked as well as praised. Fame is a shuttlecock. If it be struck only at one end of the room it will soon fall to the ground. To keep it up it must be struck at both ends.' He talked knowledgeably about tanning and butchering, about food and diet, about sermons, pugilism, duelling, ghost-writing, daggers, polygamy, gunpowder, penguins, fools, prayers and the tricks of memory, a matter which preoccupied him literarily.

In the last few pages of his *Journey*, Johnson issues a caution about the distorting effect of memory upon fact: 'He who has not made the experiment, or who is not accustomed to require rigorous accuracy from himself, will scarcely believe how much a few hours takes from certainty of knowledge, and distinctness of imagery.' A valid *caveat* – that emotion, or anything, recollected in tranquillity is usually more embellished by the imagination than controlled by record. But if Johnson hoped to plead with his readers for latitude when it came to assessing his account of Scotland, the authority of his words defeated his apologetic purpose.

A chaise, ordered by Boswell, came from Glasgow to collect them at Cameron, and they said goodbye to uneventful Mr Smollett. Excited at the prospect of getting back into 'civilisation', Johnson climbed Dumbarton Rock like a young goat. According to Boswell, Johnson throughout refused to have any acknowledgment of his age, and if they tried to treat him like an old man, he railed. Even at Iona, when shallow water kept the boat from being beached, as Boswell and Sir Allan Maclean were borne to dry land by the locals, Johnson jumped into the slack tide and waded ashore.

They stayed in the long-disappeared Saracen's Head at Glasgow, where letters awaited both. Johnson 'put a leg up on each side of the grate, and said with a mock solemnity, by way of soliloquy, but loud enough for me to hear it, "Here am I, an *English* man, sitting by a *coal* fire."' It was Friday, 28 October 1773, and Johnson, who had not received a single letter in the sixty-eight days since they went through Aberdeen on 21 August, now had six to read from Mrs Thrale. Two hours after he got to Glasgow, he wrote her a short updating letter from the Saracen's Head, but does not show that he had as yet either received or opened her letters.

From Scotland, he wrote to her fourteen times: Edinburgh, on 17 August; Banff, August the 25th; and three days later from Inverness. From Armadale in Skye he wrote on 6 September, and from Dunvegan, on the other side of the island, two letters – on the 14th and from 15 to 21 September; at Talisker on the 24th; from Ostaig on the 30th (his longest), from Mull on 15 October; back on the mainland of Scotland he wrote from Inveraray on 23 October, from Glasgow on the 28th; from Boswell's ancestral home at Auchinleck on 3 November and two final letters from Edinburgh on 12 and 18 November.

He might easily have had them published as a record of his travels, so accurately and pungently did he write. Wishing Mrs Thrale to get as close as possible to his experiences, he wrote in loose serial form. Where a long period had elapsed, he reported under the headings of the relevant dates, such as: 'Sept. 23. We removed to Talisker a house occupied by Mr Macleod, a Lieutenant colonel in the Dutch service,' and then follows a concise description of all he saw and heard there. Similar organisation appears in his reply to those six letters from Mrs Thrale; when he got to Auchinleck he wrote to her at length answering point by point, date by date, matters arising in her letters of 23 and 25 August, 8, 14 and 28 September and 7 October; then returned to his own journey: 'I am, I thank God, better than I was. I am grown very superiour [*sic*] to wind and rain.'

Mrs Thrale, his closest female friend, thereby had a pleasant and chronological account from Johnson of all his adventures, packaged in a way that she could receive them; even in his private correspondence he did his readers the courtesy of access. For example, when he wrote to her about Aberdeen and Slains, places he treated in two separate letters, the courteous preliminaries completed, he took up cleanly and exactly in the second letter where he had left off in the previous one. All neatly straddle stages of the journey – from Dunvegan, his letters cover the journey from Anoch to Raasay. Invaluably, they add little Boswellian chinks of detail. Such as: his cold made him 'too deaf to take the usual pleasure in conversation'; the Highlanders called their moorland 'mosses' and – Johnson's passion for teaching – 'Moss in Scotland, is Bog in Ireland, and Moss trooper is Bog trotter'; he knew of, but did not see, red deer and roebuck, only goats, and he believed there were 'no singing birds in the Highlands'; Peggie Boswell had warned them they would 'catch something' in Highland beds, and Lady Macdonald had told him that she and her husband came back from Skye 'scratching themselves'.

A passage in the second-longest epistle of his tour reveals, deliciously, Johnson in one particular – his difficulty with self-esteem. Half-way through the letter he interrupts himself to tell Mrs Thrale how Boswell, 'with some of his troublesome kindness', told the Macleods at Dunvegan of Johnson's birthday. Of which he did not like being reminded: 'The return of my Birthday, if I remember it, fills me with thoughts which it seems to be the general care of humanity to escape. I can now look back upon threescore and four years, in which little has been done, and little has been enjoyed, a life diversified by misery, spent part in the sluggishness of penury, and part under the violence of pain, in gloomy discontent, or importunate distress.'

The many people who knew him, and the multitudes who knew of him, would scarcely share the view that little had been done. This does not seem to have crossed Johnson's mind, nor did he want it to – because in the next sentence he reveals that this view of himself as unsuccessful, and without general fortune, acted as an engine: 'But perhaps I am better than I should have been, if I had been less afflicted.' As the letter continues, Johnson confirms that his motivation came from hope rather than reflection, from the future's promise rather than the past's achievements: 'I am hoping, and I am praying that I may live better in the time to come, whether long or short, than I have yet lived, and in the solace of that hope endeavour to repose.'

Johnson found Glasgow, like Edinburgh, not suitable for treatment: 'To describe a city so much frequented as Glasgow, is unnecessary.' Boswell had again sold tickets, so to speak, for Johnson's performances, and they met professors a-plenty. It did not go entirely well. After lunch and tea at the Saracen's Head (who *paid* for all this?) Boswell went off to write a letter, and left Johnson in the company of a couple of printer/publishers who, 'instead of listening to the dictates of the Sage, teazed [*sic*] him with questions and doubtful disputations'. Johnson, 'in a flutter', rushed off to find Boswell, who accused him mockingly of seeking refuge – to which Johnson replied, 'It is of two evils choosing the least.' Boswell's *apologia* for this treatment of Johnson says that, 'Though good and ingenious men, they had that unsettled speculative mode of conversation which is offensive to a man regularly taught at an English school and university.'

There may have been more to it than that. Johnson's opinions, expressed liberally in Scotland, did not flatter his host country. When he published his *Journey to the Western Islands*, the counter-attacks began, and contemporary Gaelic writers wrote vicious satires, later collected by folklorists:

> You are a slimy, yellow-bellied frog,
> You are a toad crawling along the ditches,
> You are a lizard of the waste,
> You are a filthy caterpillar of the stool;
> You are an ugly, soft, sluggish snail . . .
> You are the chicken in the midst of corruption,
> The badger with its nose up its arse
> Three quarters of a year.

One writer, a clergyman, gathered these rants and in assembling them, added to the attack. He quoted Johnson's remark that before the Union of Parliaments, Scottish tables had been 'as coarse as the feasts of Eskimoes, and their houses as filthy as the cottages of Hottentots'. The reverend gentleman said, not without a point, 'Anyone who has ever seen the Doctor in the act of feeding, or beheld the inside of his cell in Fleet Street, would consider the feasts of Eskimoes and the cottages of Hottentots injured by comparison.' Others reportedly painted Johnson's name and portrait on the interiors of their chamber-pots.

Glasgow had set a negative tone. They stayed Thursday and Friday nights and set out on Saturday down into Ayrshire, a detour planned so that Johnson could meet Boswell's father at Auchinleck. This had been carefully mapped out in the manse at Cawdor, where Boswell had to take a decision to get to Auchinleck before his father went to sit on the bench of the northern circuit on 18 September – which proved impractical; or aim to get to Auchinleck after 10 October, by which time the judge would have returned. They lunched on Saturday at Loudoun castle, in the wooded countryside outside Kilmarnock; the castle, still a splendid romantic ruin, bears a plaque commemorating the forces it housed in the last world war. That night they put up at the house of Mr and Mrs Campbell, Peggie Boswell's sister.

The only remarkable feature of these two days was that Johnson met two exceptional old ladies – one, the Countess mother of the Earl of Loudoun, was 95; the other, Susanna, Countess of Eglintoune was in her eighty-fifth year (Johnson says 83). 'Her figure,' says Boswell, 'was majestic, her manners high-bred, her reading extensive, and her conversation elegant.' He did not report her fully. Six feet tall in her prime, she washed her face every day in sow's milk, and kept a portrait of Bonnie Prince Charlie where she could see it first thing every morning. Her hobby had moved from running literary salons to taming and training rats; guests – but not Johnson or Boswell – reported seeing her tap the panelling of the dining-room as she sat to dinner, at which a dozen rats would emerge to be fed at her feet, then retreat into the wainscoting: she claimed they were the only creatures who ever showed her gratitude. She told Johnson she had been married the year before he was born, was old enough to be his mother, and therefore she now adopted him. He wrote to Mrs Thrale that the countess called Boswell 'the boy, yes, Madam, said I, we will send him to school. He is already, said she, in a good school, and expressed her hope of his improvement.' We may assume from Boswell's observation – 'my friend was much pleased with this day's entertainment' – that Johnson beamed.

Boswell's father built Auchinleck House, and cannily spread the construction slowly over a number of years, so that he hardly felt the expense. In excellent land, the grounds contain rugged features, such as a dangerous ravine egregious in such rich loamland. Another James Boswell, descendant of the biographer through David Boswell, James's younger brother, lives nearby; Auchinleck House, beautiful and symmetrical, though with much water damage internally, has recently been taken over by the National Trust of Scotland, and sealed, pending renovation. In a chaise hired from the nearest town, Kilmarnock, Johnson and Boswell arrived in time for lunch on Tuesday, 2 November. They stayed until they caught the post-chaise to Edinburgh on the following Monday, and the visit proved unpleasant, especially for Boswell who had to watch an altercation between his dear friend and his father. Lord Auchinleck was a year older than Johnson, and the two sexagenarians quarrelled so vigorously that Boswell refuses to give it anything but a distressed mention.

He had anticipated it; before they went to Auchinleck, aware of his father's prejudices, Boswell begged Johnson to avoid three topics – Whiggism, Presbyterianism and Sir John Pringle, President of the Royal Society, a close friend of Lord Auchinleck. Johnson, who loathed Pringle and thought him deranged, none the less said to Boswell upon this request, 'I shall certainly not talk on subjects which I am told are disagreeable to a gentleman under whose roof I am; especially, I shall not so to your father.'

Two out of the three topics came up – and went wrong; a few pages later, Boswell reports, 'In the course of their altercation, Whiggism and Presbyterianism, Toryism and Episcopacy, were terribly buffeted. My worthy hereditary friend, Sir John Pringle, never having been mentioned, happily escaped without a bruise.'

Before the argument, all had gone well. Lord Auchinleck owned a good library with a private collection of 'curious editions of the Greek and Roman classics'. Johnson even found a book he had long sought, an *Anacreon* by Richard Baxter, a clergyman writer of the previous century whose works Johnson praised without exception. So far, so good, despite the rain lashing outside. Some visitors came – to see Lord Auchinleck, rather than Johnson. One of them irritated Johnson by asking him how he liked the Highlands? 'How, sir,' he replied, 'can you ask me to speak unfavourably of a country where I have been hospitably entertained? Who *can* like the Highlands? I like the inhabitants very well.' Ouch.

Boswell's *Journal* has grown thinner since Oban – tiredness, shortage of paper, apprehension of his father? He reports one remark of Johnson's at Auchinleck which puzzles a little for its inconsistency. 'He this day, when we were by ourselves [Wednesday, 3 November] observed how common it was for people to talk from books; to retail the sentiments of others and not their own; in short, to converse without any originality of thinking. He was pleased to say, "You and I do not talk from books."'

Yet time out of number, Johnson refers to, and wrote about, and quotes from – books, usually as a means of drawing on literary opinion to furnish his own thoughts. He worked as a reviewer (beginning a critique of Blackwell's *Memoirs of the Court of Augustus* with the sentence, 'The first effect which this book has upon the reader is that of disgusting him with the author's vanity'). Johnson wrote Shakespearean prefaces, drew from all writers everywhere for his *Dictionary* definitions, became famous for his *Lives of the*

Poets. Therefore, if it may justly be claimed, as Boswell did, that when passing literary opinion Johnson brought the proceedings of his own mind to bear, it still remains too sweeping of Johnson to say he did not 'talk from books'.

Thursday, a fine day, enabled Boswell to show his great friend the grounds at Auchinleck. Now greatly overgrown, the place stll abounds in the red rock Johnson described. He devotes four paragraphs in his last three pages to his stay here, and manages to pay compliments to Boswell's father: 'He has built a house of hewn stone, very stately and durable, and has advanced the value of his lands with great tenderness to his tenants.' Boswell showed him the old castle which had a drawbridge, scene of bloody encounters of yore, they found the traces of the ancient chapel, and the day went well with no foreboding.

The trouble seems really to have begun with the arrival on the scene of the local minister, a Mr Dun, who insisted that Boswell and Johnson go to lunch with him. He then proceeded to give Johnson offence by referring to the clergy of the Church of England as 'fat bishops and drowsy deans'. Johnson told him, 'Sir, you know no more of our church than a Hottentot.' Then, with Johnson already warmed up, came the row with Lord Auchinleck, which so upset Boswell that he could not remember whether it broke on the Friday or the Saturday.

The old judge was showing Johnson his collection of medals, 'and Oliver Cromwell's coin unfortunately introduced Charles the First and Toryism. They became exceedingly warm, and violent, and I was very much distressed by being present at such an altercation between two men, both of whom I reverenced; yet I durst not interfere.' No more, that is all. Boswell, the comprehensive reporter, the copious informant, tells us nothing else – deliberately so: 'It would certainly be very unbecoming in me to exhibit my honoured father, and my respected friend, as intellectual gladiators, for the entertainment of the public, and therefore I suppress what would, I dare say, make an interesting scene in this dramatic sketch.' Poor Boswell, caught between an eagle and a lion: no matter how he wrote it, he would have had to come down on one side or the other, and he kept his silence even when both had died. That it depressed him profoundly may be gathered from the

THE CONTEST AT AUCKINLECK.

fact that the next three entries, for the Sunday, Monday and Tuesday when they left for Edinburgh, are the shortest consecutive entries in Boswell's entire *Journal of a Tour*.

Matters between the elderly brawlers did eventually cool down; and Lord Auchinleck remembering his manners – he had, says his son, 'all the dignified courtesy of an old Baron' – civilly accompanied Johnson to the post-chaise on Monday afternoon.

In Auchinleck village, a few miles away past the coal-mines of Ayrshire, near the small museum, a vault lies, containing the body of James Boswell, who became the good laird of Auchinleck. Beneath a wide trapdoor, a precarious ladder leads to the slab in the wall, in a place with none of the usual spookiness of such tombs. Here seemed a good place to end the journey, in the equally benign presence of his descendant, James Boswell, who does not in any way, except perhaps the nose, resemble the famous biographer. Boswell was 54 years and 7 months old when he died in

London in 1795, without ever having fully grasped Johnson's wonderful advice, 'Get as much force of mind as you can. Live within your income. Always have something saved at the end of the year. Let your imports be more than your exports [income and expenditure], and you'll never go far wrong.'

Boswell concluded his *Journal of a Tour to the Hebrides* by claiming the credit for it all: 'Had it not been for me, I am persuaded Dr Johnson never would have undertaken such a journey; and I must be allowed some merit for having been the cause that our language has been enriched with such a book as that which he published on his return.' Earlier Boswell remarks, 'He said to me often that the time he spent in this tour was the pleasantest part of his life.'

Johnson ended his book with the comment, 'Having passed my time almost wholly in cities, I may have been surprised by modes of life and appearances of nature, that are familiar to men of wider survey and more varied conversation. Novelty and ignorance must always be reciprocal, and I cannot but be conscious that my thoughts on national manners, are the thoughts of one who has seen but little.'

Johnson's text, though, suggests that he fulfilled his preconceived desires to some degree; he believed that what he saw in Scotland brought him closer to the past than life in London ever did, that his Scottish destination, especially the Highlands and islands, could hardly have changed at all in over a hundred years. He once observed to Boswell that 'The value of every story depends on its being true.' Thereby, in his elegantly-arranged words, even despite his prejudices (and sometimes because of them) we see the people of Scotland, not in mere objective vision, nor simply as troubled, long-feudalised, recently bloodied adjuncts of the kingdom governed from London – but as western mankind too, in a descent from the Iron-Age Celts and compared with the civilisations of Greece and Rome. Johnson's eighteenth-century travel book of Scotland is a cultural text.

For all his occasionally vile opinions, let us praise the Great Bear for intrepidity in travelling north at all. He did not have even the comfort of much precedent for such a journey. The English love affair with Scotland had not yet quite begun; the view from

THE JOURNALIST.

the south still saw tartan bandits wielding claymores. Some painters and kindred souls had already ventured 'up there', to the place
Boswell sometimes, not inoffensively, called 'North Britain', but
in general, southern explorers had not so far amounted to the
romantic flood later inspired by Queen Victoria.

Praise Boswell, too. Ever as fussy as a little boat in the wash
of a great liner, he busied himself with everything, taking up his
position generally on the upper slopes of the trivial, the lower
slopes of the profound. Moved to tears by an old soldier's account
of the battle at Culloden, or alert to a woman 'as comely almost
as the figure of Sappho as we see it painted', or pleased to meet
Highland noblefolk who might assist his social climbing back in
Edinburgh, he began in Scotland the fleshing-out service which
ultimately rendered his *Life of Johnson* unique.

Even when he causes us to disapprove of him, Boswell has a
way of re-insinuating himself with some nugget, or ridicu-
lousness, or ludicrosity. No wonder he got the clap so often: in

his writing, too, he has a dangerously promiscuous air, too easily engaged with, seductive after Johnson's demanding rigorousness. And whatever his toadying and biographical self-interest, Boswell showed his own brand of courage: he persisted with his invitation, despite his fears that Johnson would find the company north of the Border 'insipid or irksome. I doubted that he would not be willing to come down from his elevated state of philosophical dignity; from a superiority of wisdom among the wise, and of learning among the learned; and from flashing his wit upon minds bright enough to reflect it.'

A journey in their wake constitutes a marvellous introduction to them – and so captivatingly and lovingly to Johnson that it calls to mind his remark: 'He who praises everybody praises nobody' (or, as Boswell might have noted it down, 'He who prs's evr'bdy prs's nbdy'). Few literary companions, on such short acquaintance, prove so instructive. One of the earliest tasks I gave myself was an attempt to edit Johnson: I copied out several pages and soon realised that he could get more meaning and ideas into fewer words than many poets: most of the time a razor's edge will not slide between, or slim, his phrases. This excellence, his elegance and economy, his power and originality, and his heart's tenderness, and his wisdom – all go a long way towards excusing his irascibility, his indifferent hygiene, his often reprehensible manners (yet he thought himself 'a polite man'), his loftiness, his pomposity, even his xenophobia (racism, to give it its full name) which justified the heated contempt of the Scottish Gaels.

In the end, far from the little knowledge and cursory, irritated awareness of Johnson I possessed when setting out, I now find, as Macaulay did, 'in the foreground [of my mind] . . . that strange figure which is as familiar to us as the figures of those among whom we have been brought up, the gigantic body, the huge massy face, seamed with the scars of disease, the brown coat, the black worsted stockings, the grey wig with the scorched foretop, the dirty hands, the nails bitten and pared to the quick'.

On the evidence of his *Journey to the Western Islands of Scotland* it looks as if Samuel Johnson, like William Shakespeare and James Joyce, attempted to touch most corners of human experience. If he did not write upon a subject (and from my limited knowledge of him, I do not yet know how much he covered), Johnson talked about it. He looked hard at life, and was not easily fooled, unlike his admired Thomas Pennant who, on his Scottish tour, overcome by the literary blandishments of James Macpherson's *Fingal*, saw an ancient warrior floating in the air before him wielding a claymore. Such a digression from the sensible did not affect Johnson's opinion of Pennant, and ultimately this is the Great Bear's finest characteristic – his capacity for latitude, his understanding of the self-redemptive balance in human beings, as in Goldsmith, whom many considered an idiot, but whose innocence Johnson perceived, knowing, as he did, that writing is not so much what the writer does technically, as what he is spiritually. Which is why, as Robert Louis Stevenson remarked, Johnson 'retained after death the art of making friends'.

AFTERWORD

WHEN JOHNSON RETURNED TO LONDON he began without delay to write his *Journey to the Western Isles of Scotland*. He obviously trusted his own spirit and learning, or was able to think at great speed, or both. Remember that he had not contemplated turning the adventure into a book until he found himself deep in the west of Scotland. Now I discover that not only had he taken no time to prepare for writing a text before he went north, he also exercised comparatively little reflection when he came back: the book he was to write emanated from discovery and immediate response to it.

So I am looking upon a man who went forth as a tourist and returned as a traveloguist, a superior one admittedly, yet a professional, jobbing writer: Johnson knew that a traveller's tale bearing his name would find a ready public. This also stimulates the thought that those Scots who hated him for what he wrote may have had a point: that too many of Johnson's descriptions, however enjoyable and rich they now seem to us, must have sounded too superficial for them to bear. He wrote his Scottish book in a matter of months, and he meant to do so: he commenced work on the day after he returned to London, 27 November 1773. In his very first thank-you letter to Boswell, he concluded by asking him, 'Enquire, if you can, the order of the Clans: Macdonald is first, Maclean second; further I cannot go. Quicken Dr Webster' – who had promised to send Johnson some documentation on the Highlands and islands.

Throughout the next year, Johnson gave progress reports, or advanced the book's cause and information by sending other enquiries to Boswell. At the end of January he wrote, 'send me what intelligence you can: and if anything is too bulky for the post, let me have it by the carrier.' He also asked Boswell to send a box of souvenirs he and Johnson had gathered, including a small collection of horn spoons, and some branches of broom from the grounds of Auchinleck. In reverse, he told Boswell to make some enquiries regarding the most effective way of sending gifts of porter to people they had met in the Hebrides.

From his friend in Hampstead, George Steevens, the leading Shakespearean commentator of the day, Johnson requested 'Lesley's *History of Scotland*, or any other book about Scotland, except Boethius and Buchanan'. Then a letter to Boswell, dated 21 June 1774, begins, 'Yesterday I put the first sheets of the Journey to the Hebrides to the press. I have endeavoured to do you some justice in the first paragraph [the reference, presumably, to his remarks, 'finding in Mr Boswell a companion, whose acuteness would help my inquiry, and whose gaiety of conversation and civility of manners are sufficient to counteract the inconveniencies of travel']. It will be one volume in ocatavo, not thick.' A fortnight later, on 5 July, the very day he set out for Wales with the Thrales to visit Hester's birthplace near Caernarvon where she was to take possession of a legacy she had received, Johnson writes to Boswell 'I have just begun to print my Journey to the Hebrides . . .' This means that between his return in late November and the middle of the following June, Johnson started and finished the book, an economically written and stylish work of fifty thousand words.

He took great care with the protocol surrounding publication. 'It will be proper,' he wrote to Boswell, 'to make some presents [of the book] in Scotland. You shall tell me to whom I shall give; and I have stipulated twenty-five for you to give in your own name.' Regret was expressed that the distance between London and Edinburgh did not permit Boswell to have a copy of the book in proof form, and on 16 September Johnson says, 'I purpose now to drive the book forward' – as he had done throughout the year. On 1 October, back from almost three months in Wales, he chided Boswell for appending *aides-mémoires* to the list of names in Scotland to whom Johnson wanted to send copies of the Journal: 'I am not pleased with the notes of remembrance added to your names, for I hope I shall not easily forget them.' On 26 November 1774, a year to the day after he returned to London, he wrote to Boswell, 'Last night I corrected the last page of our Journey to the Hebrides. The printer detained it all this time, for I had before I went into Wales, written all except two sheets.'

The fact that he only decided to write it while *en route* accounts for some omissions of comment Johnson might have been expected to make – for example, that lack of observation on Strichen and the whole concept of the 'planned village'. His reluctance to discuss Culloden, whose borders he trod, now comes into focus for another reason, clearer after publication than before. He sent an early copy of his *Journey* to the King (George III), via a friend, Dr Hunter, who had asked, and to whom Johnson wrote, 'I am very much obliged by your willingness to present my book to His Majesty. I have not courage to offer it myself, yet I cannot forbear to wish that He may see it, because it endeavours to describe a part of his Subjects, seldom visited, and little known . . .'

Johnson would have known that any sympathetic discussion of the Jacobites must have met with royal disfavour, even perhaps (Johnson may have feared) affected his pension, and if he could not discuss the events of 1745/6 sympathetically, perhaps he preferred not to discuss them at all. Certainly the King's opinion mattered to him, however he disparaged the Hanoverians. Within days of despatching the book to the royal household, Johnson wrote in a kind of abashed glee to Mrs Thrale, 'You must not tell any body but Mr Thrale that the King fell to reading the book as soon as he got it, and when any thing struck him, he read aloud to the Queen, and the Queen would not stay to get the King's book, but borrowed Dr Hunter's.' Such nursery rhyme success, even if Johnson thought to keep it confidential, set the book on its way, and ensured that his friendly readers echoed his own opinion of his favourite travel writer, Pennant, and read it only for what was in it and not for what Johnson might have left out. (Incidentally, having sworn Mrs Thrale to secrecy, Johnson then tells Boswell in a letter, 'I sent one to the King and I hear he likes it.')

When he wrote to Boswell, telling him his copy had now been despatched, Johnson asked, 'Let me know as fast as you read it, how you like it; and let me know if any mistake is committed, or any thing important left out.' Boswell's response contained the two principal, not unendearing, types of response I have come to expect of him – adulation and self-inclusion. He received his copy four days later, on 18 January 1775, and next day he wrote to Johnson, 'Though ill of a bad cold, you kept me up the greatest part of the last night; for I did not stop till I had read every word of your book. I looked back to our first talking of a visit to the Hebrides, which was many years ago, when sitting by ourselves in the Mitre tavern in London, I think about *witching time o'night*; and then exulted in contemplating our scheme fulfilled, and a *monumentum perenne* of it erected by your superior abilities. I shall only say, that your book has afforded me a high gratification. I shall afterwards give you my thoughts on particular passages.' Then he corrects two errors: 'In page 106, for *Gordon* read *Murchison*; and in page 357, for *Maclean* read *Mcleod*.' In the meantime Johnson had written another letter which crossed Boswell's: 'I long to hear how you like the book; it is, I think, much liked here.'

Strahan, Johnson's printer, brought out and sold out four thousand copies of the book. One might consider that a distinguished result, given the population and slender literacy of the time: four thousand copies of a hardback travel book today constitutes a respectable sale. Johnson felt disappointed that he had not sold more, 'for in that book,' he said to Boswell, 'I have told the world a great deal that they did not know before.'

When Boswell next travelled south in late March, he found Johnson's book 'the common topic of conversation in London at this time, wherever I happened to be'. A variety of factors helped to keep the book alive in Johnson's circle. Johnson himself cannot have been backward in answering questions about his adventure. Some of the reaction to his anti-Scottish sentiments and opinions must by then have filtered south. Other subject matter raised enquiries: his own *milieu*, the Literary Club, had aired doubts to Boswell over Johnson's seemingly naive willingness to believe in instances he cited of 'second sight'. Most of all in the broader marketplace, and especially in Scotland, Johnson's spiky denunciation of James Macpherson's poems had re-heated the Ossian debate: 'I believe they never existed in any other form than that which we have seen. The editor, or author, could never show the original; nor can it be shown by any other; to revenge reasonable incredulity, by refusing evidence, is a degree of insolence, with which the world is not yet acquainted; and stubborn audacity is the last refuge of guilt.' Macpherson, who feared such an assault, had launched a pre-emptive strike – he claimed that he had offered Johnson sight of the originals, and suggested in public that Johnson also 'take the evidence of people skilled in the Erse language'. Boswell reported all of this to Johnson.

Macpherson then wrote to Johnson, and he must have issued some physical threat, because in Johnson's reply, which he sent to the newspapers, he says, 'Any violence offered me, I shall do my best to repel; and what I cannot do for myself the law will do for me. I hope I shall never be deterred from detecting what I think a cheat, by the menaces of a ruffian.' Johnson, who had bought a heavy stick just in case, piled it on. 'What would you have me retract? I thought your book an imposture, I think it an imposture still.' There was more – 'what I hear of your morals inclines me to pay regard not to what you shall say, but to what you shall prove,' and Johnson confirmed to Boswell that Macpherson 'never in his life offered me the sight of any original or any evidence of any kind'.

Through all of the aftermath of publication the Ossian and Macpherson question ran like a turbulent melody. Some division of opinion remained, especially in Scotland where Macpherson, whatever doubts had been aired, continued to have supporters, or at the very least, people who had not yet made up their minds to come down against him. Macpherson had a number of factors working for him – Scottish sympathies, antipathies towards Englishmen, a hankering after some antique and romantic Celtic identity, and thereby a claim to have a culture older than the Mediterranean. For instance, Lord Hailes, whom Johnson dearly liked, told Boswell he proposed to keep out of the way of the controversy.

Boswell himself had to take a position. He reveals in his *Life of Johnson* that he had been among 'those who subscribed to enable their editor, Mr Macpherson, then a young man, to make a search in the Highlands and Hebrides for a long poem in the Erse language, which was reported to be preserved somewhere in those regions'. Admitting that he contributed to the fund, he then claims to have been uneasy about the verses as they eventually appeared, even though he had earlier been captivated: 'When the fragments of Highland poetry first came out, I was much pleased with their wild peculiarity.' In February 1775, he wrote to Johnson, evidently uncomfortable at Johnson's heated repudiations of Macpherson. Borrowing from someone to whom he had recently been speaking, Boswell produced an argument that Macpherson did in fact get hold of at least one ancient Celtic manuscript, perfectly capable of being dated accurately by men skilled in the study thereof, and he concluded that if those *mss* could be claimed by such men to be 'the works of a remote age, I think we should be convinced of their testimony'.

Johnson wrote back with thunder in his ink and lightning in his pen: 'You then are going wild about Ossian. Why do you think any part can be proved?' and, notwithstanding Boswell's claim that fair scholars had agreed some authentication, insists, 'There are, I believe, no Erse manuscripts. None of the families has a single letter in Erse that we heard of . . . Do not be credulous; you know how little a Highlander can be trusted. Macpherson is, so far as I know, very quiet. Is that not proof enough? Every thing is against him. No visible manuscript; no inscription in the language: no correspondence among friends . . . If he had not talked unskilfully of *manuscripts*, he might have fought with oral tradition much longer . . .'

Over a long period, the Ossian issue abated without firm conclusion. Macpherson, a farmer's son, then a village schoolteacher, prospered, became a merchant, then a member of Parliament. Later, students of the controversy formed the view that Macpherson had recorded a small core of traditional Gaelic verse from the oral tradition but had then constructed many more in the same idiom to carry the originals forward.

In his *Life of Johnson*, Boswell calls the *Journey* 'a most valuable performance'. Justifying the comments which had given Scotland offence – and in Edinburgh Boswell was on hand to hear the condemnations first-hand – he says that Johnson bore no illwill towards the Scots, that had he done so, 'he would never have thrown himself into the bosom of their country'. And then we get some idea from the *Life* of how heatedly Johnson's book had been received, when Boswell says 'Johnson's grateful acknowledgments of kindnesses received in the course of this tour, completely refute the brutal reflections which have been thrown out against him.' He also introduces the novel suggestion that had they, the criticisers, only read Johnson's more open remarks in the letters to Mrs Thrale, they would truly have had something to complain about. It was that old excuse of the tabloid newspapers: 'If you think what we publish is bad, you should see what we don't publish.' Boswell goes on to say that 'all the miserable cavillings against his *Journey*, in newspapers, magazines, and other fugitive publications, I can speak from certain knowledge, only furnished him with sport.'

Having brought with him to London 'a great bundle of Scotch magazines and newspapers, in which his *Journey to the Western Islands* was attacked in every mode', Boswell read them aloud to Johnson and together they regretted the poor standard of the attackers' prose. One, a parody, received some of Johnson's approval: 'This (said he,) is the best. But I could caricature my own style much better myself.' Unitedly, the Scottish commentators objected to his attitude, his loftiness, his dismissals, his comments on the 'general insufficiency of education in Scotland', leading Johnson to re-affirm his opinion: 'Their learning is like bread in a besieged town: every man gets a little, but no man gets a full meal.'

The row over Johnson's remarks about Scotland seethed so heatedly that Boswell, a decade later, felt obliged to enter several pages of justification of Johnson when he published his *Life*. To do so, he drew upon the correspondence and testimonials of several witnesses who found Johnson's *Journey* 'true', 'correct', 'judicious', 'instructive', full of 'sound judgment', and possessed of 'accuracy' and 'precision' and 'justness', and 'respecting both the country and the people'. One correspondent even added how he had visited Raasay and found all there full of praise and love for Johnson. Another, with some ambiguity, said that 'Johnson treated Scotland no worse than he did even his best friends, whose characters he used to give as they appeared to him, in light and shade.'

Lord Monboddo read the *Journey* and chose to admire the Iona passages while generally condemning Johnson's language as too rich and metaphorical. Sir Alexander Dick read it and, as we have seen, congratulated Johnson for having caused the planting of millions of trees across Scotland. One of Boswell's Scottish friends, George Dempster, a lawyer and parliamentarian (whose sister had failed to teach Johnson the craft of knotting), found 'nothing amiss in the book', and, agreeing to be charmed by it, argued that, 'Upon the whole, the book cannot displease, for it has no pretensions. The author neither says he is a geographer, nor an antiquarian, nor very learned in the history of Scotland, nor a naturalist, nor a fossilist. The manners of the people, and the face of the country, are all he attempts to describe, or seems to have thought of.'

Boswell's version of the Hebridean adventure took longer to prepare. Apart from the notes he had taken so copiously while they travelled, he by no means commenced work on his own version quickly. He returned to his practice at the Scottish bar that autumn and winter. On 5 March 1774 he wrote to Johnson wondering aloud whether he should now visit London again; a shortage of cash and his wife's pregnancy gave him pause. Johnson replied in a distinction between what was useful and necessary, saying 'The reasons for which you are inclined to visit London, are, I think, not of sufficient strength to answer the objections. That you should delight to come once a year to the fountain of intelligence and pleasure, is very natural.' (And to think that Johnson had difficulty in understanding why he gave offence to the Scots! Did he ever take thought on the matter? Evidently not at all; a London newspaper recorded a reply Johnson made to an accusation; 'I do not *hate* the Scots: Sir, I do not *hate* frogs, in the water, though I confess I do not like to have them hopping about my bed-chamber.')

He pressed some more advice on Boswell; 'What improvement you might gain by coming to London you may easily supply, or easily compensate, by enjoining yourself some particular study at home, or opening some new avenue to information.' A further point still proved unpersuasive – that as Mrs Boswell 'permitted you to ramble last year, you must permit her now to keep you at home': Boswell ignored it all and came south with that armful of reviews, and thereafter, on subsequent visits to London, spent many more hours with Johnson, eventually mourning him from afar: Boswell was in Edinburgh when Johnson died on 13 December 1784, at seven o'clock on a Monday evening.

The last letter between the pair, as recorded in the *Life*, was written by Johnson on 3 November from Lichfield, where he had gone to traverse old haunts. Boswell, rampant in his emotional shiftlessness, had spent much of the year unwell; during the previous December he had contracted another bout of venereal illness, and even though he had recovered quickly, his famous melancholy was stimulated by the urethritis – and exacerbated by appalling dreams, in one of which he saw a 'poor wretch' on a dunghill in London being flayed alive by a 'blackguard ruffian' wielding a knife. Consequent upon all of this self-harassment, Boswell withdrew into deepest Edinburgh for much of the year. Johnson's letter from Lichfield begins, 'I have this summer sometimes amended, and sometimes relapsed, but, upon the whole, have lost ground very much. My legs are extremely weak, and my breath very short . . . In this uncomfortable state, your letters used to relieve; what is the reason that I have them no longer? Are you sick or are you sullen? Whatever be the reason, if it be less than necessity, drive it away; and of the short life that we have, make the best use of it for yourself and for your friends . . .'

Johnson by then felt lonelier than ever. His relationship with Hester Thrale had collapsed; when Henry Thrale died in April 1781, Hester retreated from Johnson and to his utter sadness, a bereavement as evacuating of his spirit as if she had died, she married Gabriel Piozzi, an Italian musician.

By the time Johnson wrote that sad letter from Lichfield, Boswell had almost finished assembling his own *Journal of a Tour to the Hebrides*: within a year he was ready to write a dedication – dated 20 September 1785: the book went on sale on 1 October. Enter Edward Malone, the dedicatee, a Dublin-born Shakespearean scholar, who became significant in Boswell's career and later crucial to the *Life of Johnson*. One version of their relationship had Malone encountering a page of Boswell's book at the printers and, according to Boswell's son, being so taken with a pen-portrait of Johnson that he asked for an introduction to the author. This seems odd. Malone and Dr Johnson had knowledge of, correspondence with, respect for, each other; they had Shakespeare, at least, in common. If Johnson knew Malone, how can Boswell not have? It does appear that Boswell and Malone did not become intimates until the Highland *Journal* was under way, even if they already knew each other – or else the *Journal* was at the printers for many months, giving the two men time to get acquainted before Boswell wrote his dedication. He named Malone at length as an authenticator: 'As one of those who were intimately acquainted with him . . . you have obligingly taken the trouble to peruse the original manuscript of this Tour, and can vouch for the strict fidelity of the present publication.'

The *Journal* sold out within weeks and a second edition went to the press on 20 December 1785; a third edition was published the following August. Eventually it appeared as a component volume of Boswell's *Life of Johnson*. Typically, Boswell makes a pushy claim for the *Journal*'s first impact – 'Animated by the very favourable reception which two large impressions of this work have had.' By the middle of the next paragraph, he implies a contradictory climate: he thanks those who defended the first edition and goes on to berate 'the futile remarks' caused by 'a petty national resentment', and 'the shallow or envious cavillers'. Presumably these included Thomas Rowlandson for his hooting cartoons, and Horace Walpole who called the *Journal* 'the story of a mountebank and his zany'.

The *Journal* joined what had become an instant Johnson industry. Days after Johnson's death, a printer asked Boswell whether he could assemble, and have ready within two to three months, a volume based on Johnson's conversations. Boswell refused, and declared his intention to write a detailed biography, a task he approached with some nervousness – which increased as the Johnson industry cranked itself up and began to roll. Within twelve months of Johnson's death, three biographies appeared, followed by an unflattering essay, and then came two publications much

feared by Boswell as a threat to any eventual sales of his own
Life. In March 1786, Hester Thrale, now Mrs Piozzi, produced a
collection of *Anecdotes* based on her knowledge of Johnson, for
which she received the substantial advance of £300 – and the book
sold a thousand copies in its first twenty-four hours. Exactly a
year later, in March 1787, Sir John Hawkins, one of Johnson's
circle and named by Johnson as an executor, published a full
biography. A year after that, and the year following, Hester Piozzi
published again – two volumes of letters, totalling over three
hundred items.

On each of the Hawkins and Piozzi publications Boswell went
on the offensive, most notably with an advertisement promising
his own *Life of Johnson*, which would have none of the 'light
Effusions of Carelessness and Pique [Mrs Piozzi], or the ponderous
labours of solemn inaccuracy and dark uncharitable Conjecture
[Sir John Hawkins]'.

Why did he worry so? More than one commentator has suggested that Boswell feared not rival works so much as his own
dilatoriness and indiscipline – that he might simply not manage
to write the definitive book he had planned. However, he had had
a success with the *Journal of a Tour to the Hebrides*, and as a foretaste
of the reception his *Life of Johnson* might yet have, this should
have satisfied him. But given Boswell's general emotional incom-
petence, he needed to be saved from himself whenever possible.
Here, Edward Malone's encouraging intrusion performed a valuable service to literature. Malone advised on the late stages of the
Journal, supervised the pruning, and kept Boswell on the point –
the point being Johnson in the Hebrides, not Boswell accompanied
by Johnson. Malone even saw the second edition through the
printers – and counselled a more delicate touch, including
the excision of passages which had so offended the likes of Sir
Alexander Macdonald and his wife that Boswell had almost had
to duel.

The publication of the *Journal* established Boswell at the head
and heart of the Johnson industry. If the Hawkins, Piozzi and
other lives and memoirs that appeared between Johnson's death
in 1784 and Boswell's own biography of Johnson in May 1791,
worried Boswell, they also spurred him to write his own great

work. Malone would superintend, and working together they eventually guaranteed the *Life*'s definitiveness.

Boswell gave up his practice at the Scottish Bar in 1786, a year after the Hebridean *Journey* appeared, and moved down to London. His wife joined him, in circumstances less salubrious than those in their Court off the Royal Mile. Jamie continued his grim and melancholic romps with the inevitable venereal results. Margaret's bronchial complaints had intensified, and in 1789 she died of the pulmonary tuberculosis that had been slowly overwhelming her for more than a decade. No wife, no wise old mentor on hand, Boswell's life declined, and he was bound increasingly to drink. Even the great and deserved success of the *Life* when it appeared – the King called it 'the most entertaining book he had ever read' – did not halt his thick slow downward spiral. Malone, advising all through the writing and the diligent rewriting, became increasingly involved in the second edition published two years later, in 1793, and took total responsibility for the third edition in 1799. By then Boswell was four years dead. He had managed not to capitalise, either in reputation or enhancement of behaviour, upon the literary status brought to him by the success of the *Life of Johnson*; he did not use its good outcome to anchor his existence. In June 1793, drunk, he was beaten up late at night; the watchmen took him home. On and on he racketed, seeking more and more outrageously to elevate himself, even attempting to claim a Royal Appointment to Biography, while his life ran counter to his grand words. In April 1795, he collapsed at a dinner of the Literary Club, and was carried home, feverish and vomiting. His body had taken too much of a hammering from the life he had given it – gonorrhoea, urethritis, liver assault from egregious drinking – and Boswell died in his bed at two o'clock in the morning of 19 May 1795, in his 55th year.

Other than Shakespeare or Joyce, not many figures might repay so handsomely the investigations of an inquirer who set out knowing so little about them. Stevenson, perhaps, and Coleridge, as Richard Holmes has so exquisitely shown: Wordsworth, however lovely and profound his verses, feels too forbidding; Hazlitt too coarse a companion, though endlessly lively; Byron too competitive; Dickens too diverse. These are conceits, however, and give me a moment of amusement, as I bask in the delight I have now found in the footsteps of Dr Johnson and the shadows of Mr Boswell. Likewise, the scholars whose works educated me, when I needed more than the adventures of the two men in Scotland, have not in their rigorousness daunted my enjoyment. On the contrary: it seems as if all Johnson scholarship – or the range of it I have seen – feels under some obligation to write as engagingly as Johnson himself advised, and upon which he insisted. This, therefore, has been a journey full of bonuses – Johnson, Boswell and the country of Scotland, and Stevenson and Scott, and David Thomson and John Prebble – and, afterwards, sundry biographers, historians, interpreters, novelists, poets, bards, hermits, pipers, lairds, tacksmen and Jacobites.

My mind is full of images: imagining Margaret Boswell in Edinburgh in that above-*bourgeois* house, rising to her husband's occasion with her irritableness dutifully suppressed; sundry gentlemen stepping into the hallway, then greeting the Great Bear; Johnson and acolytes in the cobbled arena of Parliament Square, with Boswell ever beaming. The imagination may follow them like a cameraman, because so many of the buildings they saw stand intact: Johnson, too, peered up at the royal ceilings in Holyrood.

From the moment they moved out and northwards, lively diversions began in earnest. Boswell at Leith tried to 'scottify' Johnson's palate by bringing him 'speldings, fish (generally whitings) salted and dried in a particular manner, being dipped in the sea and dried in the sun'. Big Sam did not enjoy. It rained on me in Leith, not much, enough to send me into a pub for an early lunch, where I met a girl who, as she served lentil soup and brown bread, told me she was 'a bonny quinie' and that I was a 'loon'. From Aberdeenshire, she spoke the Doric dialect, and she, the *quinie*, was female and I, the *loon*, male, not, disappointingly, a madman, nor, higher chagrin, a whistling lake bird from North America. I could see through the window of the pub a grey stencilled minesweeper on Leith water; outside the door floated a restaurant called The African Queen. Of all the gin-joints in all the world. The P & O vessel, *St Magnus*, waited at the quay, reminding me of Orkney and the poet George Mackay Brown. A year ago in Stromness, with the wind howling down his chimney, this most gentle gentleman recalled the brightness of the pennies he was given as a child when the summer fair came to 'Hamnavoe', as he called it in his writings, and since we were talking of childhood it seemed only fair to tell him that when I stopped a group of boys playing on the street to ask where he lived, they had never heard of 'Mr Mackay Brown', but all lit up when I mentioned that his first name was 'George'.

Some of these pubs in Leith stay open until the early hours of the morning, a facility of profound comfort since the days of trawlermen and deep-sea sailors. In this, Leith has the atmosphere of a continental port full of Norwegian sea-captains out of *Finnegans Wake*. The faces of Leith were softer than those of London, more air and space in them. On my left, a thin man, looking drained but content, sat with a woman who wore a white terylene blouse and no rings on her fingers; she had iron-grey abundant hair pinnned wandering yet firm, like a fifties *coiffure*; her heavy voice was much thicker and rougher than her rather sweet expression; her body and legs suggested that she had 'former Tiller girl' potential. Leaning back, I heard a conversation between other lunchers. 'What I cannae understand is why she cannae touch the point. It's too hot for her.' It transpires, tempering my lubricious curiosity, that they are discussing overtime and their overseer's attitude to it.

On the *terra firma* of Fife across the Firth, a field of stubble blazed with a thousand little fires in the light of an afternoon near Kinghorn, and some minutes later, the longest V-skein of wild duck I have ever seen, came swoop-stringing across the sky, looking for somebody to write a poem about them. In this same stretch of country, I also had two demoralising encounters, things that would never have happened to Dr Johnson, nor, the shame of it, even to Boswell. On the hill leaving Kirkcaldy, I asked a man in a gas company uniform how far to Cupar? He stopped and looked at me.

'Y'er goin' tae walk?'

'Yes.'

He hollered with laughter, promising to pick me up in the van if he passed; silently I told him fundamentally where to park his vehicle, and walked on, hurrying to catch up with my dignity. Yards beyond, at the gate of Ravenscraig Park, a kindly, grey-haired man directed me – unasked, unasked – to a place where I could get some good food: 'Soup an' a main course an' a cup of tea for a pound. And very good, too.' It turned out to be a church hall supplying food to the severely indigent.

In Fife live two notable travelling people, redoubtable storytellers, both now off the road and housed; one the lanky and sonorous Duncan Williamson; the other, Betsy White, with a rose-and-cream complexion unroughed by the years spent in no fixed abode. A visit to them again would surely have proven too costly to my programme of time and place: one cannot spend only a little time watching a storyteller at the loom; their brilliant garments take an age to weave. Not only that, in my sincere efforts to discover Johnson for myself, I feared letting such coloured dyes near the wash of his rigour. Likewise, I tried to imagine him sitting with Duncan Williamson who, having lived on the road, now had the dwelling of a tied bothy on a farm, for himself, his American wife and their two small children. No electricity or running water when I first saw him, amid oil-lamps, woodsmoke and whisky, he told old stories of selchies and filled my mind with kelpies, those attractive water-spirits peculiar to Scotland.

Kelpies live in rivers, and, being water-animals, gallop with the current. They toss and neigh, small dancing horses, not ponies, more elegant; if you are charmed by the kelpie's smile, and by the playful manner in which he butts you with his head, and if you climb on a kelpie's back, then beware: he will probably gallop along the top of the stream until he reaches a whirlpool; then he will strike the water with his tail, producing simultaneously both a roll of thunder and a flash of lightning into which he will disappear, leaving you struggling with the violently eddying waters. Sometimes the kelpie assumes human form, a hairy, shaggy man, who will jump up on your horse behind you, and squeeze you with his arms so tightly that you have no choice but to take him where he wants to go, no matter how far out of your way that might be. But – a trick: you can suborn a kelpie, or overcome him, by whipping off his magic bridle, without which he is powerless to do anything except obey commands like a good little horse.

Whatever anthropological interest Betsy White and Duncan Williamson would surely have generated in Johnson, and however certainly he would have been charmed by them, I could not at first envisage him taking to such stories in a relaxed fashion. Boswell's *Life* reports Johnson remarking, 'It is evident enough that no one who writes now can use the Pagan deities and mythology; the only machinery, therefore, seems that of ministering spirits, the ghosts of the departed, witches and fairies, though these latter . . . [are] every day wearing out.' When such subjects arise, Johnson emerges as a man more of rationale than excitable imagination, a man who prefers the grounding of proof to the ether of the supernatural, who prizes the thinking function above the intuitive one. He once observed to Boswell that 'The value of every story depends on its being true' – yet he allowed himself willingly to consider the second sight on Skye.

Perhaps a balance could have been struck by recalling his enjoyment of romances. He was known to read them frequently, for, he claimed, 'the fertility of invention, the beauty of style and expression, the curiosity of seeing with what kind of performances the age and country in which they were written was delighted'. But his friend Bishop Percy heard him 'attribute to these extravagant fictions that unsettled turn of mind which prevented his ever fixing in any profession'. Therefore, I summarised, Johnson would have sat contentedly by a traditional storyteller's fireside with mixed feelings, his addiction to rigour being pulled in the opposite direction by his fondness for a gaudy tale.

He would not have been the last English intellectual to take such an interest. Such folk reminiscence has all but disappeared; in an increasingly urban society, any harking back to old, unfounded customs generates suspicion, as if they represent the Stone Age of thought: they are dismissed as 'superstition'. If they vanish completely, they will take with them those instinctive faiths which, in the Celtic countries, helped to build the rope bridge from the oral to the written. A Bradford man, Robin Flower, understood this in the 1930s. He perceived the Blasket Islands off the south-west of Ireland as valuably as others saw Borneo, or the Kalahari bushmen. Deputy Keeper of Manuscripts at the British Museum, Flower translated texts from people who lived, as their daily lives, those 'superstitions', and he preserved memorable existences now vanished. Daniel Corkery, a native Irish school-teacher from the southern province of Munster, appreciated that over the half-doors of the cottages and the whitewashed thatched farmhouses up the fields, there reposed the last traces of a powerful old culture, and in his seminal books, *A Munster Twilight* and *The Hidden Ireland*, he gathered them up to show others how they could make literature from them. And they did: the three O's – Frank O'Connor, Sean O'Faolain and Liam O'Flaherty, drew on the powers and colours of the peasantry for great writing, sensing that if they pricked them they would bleed, if they tickled them they would laugh. Bryan MacMahon, q.v., followed on: he toured his own Kerry valleys talking to tinkers and celebrating their passing ways.

Here in Fife, the man who would have led me straight to the equivalent on the east coast of Scotland, another schoolmaster, died in 1987 – R.F. Mackenzie, who taught in Kirkcaldy and Buckhaven. He wrote about Fife not with the love of a native (it would probably have been unseemly in an Aberdeenshire man) but with the passionate interest of an incomer; he wrote about its saltpans, and owls, and linseed oil, and flax and close connections through fishing and shipping with the Dutch.

The east coast, hard and bright, was completely unknown to me before this trip; it has a surprisingly exotic pull, and at the same time a grimness. After St Andrews, I found my mind taken over with fiery images of oppression and religious intolerance. The last of their Protestant martyrs was burned here, and even the citizens of St Andrews, inured to burnings and gougings, felt so shocked – Walter Myln was eighty-two when Cardinal Beaton's men took him – that they refused to give ropes to tie him, or wood to burn him. I should have thought Johnson, however staunch his Anglicanism, might have dwelt on the Covenanters – flammable material for a mind equally interested in religion and the aristoc-racy. The First Covenant, drafted in honour of 'the most blessed

World of God and His congregation', had been raised by Scottish noblemen in 1557 to protect the new Protestant faith.

Throughout the next century and beyond, the boots of violence kept changing feet, as each side visited atrocities upon the other. Johnson, even though he did not specifically address such matters, had thought about underlying principles. A few months before he went to Scotland, he told a group which included Goldsmith, that 'the only method by which religious truth can be established is by martyrdom . . . he who is conscious of the truth has a right to suffer.'

Just beyond the deep blue power of the Buller of Buchan, where the cold waters of the North sea plunge and seethe in this *bouloir*, the road forks off to the prison town of Peterhead.

Slains Castle brought near for the first time the feeling of the past (Johnson's impulse handed downwards). I have a clear picture of what breakfast there must have been like – the presence of tea and coffee as revealing as a photograph; or their first afternoon there, as the Errol children were being presented. The castle is now so dishevelled that it is not easy to visualise Sam's large brown coat lumping around a corner as he looked out on the sea: yet, he almost came within reach in that breakfast scene. Was this a day on which he chose to wear clean linen? Did Joseph ever black the Doctor's shoes? At such moments, however unsanitary it might prove, I would have loved a reek of him. Following upon the massive success of *The Story of San Michele*, a woman reader wrote a fan letter to Axel Munthe, asking for a phial of his body odour. Had it been Johnson, and had there been a means of collecting his aroma, the woman might have received an odd bargain in the post – a little aromatic phial of sweat, urine, snuff, personal methane and tea.

Failing the availability of Johnson's whiff, how I wish the humanities in technology had kept pace with one another: in which case, the techniques that gave us printing, and spectacles, could also have invented the recording of sound earlier than the nineteenth century. Then I could have heard Johnson reading that dilemmatic family ode at breakfast, or *Iam satis terris nivis atque dirae* the night before – I could have played it on a Walkman, in my ear, in the shadow of Slains. An actor will not do, even were he to look similar, or to hold the page as close to his eyes as Johnson's poor eyesight must have required.

One outstanding impression of Scotland began to come to a head in Aberdeen, where I thought I began to observe it more concentratedly than in any other single location so far. I call it 'orderliness', and I suspect I mean 'efficiency' – although words such as 'prudence' and 'caution' also resonate. In the shops and in the general transactions of the day, a neatness of movement, an economy of requirement, was perceptible – no stragglings, no untidiness of person as a condition, no wasting of time or intention. The orderliness of dress along Union Street had a uniform quality; there is a particular kind of Scottish woman in whom this is noticeable – she has greying hair, is about fifty-five to sixty years old, wears a navy or grey coat; if there is colour in anything she wears it may be in a small tartan scarf at her throat, or perhaps a quiet tartan skirt, or a lavender-coloured wool jumper. She offers no exaggerated statements of her person, no suggestion of overt sexuality, all is discreet and contained; she carries a shopping bag or basket, and gets about briskly without bustling. If asked directions, she replies precisely and politely, but not extravagantly. Her husband, if she has one, will be equally neat; a grey or blue anorak, perhaps, or a sensible coat, and a tidy but never flamboyant shirt and tie. In both sexes, their shoes will be sound and clean, as if newly polished for the outing. Union Street, busy and crowded, had dozens of such folk, to whom flamboyance was a stranger, but orderliness a friend. Perennially caught between tendencies towards both, I found the repeated sight of these settled people relaxing and safe.

And then came that north coast shoulder, where two other writers, David Thomson and John Prebble, summarised it as I shall ever recall it. Thomson's *The People of the Sea* begins in Nairn, with a loving account of the house, Newton, in which I stayed. It moves to a terrifying description of the boy David encountering in the darkness of a nearby bothie a half-dead seal, a 'selchie', which is then killed brutally by the fisherman, his friend. 'Its nose was battered, its eyes closed, its whole head clotted with blood, but its smooth belly shone sleek and even in the half light, a creamy fawn in colour. Its back and flanks were mottled with dark spots, haphazard. When we took the rope off, it rolled over on its back and the two front flippers lay against its chest like hands – like human hands with five fingers webbed with skin. When the old man had his back turned, I felt the hands and stroked the long round body.'

His search for the seal, a lyrical journey, took him to the west of Ireland, and to those Hebrides Johnson never saw, South Uist and Benbecula, and to the north, to the Shetlands and Hamn Voe. Thomson met fishermen and their wives, and heard wisdom that came in a direct line straight down from mythology, and he met Duncan Williamson's selchies, or silkies, seals with human and faery souls, and the people through whose lives they swam. Oh, to search for them as Thomson did, and, growing older, increasingly to wish I had done so, to regret not having devoted a tranche of years to collecting folklore.

On account of Culloden, I return frequently to John Prebble, for snatches of everlasting impression – such as the final condition of Ranald Macdonald of Bellfinlay, 'a tall strapping, beautiful young man' whose legs had been broken in a cannonade. 'He had wrapped his plaid about him and prepared himself to die.' Or the reminiscence of Margaret Grant, a servant-girl of Inverness who saw a Cumberland freelance volunteer, James Ray of Whitehaven – 'he was a provincial snob and a great name-dropper' – ride in pursuit of two fugitives from the field. Ray yelled to her to hold his horse's bridle outside a well-house near the tollbooth where he had seen the two men run in to hide. 'She did so, and stood there while Volunteer Ray went inside, but, when she heard screams from the two men whose throats James Ray was cutting, she ran away and hid behind a corner. She saw him come out at last, with blood upon him.'

In the islands, Raasay puzzles me still: I do not know how to measure the population. A census taken in 1981 says 182; another taken in 1991 has not been published as I finish writing this book. Upon this very point history swaggers. The modern population may have been decided, or significantly influenced by, one vicious man, Captain Ferguson of the Royal Navy. In 1746, in reprisal a month after Culloden, Ferguson, abetted by a Lieutenant Dalrymple, led a rape of the women, then destroyed the laird's house and three hundred dwellings on Raasay.

The green mounds of old Kingsburgh prove moving for other reasons. Flora Macdonald was a mere twenty-four years of age when, fearless and cool, she guaranteed her place in the history books with daring protection of her Prince Charles. And once again, I see old Johnson with his big hat and his famous walking-stick, stumping and clumping along through the rain slanting across the entrance yard of Erray Farm, behind Tobermory on Mull, the tall long white house where Johnson listened to the doctor's daughter playing her guitar.

When he returned to London three months later, Dr Johnson began, through the prism of his own intelligence, to reflect upon principally, the Highlands and some islands. As we read his words, not only do we look on Scotland's history of that period with our own comparisons, we also see it through the very different glass of a learned eighteenth-century man, who, judging from the evidence of his Hebridean *Journey* alone, had the intense curiosity that defines intellectual energy – Samuel Johnson intended to use all his mind all the time. Allowing for the limitations of his age, and the fact that he took the decision to write about it rather late in the day, he attempted to decipher Scotland's past and presence, and make it meaningful in the terms of 'a good Englishman' who belonged, a political fact, in the same realm. Broader still, this general student of life and humanity brought to bear upon his Scottish experience all his reading, training, and thought, and all the tools thereof. Even from this, my first acquaintance of any length with him, it seems that he must have meant to do so in everything he wrote: should we complain if, at that age, when he was asthmatic and palsied and constantly suffering indifferent health, he fell short of comprehensiveness regarding Scotland?

Consequently, provided we make the allowances, we can, *via* Johnson, observe life through the window of that sort of classical education now rapidly disappearing from our world – so that we see not only Scotland's history, but Samuel Johnson's, and his

mind's antecedents and training, and his society's past. We walk
around and survey all the furniture in his huge mind, and we are
manifoldly informed of, and by, his great sensibility.

By going to Scotland, he permitted those of us who follow him
there, and who come from a different tradition, to include him
among our images. I remember him most on the isle of Skye, at
the house in Ullinish laying down the law on Ossian and Macpherson, and then, in his little party, and him sitting gigantic
astride a low horse, setting off down the coast heading for Talisker, with, out to his right, some of the loveliest islands in Europe
shimmering far away in the sun. As far as I am concerned – and
I concede willingly and with amusement the fancifulness of it –
he is riding down that road still. There are several caves in Scotland
– one on Mull, near Lochbuie – to which piper legends attached.
In search of gold, or underground passages, or fairyland, pipers
led people into those caves and nobody but the dog ever returned.
If you know where to go and if you listen hard, the music, faint
and recognisable, can still be heard above ground to this day. It
is the same with the booming voice of Dr Johnson.

INDEX